MARK MY WORDS

MARK MY WORDS

Native Women Mapping Our Nations

MISHUANA GOEMAN

FIRST PEOPLES
New Directions in Indigenous Studies

UNIVERSITY OF MINNESOTA PRESS

MINNEAPOLIS • LONDON

Publication of this book was made possible, in part,
with a grant from the Andrew W. Mellon Foundation.

Portions of chapter 2 originally appeared as "Re(Mapping) Indigenous Presence on the
Land in Native Women's Literature," *American Quarterly* 60, no. 2 (June 2008): 295–302;
copyright 2008 The American Studies Association; reprinted with permission by The
Johns Hopkins University Press; and as "Notes toward a Native Feminism's Spatial
Practice," *Wicazo Sa Review* 24, no. 2 (Fall 2009): 169–87.

Excerpts from "Mark My Words" by Diane Schenandoah from
*Iroquois Voices, Iroquois Visions: A Celebration of Contemporary Six
Nations Art*; reprinted by permission of Bright Hill Press and Literary
Center. Excerpts from *From the Belly of My Beauty* by Esther Belin;
copyright 1999 The Arizona Board of Regents; reprinted by permission
of the University of Arizona Press. Joy Harjo, "We Must Call a Meeting"
from *In Mad Love and War*; copyright 1990 by Joy Harjo; reprinted by permission
of Wesleyan University Press. "Letter from the End of the Twentieth Century,"
from *The Woman Who Fell from the Sky* by Joy Harjo; copyright 1994 by Joy Harjo;
reprinted by permission of W. W. Norton & Company, Inc. "The Path to the Milky Way
Leads through Los Angeles," from *A Map to the Next World* by Joy Harjo;
copyright 2000 by Joy Harjo; reprinted by permission of W. W. Norton & Company,
Inc. Heid E. Erdrich, "The Girl in Geography Class," reprinted by permission
of the authors and by Salt Publishing, Ltd.

Published by the University of Minnesota Press
111 Third Avenue South, Suite 290
Minneapolis, MN 55401-2520
http://www.upress.umn.edu

Library of Congress Cataloging-in-Publication Data

Goeman, Mishuana.
Mark my words : native women mapping our nations / Mishuana Goeman.
(First peoples: new directions in indigenous studies)
Includes bibliographical references and index.
ISBN 978-0-8166-7790-0 (hc : alk. paper) — ISBN 978-0-8166-7791-7 (pb : alk. paper)
1. Indian women—North America—History. 2. Indian women—North America—Social
conditions. 3. Indian women—Political activity—North America. I. Title.
E98.W8G64 2013
920.72089´97—dc23
2012043832

To my mom,
DEBRA JEAN RE,
and my family,
KEITH SHULSKY, SEDONNA, *and* THEO

Contents

Introduction:
Gendered Geographies
and Narrative Markings

THIS PROJECT WOULD BEGIN BEFORE I WAS EVEN COGNIZANT OF THE power of place and its relationship to colonialism, race, and gender. Yet, even as young children, many of us learn the constraints and limitations of the socially constructed spaces we find ourselves in. While I may not have known the history of how reservations came to be or how colonial governments enacted power in that space, I was deeply aware of the difference when I passed the lines of trees that mark the territories between off-reservation and on-reservation. I knew, on a deeply emotional level, that this was sovereign land without knowing the precise legal history. In my childhood migrations, I learned at a young age what it meant to be and how to act as a young Native girl in small-town rural Maine, or white suburban Connecticut, or a predominately black part of the city of Apex, North Carolina—and I knew it required adaptability and awareness of my own embodiment as I moved through tumultuous geographies constructed around differing and constantly shifting power structures. Yet I would not consciously reflect on these geographies and what they meant for years to come, even as I navigated them throughout the various stages of my life. In many ways this book theorizes my encounters within these spaces and what the geographies and maps we have created mean for the past, present, and future of not only Native people, but all of us.[1]

In this book, I interrogate the use of historical and culturally situated spatial epistemologies, geographic metaphors, and the realities they produce; examine the discourse of spatial decolonization; and trace a trajectory of spatial configuration in Native women's writing. Yet this is not a treatise on Native women's construction of self, nor do I believe that such a text would be appropriate apart from a lengthy discussion of individual cultural construction that coincides with tribal specificities as well as those that interrogate how the United States, Mexico, and Canada map difference. The texts with which I have chosen to work are documents: they provide evidence of the reality of Native women imagining and partaking in a future that produces possibilities for Native people. Rather than stand on the periphery, Native women are at the center of how our nations, both tribal and nontribal, have been imagined. The Native literature I discuss reorganizes a space that was never blank or fixed in time or space. Examining discourses of spatialized power dynamics in literature was a strategic move on my part. The imaginative possibilities and creations offered in the play of a poem, imagery of a novel, or complex relationships set up in a short story provide avenues beyond a recovery of a violent history of erasure and provide imaginative modes to unsettle settler space. That is, the literary (as opposed to other forms of discourse, such as journalism, surveys, BIA/field reports, Indian agents' diaries, etc., in which Native women are continually a shadow presence) tenders an avenue for the "imaginative" creation of new possibilities, which must happen through imaginative modes precisely because the "real" of settler colonial society is built on the violent erasures of alternative modes of mapping and geographic understandings.[2] The Americas as a social, economic, political, and inherently spatial construction has a history and a relationship to people who have lived here long before Europeans arrived. It also has a history of colonization, imperialism, and nation-building.

The authors I examine in this project employ elements of Native conceptions of space in their narratives to (re)map a history of what Mary Louise Pratt terms a "European planetary consciousness," a consciousness that is deeply patriarchal in nature.[3] This "planetary consciousness," which still largely orders the world, has had major implications for Native and non-Native communities alike. It has its historic roots in early geography and travel writing, a point I attend to in my last chapter, on Leslie Marmon Silko's *Almanac of the Dead*. Colonization resulted in a sorting of space based on ideological premises of hierarchies and binaries, and Indigenous women did not fare well in these systems of inequity. Settler colonialism continues to depend on imposing a "planetary consciousness" and naturalizing geographic concepts and sets of social relationships. Yet geography and the language we use to order space are formed in a "contact zone" in which various cultures interact. A main point of this book is to examine Native narratives that mediate and refute colonial organizing of land, bodies, and social and political landscapes.

(Re)mapping, as a powerful discursive discourse with material groundings, rose as the principal method in which I would address the unsettling of imperial and colonial geographies. The various intersections constructed by the colonial geographies enframe the boundaries of the state and manage its population, thus affecting our current actions in the world. Aboriginal scholar Linda Tuhiwai Smith reminds us about the connection among policy, people, and the mapping of space: "Imperialism and colonialism brought complete disorder to colonized peoples, disconnecting them from their histories, their landscapes, their languages, their social relations and their own ways of thinking, feeling, and interacting with the world."[4] The relationships among Native peoples and between others begin to be ordered along gender, sexuality, and racial regimes that exert power and bring into being sets of social, political, and economic relationships. (Re)mapping, as I define it throughout this text and in my previous work, is the labor Native authors and the communities they write within and about undertake, in the simultaneously metaphoric and material capacities of map making, to generate new possibilities. The framing of "re" with parentheses connotes the fact that in (re)mapping, Native women employ traditional and new tribal stories as a means of continuation or what Gerald Vizenor aptly calls stories of survivance.

My objective to chart women's efforts to define themselves and their communities by interrogating the possibilities of spatial interventions, such as those found in literary mappings, reflects my belief that power inheres in our stories. My aim here, however, should not be mistaken as utopian recovery of land through mapping pure ideas of indigeneity (which I find troublesome) on top of colonial maps. Even if we were to recover the historical and legal dimensions of territory, for instance, I am not so sure that this alone would unsettle colonialism. Recovery has a certain saliency in Native American studies; it is appealing to people who have been dispossessed materially and culturally. I contend, however, that it is also our responsibility to interrogate our ever-changing Native epistemologies that frame our understanding of land and our relationships to it and to other peoples. In this vein, (re)mapping is not just about regaining that which was lost and returning to an original and pure point in history, but instead understanding the processes that have defined our current spatialities in order to sustain vibrant Native futures. I will examine the consequential geographies, a term Edward Soja uses to fore-ground a concept of spatial justice, albeit one that problematically does not address settler colonialism, in order to examine "spatial expression that is more than just a background reflection or set of physical attributes to be descriptively mapped."[5] As such, my interests lie in examining the theoreti-cal dimensions of power that struggle over geography's hold, rather than a recovery project. What are the relationships set forth during colonialism that continue to mark us today? What happens when non-normative geographies are examined? I use the parentheses in (re)mapping deliberately to avoid the pitfalls of recovery or a seeming return of the past to the present. (Re)map-ping is about acknowledging the power of Native epistemologies in defining our moves toward spatial decolonization, a specific form of spatial justice I address throughout. It is about recognizing that "our geographies, like our histories, take on a material form as social relations become spatial but are also creatively represented in images, ideas, and imaginings."[6]

For me, Native women's literature presents ways of thinking through the contradictions that arise from the paradoxes and contradictions that colonial-ism presents and that Native people experience on a daily basis. Whether it was within the crisp white pages of Joy Harjo's book *How We Became Human*, or my musty working copy of Leslie Marmon Silko's *Almanac of the Dead*, which traveled with me across the country four times, accruing black coffee stains, strange smells, and creased corners, I begin to see a pattern of con-fronting the epistemologies that sought to incorporate Native people through their disappearance or social deaths. As I wrote the chapter on *Almanac* (par-ticularly on the "Five Hundred Year Map"), I began to unravel more of my own stories. As a Seneca woman from a family that moved and migrated around the East Coast, these experiences made the nodes, centers, and webs formed in *Almanac* comprehensible. The layered geographies in Native liter-ature intersect with many of my own experiences and understanding of social, cultural, and political space. My dad, a "traditional" Iroquois ironworker, would pack up our gray Chevy pickup and make my brother and me a cozy spot in the bed of the truck among all our belongings: our clothes, my mom's cookware and beadwork, my dad's tools, and an odd piece of furniture or two that always changed with each move.[7] We would drive for hours huddled up in the back of the truck, fighting and playing until we arrived at a new des-tination or one of our home bases. We would go either to Tonawanda or, more frequently, to northern rural Maine, a place called Twelve Corners named and claimed by my grandfather. Much of this depended on where my father had a paying job. The literary narratives involved in Silko's compiling a story about History (capital H intended) and its visual representation catalyzed my introspection into the geographies that prevail in my own life and my navigation through these very different terrains. Unlike the maps that designate Indian land as existing only in certain places, wherever we went there were Natives and Native spaces, and if there weren't, we carved them out.

Critical explorations of space, as figured in feminist geographer Doreen Massey's book *For Space,* delineate the possibilities that space holds rather than glance over it as a surface upon which we act. Much about Native mobility sees space as such, whereas in my experience we literally influenced the spaces and people around us as much as these spaces imprinted upon us. So, what exactly is space, and how do we pin down a definition when we have been conditioned to think of it as a surface of expanse and enormousness? Even if we delimit our definition by the modifier of Native spaces, the term still holds up as boundlessness. In fact, I struggled with constraining the geographies in this book until I settled for a discussion of the spaces between Mexico's northern border and Canada's southern border for pragmatic reasons, but I am well aware that these spaces are influenced by and intersect with much broader spaces. Massey's turn to uprooting normative modes of thinking of space defined as that which becomes "obvious" in the "tellings" that position space as "an expanse we travel across" is helpful as we progress throughout this text that wishes to (re)map our geographical knowledges. In order to reconceive space, Massey opens with a telling of arrival to "new" spaces that will be named the Americas, formed through the "crossing and conquering [of] space."[8] Specifically, she begins her exploration with stories of the Spanish conquistadors and the positioned narratives of "discovery." The "we" implied in this instance is that of Europeans, for as Massey's analysis of this moment continues, this depiction of space "immobilizes" and "differentiates" Europeans as the history and mapmakers carrying with it "social and political effects." Massey asks to reimagine space and "to question that habit of thinking of space as surface" and instead think of it as a "meeting-up of histories." In many ways this project is interested in the constant meetings that compose space: meeting between Native peoples, between Native and non-Native peoples, between people of color, between different migrating populations and especially meetings of different conceptions of land and ways of being in the world. As such, Massey's work with space is incorporated throughout the following chapters as she distills space into three functions that I posit are of utmost importance in decolonization projects: first, space can be defined "as the product of interrelations"; second, "as the spheres of possibility"; and third, "as always under construction" or a "simultaneity of stories-so-far." This definition moves us from essentialism, a common accusation made of Native scholars as we labor to maintain tribal traditions, political ground, and our lands, in that alternative spatialities are not mired in individual liberalism, but maintain their political viability. Alternative spatialities that I examine in this book imagine that many histories and ways of seeing and mapping the world can occur at the same time, and most importantly that our spatialities were and continue to be in process. As Massey effectively contends, "only if the future is open is there any ground for a politics which can make a difference."[9]

As I thought through space, I kept returning to Silko's map of characters, Tucson, and the borderlands that in no way present as a realist map, one that we too often take for a transparent form or depiction of objective reality, nor did the "Five Hundred Year Map" act as a stabilizer of space-time. That is, the map itself made no gestures toward veracity or Truth (intended with a capital T) in its representation. The map and its accompanying text complicated the narratives of what it means to live in this land. The spatialities I navigated through daily were complicated as well—the maps of my experience did not reflect those learned in grammar school or mediated through pop culture. What would a map of my trajectory look like if I set aside prescribed notions of what it means to be Indian, a woman, light-skinned, non–Seneca speaking, and other such constructed but materially real modifiers? How would the multiple histories it would take to create a representative map affect its comprehension? What power structures have deterred certain maps and produced others through the choices I have made or through others with whom I have come into contact or through those who have preceded me? Most importantly, I questioned what it would mean not to have the stories to accompany a map that represented my location.

I am the daughter of a Seneca man whose job as an ironworker resulted in migratory patterns of movement on and off our home bases. Gender was a significant aspect of our family's movement and tribal histories. We did not live on the reservation, as my mom was white, and in my Nation, women largely govern the land. So we—and I mean entire sections of my family— moved from city to city to rural areas, from place to place. Unlike many narratives would have us believe, I did not feel isolation from Native communities, even though I lived on my small reservation of Tonawanda in upstate New York only briefly when my father's job site was near, or when my aunt invited us. I was encircled by extended family, adopted uncles, and many, many cousins who also moved to their fathers' ironwork sites, or I was surrounded by the Natives who already lived in the area who gravitated toward hanging out with other Natives. This experience reflects the fact that in these cities and places are many Native people, often only brought up in our field of study in relation to the 1950s construction of the urban Native. According to the 2000 census, 60 percent of Native people reside in areas off-reservation, but many of the models map research into tight constraints of reservation bases or urban relocation centers.[10] Our family's mobility causes me not only to pause at the dichotomy of the urban/reservation Native, as we exist somewhere outside that paradigm, but also to question the very acceptance of colonial spatialities that, rather than reflect deeper meanings of spatialities, look at distance and closeness in terms of dichotomous differences.

My own "directional memory," a term coined by Esther Belin that I address in the second chapter, (re)maps my trajectories and was formed from early migratory patterns. Most importantly, the stories I heard about who we were provided me strength and remained with me as we moved from place to place. The stories we continue to make reflect these earlier stories and influence our everyday practices. I start with this reminiscence about the origins of this project and its personal trajectory, because, like Native writer and academic Gloria Bird, "I am motivated . . . by the belief that it is only through a critique of where I come from that the act of witnessing and the testimony I offer can become a decolonizing strategy."[11] Addressing the way the literal and figurative production of space constructs my realities quickly arose as a primary concern in this book. Rather than my story not fitting the mold of geographical imagining of Native people—or at times even Native peoples' imaginings—I instead believe it is a story much more prominent than the mapping of Native bodies and place reveals in the current research. Much of the work in Native literary studies did not present an analysis of intricate mobility and only now is beginning to do so.[12]

To further complicate ideas of space that figure so prominently in the way Native people construct their politics, identity, and strategies for dealing with the pressures of colonization, there were my grandparents, Vera Swanson and Theodore Goeman. Originally from Minnesota, they imagined and constructed their own Native landscapes in Penobscot territory, or what is now known as Maine. In the mid-1960s, my grandfather bought two hundred acres of land and proceeded to build a house for his family—my great-grandmother and my several aunts and uncles. It was a tarpaper house with cement floors, built briskly and not very well, and thus holding an air of impermanency around it. There was a kitchen, one back room, and the living room—no bathroom, as we hauled our water from the undrinkable well about six hundred yards away at the bottom of the hill. In this small house lived multiple families and multiple generations—it was never quiet or a place of respite; one went into the woods to play, hunt, fish, or wander for that. Eventually, another room was added, meant to be an Indian jewelry store, which then turned into a convenience store. This capitalist endeavor best describes a meeting space in which we interacted with old Mainers, other Indians, tourists, or Europeans who fascinated me with their strange ways. These failed endeavors lapsed either when Indians went out of fashion in the 1980s or because it was too provisional to make any money. The room was then used to accommodate new cousins and eventually my great-grandmother as she grew elderly and needed care. This was the only room built with wood floors, a place where we huddled to avoid the lightning strikes that bombarded the bottom of the valley and the bottom of our feet on cold cement. Twelve Corners drew many forms of lightning to it.

Twelve Corners was the most vivid place of my childhood memories and consciousness of who I was as a young Indian girl. It was our imagined space of the rez, complete with aunts and uncles who eventually built on various sections of the land and whose land was invariably lost after my grandfather's passing when it was sectioned into private lots. In the early 1970s, a large canvas hung in the front, prominently displayed with its red-lettered words on white backdrop that stated my family's politics, "WE SUPPORT WOUNDED KNEE." It looked like the rez, too, with its beat-up cars, free-ranging dogs, and unwelcome cats. It was a safe space for Indians traveling from Canada down to Boston or New York in the 1960s and 1970s, or wandering hitchhikers from Europe, or drifting hippies enthusiastic to be picked up by one of my long-haired, good-looking Native family members, who would bring them home and play with their imaginings of Indians. It was a place of stories, laughter, anger, incredible turmoil, unimagined strength, and a deep sadness that spanned generations. In all aspects, it wasn't just a surface we crossed, but a place built through intersecting histories, longings, and belongings.

This home base for me in rural Maine provided much of the little stability and simultaneous instability I felt growing up. Twelve Corners, while it was marked as individual property by state authorities, was more than a piece of land owned or occupied. It was a stretch of land I knew completely and a place to which family would always return even if they left for a while. Native people from Canada and the United States, from a number of tribes, stayed with us at various times. Passamaquoddy and Penobscot folks from the reservations closest to us, whose lands constitute what is now Maine, would stop by and swap goods for artwork or stories for laughter. The decade of my first memories was a politicized time, and my aunts and uncles were young and hopeful about changing the world in which we lived. Before coming to Maine, where my parents had met, they had lived in cities and Indian ghettos as well as on Tonawanda until my grandparents split. Maine was supposed to be a place to get away, but upon arrival, with their long hair and tough beauty, they quickly realized the inherent racism that knew no borders or specificity in place. My family was the closest most people in Maine would come to encountering the racial conflict that was taking place on a national level. This was a time when Native people were organizing across national borders (both in terms of the larger nation-states of Canada and the United States and in terms of tribal Nations' borders), and my family was quick to participate. Even as a young child, I felt the tension, excitement, and air of possibility.

While place here references the point on the map in terms of latitude and longitude as well as a locale, or a definition of place where material setting provides a mechanism for social relations to take place, I conceive of Twelve Corners as a place of belonging connected to other such places of belonging, such as Tonawanda. This sense of place becomes more than a fraction of space and/or a historical or material construction. Yet my affective attachment to this place is also accompanied by an acute awareness of what it meant to grow up in rural, predominately white, poverty-stricken Maine where everyone knows who belongs and who doesn't. In this spatial schema, Twelve Corners was criminalized in the outer community. At play here was more than the material location or even more than the present material social relations; instead evident here was the idea of Indians as criminals already, in a long history of colonial/Native relationships. All the same, this made my family's attachment to place, to Twelve Corners specifically, all the stronger, as it was protection against violence that accompanied us outside of these lines, even while at times violence took place within them. Place, and the way I will speak of it throughout this book, follows along the lines of geographers who have worked to expound the boundaries of place as more than just the point on a graph or locale, but that which carries with it a "way of being-in-the-world."[13] As mobile Indian bodies, we did traverse the safe—and at times not so safe— parameters and boundaries of the reservation or Twelve Corners, carrying with us these epistemologies that helped us navigate settler terrains. In a state where the murder rates are continually in the lowest one-eighth in the United States, two of my uncles have been brutally murdered and their aggressors received minimum jail sentences.[14] Racialized violence was a common occurrence in my family's experience, and often still is as we were the only people of "difference" from the 1960s through the 1980s. Understanding spatiality and the places you occupied were and continue to be a significant means of survival. The demographic makeup of this area would evolve as changes were implemented in urban and immigration policies in the 1980s, which I discuss in relation to Joy Harjo's work. I use the personal here, to theorize place in terms of humanistic geographers, because it complicates notions of place as purely locale and the site of our identity formations, a mutually constitutive definition particularly problematic for hyperspatialized Native people. Too often in this hyperspatialization, we are left with little room for imagining connections to other people, alternative histories, places, or even futures.

While my story may be very different from that of other Native people (though I suspect it is not as rare as might be believed, and it is becoming much more common), the construction of the geographies at various scales and its impact on our family and cultural relationships have remained the cornerstone of my politics and who I am as a scholar, friend, mother, and family member. I speak of the place from which I come because it is the base of my memories and politics of location; it is also what forms the base of my academic work. Again, Bird's words best summarize why I am telling my story, which is much more complex than I could possibly delve into in this introduction:

> In and of itself my story is not important either. What makes it important are the other relevant issues that surround us as Native people and that are the context in which I am presenting my story. Without that discussion, telling my story would be parading my ethnicity. I need to believe that my story serves a useful purpose.[15]

Often my memories correspond with places, movement, and my own gendered and racialized, or tribal, identity. My personal geographies or politics of location in reference to feminist Adrienne Rich intimately tie the spaces of body, Twelve Corners, the reservation, region, state, and nation together to map a place. When I speak to the spatial discourses (re)mapped by Native women, I also encourage us to move toward spatialities of belonging that do not bind, contain, or fix our relationship to land and each other in ways that limit our definitions of self and community. I rely on the creative strength my grandparents taught me as they tried to imagine a safe place for our family, even if the ruptures at times were powerful. I also carry forth the responsibility they taught me about the politics of language, for instance, asserting sovereignty through language by choosing not to use "tribe" and only referring to Tonawanda as a nation. This reference to locating myself was an early lesson in the power dynamics of spatial metaphors.

Unsettling colonial maps is what drives this study of colonial spatial violence in twentieth-century Native American literature. The stories fill in the spaces between Native lives mapped onto reservations or urban centers or somewhere in between, or those lives relegated to a romanticized American past; the stories I am attuned to provide a window into the complexities of spatial subjectivities and geographic histories, giving us a richer understanding of how Native people imagine community and create relationships. My personal story ties the multiscalar spaces of body, Twelve Corners, the reservation, region, state, and nation intimately together. By accounting for the various scales of geography in relation to Native peoples and a history of conquest, we can begin to understand the relationship between lands and bodies as more than just a surface upon which we travel or a descriptive geography. "Multiscalar discourses of ownership," contends Katherine McKittrick, who examines black women's geographies during the transatlantic slave trade, is "one of the many ways violence operates across gender, sexuality, and race . . . having 'things,' owning lands, invading territories, possessing someone, are, in part, narratives of displacement that reward and value particular forms of conquest."[16] When I speak of the (re)mapping discourses created by the women in the pages of this book, I am speaking of the move toward geographies that do not limit, contain, or fix the various scales of space from the body to nation in ways that limit definitions of self and community staked out as property. My intervention into these various colonial scales and my interrogation of Native women's geographies should not be read as a longing to further construct or revamp that elusive "Indian" that is propped up through racial and gender codes, nor is it a putting of Indians in place or taking them out of it temporally and geographically. Instead, I am concerned with producing decolonized spatial knowledges and attendant geographies that acknowledge colonial spatial process as ongoing but imbued with power struggles. I ask a similar question to that of aboriginal scholar Irene Watson: "Are we free to roam?" and if so, "do I remain the unsettled native, left to unsettle the settled spaces of empire?"[17] Rather than construct a healthy relationship to land and place, colonial spatial structures inhibit it by constricting Native mobilities and pathologizing mobile Native bodies.

Embodied geographies thus become pivotal to address in decolonization projects, and it is here that Native feminisms can play a major role in our thinking about the connections between land, individuals, and constructions of nations. Bodies that are differently marked through the corporeal or through a performance—whether through gender, race, sexuality, or nationality—articulate differently in different spaces. As Native bodies travel through various geographies, they are read differently and thus experience lived realities that are constantly shifting. For as Michel Foucault and ensuing scholars have argued, the body never exists outside of space and is connected to other indicators that are used to relegate power relations between the bourgeois and those deemed as degenerate subjects.[18] For Indigenous people traveling through constructed colonial and imperial spaces, the body can be hypervisible as the abnormal body, and at times hyper-invisible as it becomes spatially disjointed from the map of the nation in both physical and mental imaginings. In "Fatal Couplings of Power and Difference," geographer Ruth Wilson Gilmore speaks about "the range of kinds of places—as intimate as the body and as abstract as a productive region or a nation-state,"[19] and it is in this range of connected places that I will discuss how Native women have mapped their lives.

In much Native American cultural production, place continues to hold these fragile, complex, and important relationships. But as Foucault's work with space and the body indicates, the state and citizen subjects' roles that come into being also had to perform a self-regulating mechanism in a field of surveillance. I contend that instead of ingesting the norm of immobile Native women, we open up the possibility of (re)mapping the Americas as Indigenous land, not only by rethinking dominant disciplining narratives but also critically examining how we have become a self-disciplining colonial subject. How might our own stories become the mechanism in which we can critically (re)map the relationships between Native peoples and communities? As Gilmore states, "if justice is embodied, it is then therefore always spatial, which is to say, part of the process of making place."[20] In examining Native women's (re)mapping of the nation-state, my intention is not to focus on previously neglected texts, though I do believe the texts I include deserve more attention in the field of American literature and in race and ethnic studies as well as in cultural geography. Neither do I aim to create or affirm an essential "female" or essential "Indian" category to address "common oppression." Rather, the focus on the gendered body in these texts provides sites in which we can examine gendered, sexualized, and racialized differentiations in relation to imagined geographies that buttress colonialism and enact violence in our daily lives.

Secondly, my focus on Native women's texts and the gendered scenarios they present takes into account Robert Warrior's foundational work in *Tribal Secrets*. In particular, I take seriously his call to examine the intellectual histories of Native writers and put forth a "generational view . . . [that] provides a new historical and critical site that invites us to see contemporary work as belonging to a process centuries long, rather than decades long, of engaging the future contours of Indian America." Warrior's work demonstrates the vitality of Native literatures to imagine a future for Native peoples who are not simple, exotic, insubstantial, or easily erased. Rather, Native stories, generations old and often labeled traditional or pure even when they are not, and new stories too often dismissed as tainted by Western literacy so therefore not Native enough, incite us to imagine literary possibilities that deconstruct tired colonial paradigms. My choice to put forth Native women's literary engagement with space and politics at various scales was very much influenced by Warrior's assertion that determining our future depends on "critically reading our own tradition[, which] allows us to see some of the mistakes of the past as we analyze the problems of the present."[21] Though some critiques suggest there is an element of essentialism because of an emphasis on literary nationalism, they too often overlook Warrior's careful assertion that we must contextualize the writers as engaging with the world around them. A fruitful acknowledgment of the pain and chaos of colonization provides the fertile ground needed for decolonization. By "making ourselves vulnerable" and recognizing how "outside influences" have affected "our consciousness, and our imaginations," Warrior insists on an intellectual sovereignty as "a process of asserting the power we possess as communities and individuals to make decisions that affect our lives."[22] The women whose texts I have chosen assert a spatial sovereignty literally grounded in their relationships among land, community, and writing. It is not a remythologizing of space that is occurring, such as that often performed by nationalist groups, but a (re)mapping that addresses the violent atrocities while defining Native futures.

My choice to concentrate on Native women's literature in relation to mapping new spaces is threefold. First, by examining Native women's engagements with twentieth-century spatial restructuring, I am able to delve critically into the construction of gender, heteropatriarchy, and race categories as instrumental to colonial logics. Rather than privilege writing as a hegemonic form of resistance, I contend that the Native women's writing I have included reflects the instability and mobility of the categories of race, gender, class, and sexuality at times when these intersections were most operable in colonial spatial restructuring. Kimberlé Crenshaw's feminist theory of intersectionality as a method to examine power relations influences much of my analysis. Although speaking to violence against women of color in general, Crenshaw's problematizing of the way identity has been conceived as a method of analysis is useful to my own thoughts on the spatial violence inflicted on Native communities:

> In the context of violence against women, this elision of difference in identity politics is problematic, fundamentally because the violence that many women experience is often shaped by other dimensions of their identities, such as race and class. Moreover, ignoring difference within groups contributes to tension among groups, another problem of identity politics that bears on efforts to politicize violence against women. Feminist efforts to politicize experiences of women and antiracist efforts to politicize experiences of people of color have frequently proceeded as though the issues and experiences they each detail occur on mutually exclusive terrains. Although racism and sexism readily intersect in the lives of real people, they seldom do in feminist and antiracist practices. And so, when the practices expound identity as woman or person of color as an either/or proposition, they relegate the identity of women of color to a location that resists telling.[23]

By examining Native women writers through an intersectional approach, I am choosing a feminist method of analysis that presents us with a multiple grounded "telling" of violence and its impact on the structural, political, and representational lives of Native peoples and their communities.

Second, Native women's alternatives to heteropatriarchal representation of national space, referred to as traditional geography, are fundamental to understanding the ways in which nation-states in North America have built themselves through gendered spatial metaphors of dominance. For instance, civilization and frontier are metaphors that are engrained in Americans' imagining of their place in North America and on the global stage. Instead of presuming the naturalness of "Indians' relationship to the land" and Indians' victimization from land theft through masculinized Indian wars, I explore how E. Pauline Johnson (Mohawk), Esther Belin (Diné), Leslie Marmon Silko (Laguna Pueblo), and Joy Harjo (Muscogee Creek) attend to gender and land contesting U.S. nation-building *while they imagine a future for Native nations*. The patriarchal and racist nature of displacement becomes very clear in such policies as the Indian Act and relocation, which I discuss in the first and second chapters, respectively. Understanding these categories as stemming from the project of Enlightenment and tied to contested spaces enables a rethinking of settler nations by exposing the worldviews that rationalize the settler state and the project of liberal democracies, which rests on the individual.

Third, this approach to the relationship between gender and space demonstrates that Native people have had and continue to have their own discourses regarding the production of the world around them—discourses that produce a different set of economic, political, and social relations than the ones intended by implementation of various Indian policies in the twentieth century.[24] My intent in mapping twentieth-century geographic imagining by Native women is to put forth sets of social relations that lead us in directions beyond a settler heteropatriarchal mapping of space. In thinking through the poetics involved in imaging new landscapes, I find Édouard Glissant's work important, though he is speaking to transatlantic blackness in the Caribbean and American South.[25] For Glissant, who speaks to black alienation from the land, poetry and the narrative open up the production of space, providing alternative geographies. These alternative geographies contest dominant histories and geographies, even if they do not displace the regimes of power that assert spatial hierarchies. The Native women's texts with which I work are documents of the violence inflicted on their communities and a critique of the spatial restructuring of their lands, bodies, and nations; they are what Glissant refers to as a grammar of liberation that seriously engages alternative spatial practices to that of making land into property or treating land as purely a surface upon which we act. These women's stories and my Native feminist analysis are not testaments to geographies that are apart from the dominant constructions of space and time, but instead they are explorations of geographies that sit alongside them and engage with them at every scale. Even though these geographies may be marginalized, dismissed, concealed, or erased, they still constitute a part of our daily lives. These women's imaginative geographies are the stories that construct, contest, and compose a mapping of the Americas.

Mapping Empires

In these pages, I reiterate past concerns and link them to contemporary mappings of indigeneity, race, gender, and nation to unsettle the spatial ideologies at the foundation of nation-states. Maps, in their most traditional sense
as a representation of authority, have incredible power and have been essential to colonial and imperial projects. The commission of surveying projects
by both the Canadian and American nation-states was not a simple act of
scientific research, but implicit involvement in creating empire. While many
authors have examined this earlier period and mapping of the Americas as
a colonial project, I argue that these mappings of Native land and bodies continue well into the contemporary time.[26] I intend to interrogate the process
of mapping, both as a metaphor and as the physical mapping of lands and
bodies, as one that supports and naturalizes race, gender, heteronormativity,
and colonial power relations. The mapping of settler nations is too often mis-
understood as a "deceptively simple activity," while the power exerted through
state structures is made normative through this deceptiveness. As human
geographer Dennis Cosgrove tells us: "To map is in one way or another to take
measure of a world, and more than merely take it, to figure the measure so
taken in such a way that it might be communicated between people, places,
or times. The measure of mapping is not restricted to the mathematical; it
may equally be spiritual, political, or moral. By the same token, the mapping's
record is not confined to the archival; it includes the remembered, the imagined, the contemplated."[27] As "a spatial embodiment of knowledge," maps can
reveal much about the processes of producing settler colonial nations. As a
"stimulus to further cognitive engagements," the mappings in Native women's
literary texts challenge the organization of land and bodies into categories
generated during the age of enlightenment, past surveying of Native land;
and the continued use of these categories, albeit in different forms, sustains
the settler nation-state. The literary mapping in the texts I work with in the
following chapters represents and "communicates" a Native ethics and politics of their place in the world with potential to contest the ever-developing
settler/imperial nations.

While the literary works I discuss begin in the twentieth century, I would
like to step back a bit further into the eighteenth and nineteenth centuries,
when European nations sought to solidify power, and newly forming nations,
such as the United States, Mexico, and Canada, sought economic independence. It is no surprise that maps were instrumental to these projects, just as

they were to early empires that sought domination of Native land in the Americas. Ricardo Padrón, in his book *The Spacious Word*, investigates the trajectory of cartography, specifically of the Spanish empire, as foundational to modern conceptions of space and the "invention of America" by the West. He traces not just the practical use of maps, such as planning of military operation, delineating control, or even those that laid out "the faithful or idolatrous" Indigenous peoples in order to proselytize them, but also the ideological uses of maps in early modern Spain. It is the residue of these ideologies that continues to influence contemporary understanding of space and authorize state force over Native land and bodies.

In speaking of the aesthetics used to "flatter" a monarch or contemporary uses of the "image of territory that inspires our affection, demands our loyalty, calls us home," Padrón discusses the ideological purposes of cartography at a time when European empires "were only beginning to learn how to imagine their world, relate to it, and transform it in ways that depended upon the unique conceptualization of space that lay at the heart of modern map."[28] Padrón makes clear that in the Middle Ages the words "map" (*mappaemundi*) and "space" (*spatium*) were rarely found or used outside the context of traders and mariners, and, in fact, maps were limited to a few uses and not used by many people. The conception of space and "the cartographic revolution" ushered in new notions of space that would hold sway as America became invented in the European imagination. In this book, I aim to look at the ideological mapping that continued from these early formations. The development of the "scientific" modern map—one of geometric, abstract grids—is a development that coincides directly with Europe's war on Indigenous people. As Padrón, invoking Said's *Orientalism*,[29] makes clear, however, and as I examine in my reading of Leslie Marmon Silko's novel *Almanac of the Dead*, the "invention of America" through the trajectory of cartographic development did not just reflect the Americas as "a purely natural object" but also defined Europe and its colonies. Padrón states, "America is indeed a slice of the natural world, but it is one that has been cut from the globe by a particular people, at a particular time, interested for particular reasons in carving the world up in the first place . . . this process of 'inventing America' can be understood as the process or 'remapping' the European imagination in ways that bring to light the connections between the early modern cartographic revolution, a larger process of cultural 'mapping,' and deep change in Europe's conception of itself and its world."[30]

While maps were essential to earlier projects of exploration as well as the documentation of explorers and literate traders before the nineteenth century, it was in the 1800s that maps were understood by many to simultaneously represent the "real" as they symbolized the destiny of settler states. These early maps differed from their predecessors and were often naturalized and understood to project the real through the use of grids and mathematics. No longer were the maps laden with religious icons or pictorial symbols of the aristocracy that commissioned their making, yet the ideology behind the earlier forms of these maps remained. Hidden in the rhetoric and its visual presentation—in particular in the intent—was still the imagery of colonial empire. Exploring the discourses of mapping is necessary in understanding the way worldviews are represented. Maps exert political control by manipulating the representation of space into a language of normativity. For instance, the Louisiana Purchase as an inventive claiming of territory is still rarely questioned in the public imagination. Though we know that Sacagawea met with other Nations and translated languages, the relationship of Native people to place is absented and obscured. Without these stories, or in the suppression of them, the entire West is depicted as a blank slate, even though Native people were and are acknowledged as inhabiting the land. There remains a spatial imaginary of vast landscapes filled with flora and fauna. Native people in this unjust spatial imaginary become part of the flora and fauna open to settlement, while the state supports its fantasy through the law.[31]

The development of modern nation-states depended on sending out official mapmaking expeditions as a state tool to find information that would enable the assertion of political force over territories and all contained within. For instance, it was President Thomas Jefferson who commissioned the famous mapmaking Corps of Discovery expedition led by Lewis and Clark. Interestingly, Jefferson was inspired by Enlightenment tales of the West and sagas of those who traveled to hostile lands, yet he was also prompted by the threat that the British were sending expeditions to Western lands.[32] The famous expedition arose from the geographic imaginings of Jefferson, who often engaged in voyage and travel literature and for whom territorial accumulation was pivotal. His assignment to Meriwether Lewis reflects the goals of empire; the future of Jefferson's fledgling nation meant expanding the territory and exploring "for the purposes of commerce." In the instance of the Great Basin Indians, Ned Blackhawk contends that these early mappings were crucial to conquest: "Their maps, reports, and journals ultimately carried greater influence than the thousands of beaver pelts and horses ferried to market in St. Louis. By producing the knowledge from which conquest could flow, those who extended American claims in the region became agents for the most violent forms of imperialism. The settlement, law, policing, and governance—the mechanics of colonial rule—that followed within a generation overturned the worlds of Great Basin Indians forever."[33] While Lewis and Clark's journey has perhaps been the most celebrated in United States history as an event that opened up the West to incorporation into the nation-state, there were many other cartographic projects that sought to survey and explore lands as the Indigenous world was carved up in settler imaginations and writings in a push to map and consolidate empire.[34] In the imagination of Jefferson and his companions, these early expeditions into the West laid claim over the land and resources. While several studies have connected the geographical knowledge produced during colonization with that of the making of the modern nation-states and the advance of capitalism, I am also concerned with how these early events have set up gendered colonial structures that continue to dominate and enact violence at both the interpersonal and state level on Native peoples.[35] The spatial violence asserted through the geographical imaginings and subsequent mappings would be tremendous throughout the West in what is now Canada, the United States, and Mexico securing an ongoing and violent spatial legacy.

Native nations, however, had and still have their own claims on the land, beginning with creation stories. Colin Calloway opens his book *One Vast Winter Count: The American West before Lewis and Clark* with a mapping of Native nations' place-based creation stories in the West. By centering these stories in relation to the Bering Strait theory's assumption of a land bridge in the context of a history of this region before Lewis and Clark's mapping expedition into those lands, Calloway adeptly tackles ongoing disputes over representations and relationships to time and space, or to history and place. He asserts: "Often in history what we think we know turns out to need revision and what we dismiss as nonsense proves to make a lot of sense. 'Other' stories of coming into America—whomever may be telling them—may not be any more or less 'accurate' than those we think may be true. Indian peoples had many stories to explain their presence in the West." He provocatively proposes a reconsideration of the archeological, historical, and anthropological narrations of understanding Native people as "first immigrants" by shifting the paradigm, suggesting that "perhaps the first pioneers did not come to the West; perhaps they were made in the West."[36] Oral stories, often

embedded in contemporary literature, predate the European maps made by
Lewis and Clark and other early surveyors of the East and West who sought
to claim land for their respective nations.

These colonial maps were instrumental in treaty making and creating
national boundaries; they are still used to regulate and determine spatial practices. Dispute of these maps was not uncommon, and tribal leaders would
often draw on their own geographical interpretations to dispute the treaties.[37]
Native scholars, researchers, and mapmakers who now have more access to
the archive are also using maps and documents as sources for land reclamation. The exchange of knowledge that took place in the early years was
common, as Malcolm Lewis acknowledges in his essay "First Nations Mapmaking in the Great Lakes Region," though, in fact, acknowledgment wasn't
often given, and when it was, "ambiguously so."[38] In fact, it was the oral stories or words that would convey distances, villages, landmarks, and so forth.
The additive oral component, according to Lewis, could be beneficial and at
other times could lead to omissions or errors. At any rate, what is made clear
in cartographic historians' engagement with colonial maps was the power that
they would continue to have after these early years. Cole Harris situates domination in the early surveying of Native territory: "My conclusions are these:
the initial ability to dispossess rested primarily on physical power and the
supporting infrastructure of the state; the momentum to dispossess derived
from the interest of capital in profit and of settlers in forging new livelihoods;
the legitimating of and moral justification for dispossession lay in a cultural
discourse that located civilization and savagery and identified the land uses
associated with each; and the management of dispossession rested with a set
of disciplinary technologies of which maps, numbers, law, and the geography of resettlement itself were the most important."[39] Harris continues with
his investigation by turning away from cultural studies discourse, or what he
frames as a concentration on the word, and by concentrating on the "disciplinary technologies" of mapping as the instruments of colonialism and later
empire that *do* the dispossessing.

While I agree that to understand colonialism we must begin with asking the question of how colonial power was deployed, it is important to
see mapping as a means of discourse that mapped an imperial imaginary.
Later it would map discourses of spatial identities that would have the real
effect on access to resources, such as on-reserve/ation or off-reserve/ation.[40]
Native people did resist the technologies of colonialism, as Harris reminds
us: "Like oppressed people everywhere, they engaged in a virtually constant

micro-politics of resistance: moving fences, not cooperating with census enumerators, sometimes disrupting survey parties. There was a stream of letters and petitions, often written with missionary assistance, to officials in Victoria, Ottawa, and London, and meetings with cabinet ministers, prime ministers, and even, on one occasion, the king."[41] Yet, in the end, it was the power of the word and marking of Native place passed on through stories that refuted settler power.

I start this book shortly after the signing of the 1870s Medicine Treaties and the corralling of Native people onto reservations as if they were wild animals needing containment. Not coincidently, it was also in 1876 that Canada became a confederation, severing its ruling ties to the metropole of Britain. Academics have too often separated the Native policies of Canada and the United States and not explored junctures of power that support ongoing spatial violence. I contend that, while we must scrutinize the particularities around how each nation-state has incorporated and expunged Natives, and must do so at the local scale as well, it is also important to examine how inflicted violence supported suppression and colonization *throughout the Americas*. In this instance, the brutal physical violence inflicted by the U.S. Army led to signing of treaties and brutally forcing Native people onto reservations. Many of these Native nations' traditional homelands spread into what is now known as Canada and Mexico. The restrictions placed and enforced by the U.S. Army helped to settle the southern borderlands of Canada and the northern boundary lands of Mexico. Cities grew, white immigration flourished, and the colony no longer needed to rely on Britain for military protection. The settler nation-states of the Americas, in recognizing one another's boundaries and overlooking colonial violence, legitimate the settler state as an entity while overlooking the injustices toward Native people under its guise of the affairs of a sovereign nation. While mapping was indispensable to brute colonization of Native land in North America through genocide, it is at this point colonial logics took a spatial turn that changed the everyday practices of Native people. Colonial governmentality articulated and implemented structures that would regulate Native spaces and Native bodies through a variety of state practices. Family, clan, and intra- and intertribal relationships were reformulated in ways readable to the state. The authors with whom I work address the severing of these relationships by the pounding discipline of state force. Once territories and land were claimed by Western empires turned settler states, violent state practices were read as internal affairs. It is in this era I begin my project.

By drawing the connections between maps and what Andrea Smith refers to as the three pillars of heteropatriarchy in the forms of colonialism, slavery, and orientalism, we can think about Smith's call for us to combat heteropatriarchy by seeing beyond assertions of a "common property of all oppressed groups," which in many ways has become operating controlling spatialities such as the urban, ghetto, barrio, and reservation.[42] Maps were instrumental in the navigation of the slave trade in the Black Atlantic that provided labor instrumental to conquest, maps erased Native land claims and sacred sites, and maps situate the borderlands that mark the immigrant as a foreign body to be policed and disciplined. So, while this project examines Native peoples in particular, it also is concerned with interlocking systems of oppression and other locations. The mapping and invention of America required the brute force of slavery and colonization and the ideological framework of orientalism—all of which were and are gendered forms of violence. Mapping as a tool of traditional geographies, then, becomes a site in which to explore the exchange of power and struggle over the ordering of cultural, physical, and embodied space and explore heteropatriarchy.

While I have spoken above of historical processes of mapping, and the book itself is arranged in chronological order, my aim is not to document a stable, historical, geographical discourse in the history of twentieth-century Native women's writing. Rather, I posit a study of spatial discourses that are always in movement and colonialisms always in contradiction in order to illuminate the fact that space is shifting, layered geographies with connecting and complex histories, histories that are too numerous to discuss in one book. My decision to strategically address historical elements that provide important context is meant to strengthen a social criticism of our approaches, which are too often spatially bounded. This book is not meant to be a decisive history of the spatial construction of our nations, but rather a social criticism that opens up and questions, through a study of the language and physicality of geography, normative nation-state maps that inform the present. Writers and artists work to free us from imposed rigid definitions set in place through Western interpretations and definitions of "Native," "Native land," "Native Sovereignty." The attempted interruption and displacement of Native spatial concepts by colonization has had a profound impact on our communities. By placing Native women's writing in a historical context, alternatives to the normative arguments arise. Ever present is the flexibility of tribal stories to hold communities together despite displacement from lands, the corroding of tribal ways of thinking, and a litany of Indian policies that produce self-surveillance and community inter- and intra-tensions.

READING NATIVE MAPS

The Native women writers discussed in the following chapters challenge the seemingly objective and transparent forms of Western mapping by including narrative experiences and cultural systems that tell and map a story of survivance and future. This literary work challenges hegemonic conceptions of race, gender, and nation too often mapped onto Native people both ideologically and physically. The material reality of inequities and hierarchies result from the mapping process of naming and symbolically defining and enframing land. Cosgrove, in speaking about the history of maps, finds the key to distinguishing "variations" in histories and the different "intellectual and visual universes" is to consider the map beyond "the frame of the history of sciences and of geographic knowledge *stricto sensu*." He states that the map "encompasses many other components of a culture: its conception of the world, physical and metaphysical, its cognitive categories that bring truth within reach of the human mind, the social construction and sharing of such knowledge about the world."[43] To unmap these settler maps is to decolonize "social constructions" and "such knowledge." While critics such as Edward Said, Eric Bulson, Allan Trachtenberg, and Richard Phillips have examined literary mapmaking and its importance in supporting nationalism at home and empire abroad, their projects are mainly concerned with European or settler-nations literature.[44] These discussions of empire in relation to the literary canon, while important contributions that have influenced this project, leave out the voices that have also shaped our current world. Absent in the discussion are the hopes of those who are claimed in the rhetoric of empire. This project turns to an examination of the steps that Native people have taken to mediate the maps of colonial and national imaginative geographies. To begin to (re)map the settler nation, we must start with Native forms of mapping and consider Native-made spaces that are too often disavowed, appropriated, or co-opted by the settler state through writing, imagining, law, politics, and the terrains of culture.

In speaking of normative maps used in colonial processes, J. B. Harley states that "the social history of maps, unlike that of literature, art, or music appears to have few genuinely popular, alternative, or subversive modes of expression. Maps are preeminently a language of power, not of protest."[45]

Harley's failure to recognize that Western literature and maps have often formed a nexus, supporting and inspiring exploration, conquest, and imperial projects, perhaps led to his inability to distinguish Native stories and forms of telling as maps.[46] These are maps that have contested power relations in the Americas even before European settlement. Harley, though instrumental in upsetting the modernist notion that maps merely reflected "reality," fails to recognize the intricate relationship between maps and literary discourses that protest settler ideological and physical dominance in the Americas. Concerned largely with Western forms of representing and marking space, he overlooks forms of spatial production that existed before Europeans arrived. The literary maps of Native people presented in oral stories, or later in writing, are the subversive or alternative geographies I will engage in this book.

Alternative mapping projects, the focus of scholars such as Matthew Sparke and Marc Warhus, do exist as counter projects to colonial narratives and capitalistic endeavors. Even the western mapping project is to some extent affected by these alternative maps as demonstrated in the earlier discussion of Sacagawea and the role of coureur des bois. After all, explorers produced many of the earliest maps, and their main source of knowledge resided in the Indian guides, many of them women, who helped navigate through terrain these newcomers found foreign. Sacagawea, one of the few Native women who occupy space in the cultural imagination of most Americans, was instrumental to the Lewis and Clark trip. Without her knowledge of the land and its resources, translation abilities, familial relationships, and overall presence, the Corps of Discovery would have surely faced death. Native people have always had maps of their own, and women in the earlier years, as spouses, companions, and day laborers, were part of this exchange of knowledge.[47] Native peoples' knowledge, relegated to the realm of the primitive, was not acknowledged and made absent on the "official" maps of the state. Native women, however, were doubly excluded from the realm of a seemingly objective and masculine world of science and cartography. These erasures have had an enormous impact on the archives of colonial maps.

Historian of cartography Marc Warhus, however, was able to collect various such forms of Native maps dating from before 1492 to the present, though most were made by men. These stunning visual maps have several different formats and are printed on various materials, such as bark, hide, and paper. The maps in *Another America* present unique constructions. Warhus articulates the methods for understanding Indigenous maps:

To read these Native American maps it is necessary to suspend western preconceptions of what makes a map. Unlike western cartography, where the primary document is the physical map and the conventions of scale, longitude, latitude, direction, and relative location are believed to "scientifically" depict a landscape, Native American maps are pictures of experience. They are formed in the human interaction with the land and are a record of the events that give it meaning. Far from being unsophisticated or "primitive," these Native American maps were as functional and transmissible as the products of *Rand McNally* or *National Geographic*.[48]

I stress that elements of these maps remain today in oral traditions, contemporary stories, and experiences conveyed through story, and these stories are often carried on through women. These mental maps found in the stories shape relationships around us and serve to imagine identity and community differently. They are a significant component of Native survival: "Unlike western society, maps were not created as permanent documents in Native American traditions. The features of geography were part of a much larger interconnected mental map that existed in the oral traditions. The world was experienced and perceived through one's history, traditions, and kin, in relationships with the animal and natural resources that one depended upon, and in union with the spirits, ancestors, and religious forces with whom one shared existence."[49] Even though Warhus refers to "the missing oral components of the map," I contend that they are not missing, but may have changed form just as changes in cartographic practices have produced new forms of maps that differ greatly from their early roots.

The stories, songs, and rituals still remain and continue to be passed down through the generations. Unlike Western maps whose intent is often to represent the "real," Native narrative maps often conflict, perhaps add to the story, or only tell certain parts. Stories and knowledge of certain places can belong to particular families, clans, or individuals. These maps are not *absolute* but instead present multiple perspectives—*as do all maps*. While narratives and maps help construct and define worldviews, they are not determined and always open for negotiation.

While explorers and later government agents relied on these maps made by men of empire to assert truth claims that rhetorically assert power over the land and those living in those spaces, it wasn't too long before Native people recognized their power to hold onto their land and the relationships it engendered. From the earliest moments of contact, Native people understood the power of Europeans' production of physical maps and written literary accounts to reinforce colonial claims and the importance of Natives' own Indigenous forms of cartography and knowledge to dispute territorial takeover. Production of Native maps is quite different from European forms, as the work of many geographers, including Malcolm Lewis, Matthew Sharpe, and Mark Warhus, has pointed out. Lisa Brooks, in *The Common Pot*, writes at length about the symbolic and formal ways that Native New Englanders claimed space, rebuffed colonial claims on their land, and maintained relationships to each other, other nations, and the land by examining texts written by from the eighteenth and nineteenth centuries. Her examination of writings, such as treaty petitions, treaty literature, journey journals, letters, and diaries, engages with a recovery of space putting forth an analysis of how writers in the nineteenth century imagined themselves in New England.[50] This "recovery of space" largely depends on those stories that accompany the normative maps put forth. This project differs from those of Brooks, Warhus, and Lewis, not only in the time frame, but in my approach to interrogating the geographical power/knowledge of the map itself and the sets of relationships that change in the contestation over space.

Mark Our Words: Maps and Decolonization

How do poetry and literature intervene in the colonial logics that continue to erase Native presence on the land and continue to accumulate Native land and bodies into the imaginative geographies of empire? A spatial analysis of the social and geopolitical imagining of the colonial nations of Canada, Mexico, and the United States is pivotal in answering these questions that make up a critique of settler nation-states. The works of Native women writers address the intersections of economic, social, political, and cultural institutions that are mapping out their surroundings and constituting their lived realities. Native women, however, have engaged a changing geopolitical field by narrating geographies that unsettle the heteropatriarchal institutional structures that use race and gender as tools to support settler colonialism. Just as the colonizer never left the Americas, neither did the Native people who continue to engage with land, nation, and community in their own tribally specific and gendered ways.

In the excerpt below from the poem "Mark My Words," Diane Schenandoah (Oneida, Wolf Clan) marks Native existence on the land, reclaiming it from "a wally world that would peddle clothes made by small / children in

some foreign country that truly reeked of / poverty." She begins by marking
the "cycles" of collective Native harvesting and care for land:

> as i walked past the storage pits thinking of all
> the hands that helped dig and fill this deep hole every
> harvest hoping it was enough to last the winter until
> spring would provide the necessary sustenance to continue
> the cycle of survival in a spiritual existence . . . i saw the
> bulldozer ready to erase the way of life that had been the
> only supermarket in town for centuries . . .[51]

Most importantly, Schenandoah maps a Haudenosaunee existence that pre-
dates "all the surrounding communities [who] will come to the grand opening of red white and blue balloons." As a contemporary Native woman writer,
Schenandoah uses "words" to (re)map sets of Native relationships to the land
and to those who seek to develop it without regard to human relationships.
She claims the land as Haudenosaunee, reflecting on the hands that worked
the earth through multiple generations, juxtaposing alongside and against the
United States or commercial entities' stake on the land that is as fleeting and
fragile as a balloon.

Across disciplines, Native American literature is often spoken about as
signifying Native relationship to the land. Interpretations of these spatial
moments in critical articles abound in discussions of Native American literary
production in both its oral and written forms. In academia, the relationship
between land and Native people is often evoked in discussions of histories, legalities, cultures, and the consequences of environmental destruction.
While there are books and articles that analyze specific cultural relationships
between specific tribal literature and tribal concepts of the land, most do not
engage the complex relationship between changing cultural practices of producing Native spaces and the pressure of colonization and the rise of nation-
states and capitalism. By thinking through critical geographies' assertions
that the nation-state uses nationalism to make place out of space, we can begin
to think of the power of cognitive maps produced through narrative. Peter
J. Taylor's work in particular is useful to an analysis of how colonial spatial
structuring depends on nation-states and their use of certain geographical
technologies such as maps, jurisdictions, education, community descriptions, and statistics to create "deeply felt emotions of place." Taylor addresses
the move in the nineteenth century, the point where this book begins, by

states to use affective narratives and mythologies to create allegiance to place. Yet as Taylor states, even twentieth-century politics of inclusion did not move regimes of spatial production, "becoming a national place made no difference to the fact that the state was fundamentally dis-enabling, a de-humanizer of places as a producer of spaces."[52] Certainly part of what Schenandoah's community is experiencing is the restructuring of space around dominant modes. Yet, Schenandoah's narrative destabilizes nation-state place-making by revealing the act of producing abstraction. She invokes the temporality and construction of the U.S. nation through the balloon colors "red," "white," and "blue," which make up the American flag and are symbolic of a deeply driven nationalism dependent on colonial erasure and the myth and practice of American exceptionalism.

Describing Native relationships to land is riddled with pitfalls and paradoxes, many of which are impossible to avoid given the nature of power and colonialism. I do not take the phrase "relationship to the land" as a given, unchanging, and naturalized part of Native American identities, especially as capitalism and colonization have produced new ways of experiencing time and space as exemplified above. On one hand, Native relationships to land are presumed and oversimplified as natural and even worse, romanticized. In this, the politics of maintaining and protecting tribal lands drop out of the conversation. Notions of the warrior on the plains, the medicine man communing with nature in solitude, or Iron Eyes Cody with one tear in his eye as he surveys the destructive world that capitalism produces, appeals to the realm of the emotional, rather than reflecting on the intellectual and critical work that Native people undertake to pass on these sets of relationships for generations and generations. Respecting the environment is not encoded in the DNA. In fact, tribes have experienced many travesties of justice in regard to environmental destruction.[53] We also have a tendency to abstract space—that is to decorporealitize, commodify, or bureaucratize—when the legal ramifications of land or the political landscape are addressed; too often we forget that reserve/ations, resource exploitation, federal Indian law, and urbanization are relatively new phenomena. The stories that connect Native people to the land and form their relationships to the land and one another are much older than colonial governments, such as conveyed in the poem above. Stories create the relationships that have made communities strong even through numerous atrocities and injustices.

Schenandoah's poem marks the transformation of human and land relationships from harvesting to a consumer society that unravels and abstracts those connections by reorganizing human relationships and geographies on a variety of scales. Schenandoah is from a community where women were the farmers, harvesters, and delegaters of the resources within their communities—the longhouse, the storage space referred to in the poem, was a substantial space used as a framework for community relationships. The changing distribution to an abstract producer of goods undermines these gender roles. The mediation between Native peoples and colonial entities throughout twentieth-century spatial restructuring has reframed and gendered our "relationship to the land." This book aims to think through the gendered colonial constructions of space and place in order to address regimes of power that have positioned Native women as insignificant. Maps reflect and constitute geographical imaginations defined by Derek Gregory "as sensitivity towards the significance of place, space, and landscape in the constitution and conduct of social life."[54] Native maps perform similar functions, as we see in the importance of marking the harvest pit and warning against desecration in the construction of a supermarket. If, according to Harley, "cartography remains a teleological discourse, reifying power, reinforcing the status quo, and freezing social interaction,"[55] then Native maps are writing against this traditional geographical grain. We need to complicate our conceptual maps in Native nation–building as they are necessary in defining new terrains that move away from an ordering of abstract nation-state space and the asymmetrical relationships they produce.

Remembering important connections to land and community is instrumental in mapping a decolonized Native presence. The poem is an example of making visible colonial and imperial maps and (re)mapping our relationships. Alternative conceptions of borders, nations, and place are subversive to the masculine project of empire building. American Indian women are seeking to (re)map first encounters and mediate ongoing spatial projects seeking to solidify nation and power relations by writing in the form of these alternative maps. While maps are often understood as "a drawing or other representation of the earth's surface or a part of it made on a flat surface, showing the distribution of physical or geographical features (and often also including socio-economic, political, agricultural, meteorological, etc., information), with each point in the representation corresponding to an actual geographical position according to a fixed scale or projection; a similar representation of the positions of stars in the sky, the surface of a planet, or the like Also: a plan of the form or layout of something, as a route, a building, etc.," according to the *Oxford English Dictionary*. I expand that notion to coincide with the strategies Native people used and developed to map space and how they are still present in our everyday lives.[56] Considering discourse as a type of mapping is crucial to understanding Native peoples' conceptions of space and their place in the world. In order to speak of the power relations involved in mapping space, it is important to reframe place-based discourse, which has tended toward ethnographic readings of local Native places, and instead look at these discourses as engaging with the forces that construct our understanding of space—whether it is at the scale of the Nation, a sacred site, or the body. Maps produce wider realities and gesture outward.

For instance, Schenandoah's description of the opening of a Kmart on Oneida land and a culturally marked area moves beyond the mere destruction of this important site as well as the political moment or event of the construction of a Kmart. The poetic imaginings address the fact that settler colonialism sets up a structure that undermines a way of life. In "Settler Colonialism and the Elimination of the Native," Patrick Wolfe positions settler colonialism as a continuous structure rather than an isolated historical event that "employs a wide-range of strategies of elimination that become favoured in particular historical circumstances."[57] Thus, the production of space, referring to landscapes that arise out of social practices and geographic forms of organization along the lines of gender, race, and class, are structured to maintain a sense of stable colonial histories and power.[58] In relation to settler colonialism imposing colonial geographies must be understood *as yet another method to eliminate or eradicate or absorb that which is Native.* If applied to geographies, we can come to understand the simultaneous unmarking of the area as Native land with a mapping of it as private corporate property as part of the geographic knowledge regimes. Early Native writers often wrote and pleaded with the public and the government about the effect of a newly mapped-out social order.[59] Current writers and contemporary Native communities continue to struggle with the legacy of U.S. land acquisition and the development of unstable colonial policies and their uneven implementation. Various forms of territory—from that of the body of the individual, to the tribal nation, to colonial nation-state—become contested in the struggle with competing concepts of social ordering. The implementation of colonial geographies into Native spaces are critical to address as "depending on the historical juncture, assimilation can be a more effective mode of elimination than conventional forms of killing, since it does not involve such a disruptive affront to the rule of law that is ideologically central to the cohesion of settler society."[60] Stealing land, or property, is unacceptable in a liberal democracy, but structuring Native lands as part of the abstract space of the nation eases public outcry. Native experiences are too often marginalized in the colonial processes, and the use of geographical power to limit or expand a territory is too often disguised as a simple, transparent process. Also is the way our minds are assimilated to believe our place, literally and figuratively, in the world.

Schenandoah's poem opens up the question of property as stable, calling for us to consciously assess our relationships to capitalism and the land. Her knowledge of the land stems from the mental maps of her community that Warhus speaks to above, maps that make possible different visions of the world. For Schenandoah, memory is mapped in the locale of the poem, recalling the importance of that place along with the sets of social, political, cultural, and economic relationships that comprise a community. Yet this place is not just closed off, nor is it just a Native issue or just a Haudenosaunee issue. This particular erasure of a way of life is deeply tied to economic exploitation in other global spaces. Schenandoah's marking of place connects exploitations of the nation-state to those structured beyond the borders it seeks to ideologically maintain, thus elucidating the connection between imperialism and colonialism: "the surrounding communities . . . throw their cigarette butts on the ground and / not give a second thought to the race that existed / just below their feet and not give a second / thought to the small hands that toiled over / their blue light special."[61] The disrespect, emphasized through the misuse of tobacco in the form of cigarettes and then abuse of the environment in the fact that the butts litter the ground versus tobacco's use in prayer, extends to disrespect for human life and the earth in the name of capitalism. While this poem reflects the local displacement of land, it also troubles the nation-state's transnational ties to exploitation, a point that will be further elaborated on in chapters 3 and 4.

What happens when you map out a place in the form of a poem that recalls its meaning to Oneida people, such as in "Mark My Words"? The words in the poem "mark" the place of harvest, recalling the stories tied to it, and remind the reader of the importance of place-based relationships. Like so many Native authors before, this Oneida woman (re)maps a relationship to land, community, and memory to defy imperial geographies of closure. The literary (re)mapping of land at the opening of a new Kmart unsettles the idea of blank space waiting to be transformed or *terra incognita*. She ends the poem by reminding us of our responsibilities, because "somewhere, somehow, / someway, there will be a time when we will be asked why." Throughout the twentieth century, Native women's writing has asked "why" as colonial spatial restructuring constructed borders, maps, places, and nations to displace Native people and possess water and land.[62] The poem "Mark My Words" not only protests the building on an important Haudenosaunee site, but its figurative map creates geographical imaginations that undermine the settler state and refuses to silence global exploitation. By deconstructing the ground of Kmart, and moving into a new space that accounts for a past and forewarns of a future that must be reconciled, Schenandoah and the Native American women in this book open a space where a new kind of spatial politics is possible.

DECOLONIZING SPATIAL RELATIONSHIPS

A spatial analysis of the social and geopolitical imagining of the colonial nations of Canada, Mexico, and the United States is pivotal in a critique of settler nation-states. The works of Native women writers address the intersections of economic, social, political, and cultural institutions that are mapping out their surroundings and constituting their lived realities. Native women, however, have engaged a changing geopolitical field by narrating geographies that unsettle the heteropatriarchal institutional structures that use race and gender as tools to support settler colonialism. Just as the colonizer never left the Americas, neither did the Native people who continue to engage with land, nation, and community in their own tribally specific and gendered ways.

As Native nations maneuver for power in the liberal nation-state, it is important not to be coerced by the power of abstracting land and bodies into territories and citizens. Henri Lefebvre's pivotal work warns about the roots of the abstract space of capitalism and the alienation of individuals from the everyday reality of living on, or with, the land: "As a product of violence and war, [abstract space] is political; instituted by a state, it is institutional. On first inspection it appears homogenous; and indeed it serves those forces which make a *tabula rasa* of whatever stand in their way, whatever threatens them—in short, of differences."[63] Native people in North America have not only been made a tabula rasa, but also have been incorporated into national discourses in often unrecognizable forms. Liberal discourses that arose along with a budding nation-state have recently recognized past wrongs and past Native presences on the land, and, at times, current issues as well. Yet these discourses, rather than serve Native people, become incorporated into settler myths. Land remains the territory of the settler nation, and the stories of its birth are celebrated; this occurs simultaneously with the recognition of Native peoples' loss of land, political control, and many relatives—all of which are conceived of as an unfortunate *national* past even though colonization is ongoing. Bolstered by ideas of progress, both moral and in terms of the nations coming into adulthood, time and space are mapped, as are the material realities of Native people whose few small land holdings and lives remain threatened.

Native space is delegated to exist outside national settler terrains, even while it is controlled and manipulated by settler governance. As Native bodies are constructed as abnormal and criminal, they, too, become spatialized. Natives occupy certain spaces of the nation and are criminalized or erased if they step outside what are seen as degenerative spaces. Colonialism is not just about conquering Native lands through mapping new ownerships, but it is also about the conquest of bodies, particularly women's bodies through sexual violence, and about recreating gendered relationships.[64] Thus, the making of Indian land into territory required a colonial restructuring of spaces at a variety of scales. Native bodies, as I speak to in relation to allotment in Joy Harjo's work, were conceived of as part of the flora and fauna. This animalization of Native bodies and subsequent codification of the doctrine of discovery during the 1830s that resulted in legalizing conquest and incorporating Native lands into the regimes of geographical knowledge produced by the state may not be apparent consciously, but they do order our reactions and relationships to those around us.

In *Human Territoriality,* Robert Sack, a foundational scholar in the field of human geography, denaturalizes territory by looking at its processes. It is not "biologically motivated . . . but rather . . . socially and geographically rooted."[65] Humans do not ally themselves naturally along nation-state borders or contain themselves within those borders. The narrations of national myths normalize colonial closures, but the many creation and migration stories of Native people attest to their presence. This "deeply spatialized" story of the settler states "installs Europeans as entitled to the land, a claim that is codified in law."[66] Sack uses the Anishinabeg band systems as an example of the social and geographic processes and sets out to discuss conceptions of the "modern" versus "premodern." Imposing European concepts of territory was a strategy of control and a method of creating empty space. While I appreciate this intervention, Sack detracts from his argument by not considering the storied relationships to the land that intricately tied together what Sack perceived of as "minimally territorial" bands. The power contained in stories of the Manitous, for instance, exert a control and regulation of human relationships to one another and the land beyond that of law and continue to do so.[67] The Native literature I discuss does not portray land as blank, fixed, and linear in time, nor is it aligned mystically to Native people. Stories teach us how to care for and respect one another and the land. Responsibility, respect, and places created through tribal stories have endured longer than the Western fences that outlined settler territories and individual properties that continue to change hands.

Territory is not a simple artifact, impenetrable in the wave of economic and political power, but rather is constitutive of cultural, political, and economical practices. By recognizing the historic processes of enframing space and its corresponding cyclical turns and layering, the tangled threads produced in the claiming of Native lands and erasure of bodies begin to unravel.[68] Walter Mignolo's definition of territoriality "as the site of interaction of languages and memories in constructing places and defining identities" speaks to the way Native stories create a literary map.[69] Like Mignolo, I argue that territoriality develops not only through geographic place but also through time. The process of making territory extends beyond legal court systems that set in place political authority and borders, and relies on narrations and mythmaking. By proposing to examine the historical engagement among Native nations and the United States, Canada, and Mexico as it concerns the various overlapping, contested, and agreed upon concepts of geography, I am proposing that we need to see *through* the concept of territory and understand the processes and concept as a social product. Native literature provides a mechanism to see the limits of territory, as it is legally interpreted from original treaties, and give sustenance to Native people's relationship to the land. The scales of the interpersonal to the international in the texts I have chosen reflect a wide array of possibilities for political and social movements in Indian Country.

I am advocating that we take into account territories narrated through stories—both contemporary and those, much, much older—that interrogate and complicate state-bounded territory by examining the social orders expressed and denied in its representations. As one aboriginal scholar concludes about the possibilities of reconceiving territory for both Native and non-Native sums up: "Is aboriginal sovereignty to be feared by Australia in the same way as Aboriginal people fear white sovereignty and its patriarchal model of the state—one which is backed by power or force? Or is aboriginal sovereignty different . . . for there is not just one sovereign state body but hundreds of different sovereign aboriginal peoples. Aboriginal sovereignty is different from state sovereignty because it embraces diversity, and focuses on inclusivity rather than exclusivity."[70] A spatial and literary analysis of settler colonial nations as examined in Native women's literary maps will put some teeth into Native political and social movements by exposing spatial practices that construct and maintain a white settler society.

Conceiving of land through narrative process, however, is not unique to Native people. Property law, European concepts of environment, and concepts of Nation all rely on tales to lend meaning to nature and ordered space. It is for this reason that James Scott opens with lines from the epic of Gilgamesh to talk of the "tunnel vision" of a "fiscal lens" by which the early modern state viewed its forest as revenue and created a "vocabulary used to organize nature . . . focusing on those aspects of nature that can be appropriated for human use."[71] Colonial ideologies make truth claims and attempt to empty Native people's relationship to land and place through naturalizing of the relationship of people to land and naturalizing the conquest of both.

J. B. Harley and Denis Wood explore mapmaking cultures' obsession with terra incognita, particularly as it is narrated and represented in Joseph Conrad's *Heart of Darkness*. Terra incognita, a concept of blank space in European thought, disavows Natives' socio-relationship with land and the communities that spring forth from this relationship. Blank spaces not only "stir the geographical imagination," but provide the means of "opening up" new territories: "But [a passage from Conrad] demonstrates the map's double function in colonialism of both opening and later closing a territory," Wood notes, and continues on to "argue that Conrad's thirst for blank spaces on the map—like that of other writers—is also a symptom of a deeply ingrained colonial mentality that was already entrenched in seventeenth-century New England. In this view the world is full of empty spaces ready for taken by Englishmen."[72] Maps in this case also provide the narrative backbone of conquest. In this narrative of conquest, maps have affirmed "the truth" of territories. The "closure" of blank spaces or mapping of territories is a strategy to limit Native legal rights, ownership of land, and tribal imaginations. It is a means of transfiguring Native land into colonial territories in the socio-imaginary. As those imagined territories become liberal nation-states, the mythic narratives of exploration and heroic achievement remain part of the national terrain. Inclusiveness of a Native past becomes celebrated under multiculturalism, yet, as my work with the authors in this project demonstrates, the national space does not become imagined as Native space. If anything multicultural narratives serve to undermine the Native subject, and her land becomes abstracted and incorporated in the national polity.[73] And, as Andrea Smith demonstrates by showing patterns of interpersonal and state violence in her important treatise *Conquest: Sexual Violence and American Indian Genocide,* gender violence functions as a tool for conquest.[74] Conquest of land required a conquest of Native bodies both in its physical manifestation and in in the mental maps produced.

By examining the writing of Native women, I unmoor settling narratives used to dislocate Native people and address concepts that extend from land that move us beyond simplistic and naturalized notions of "Indians" that began with contact. National mythmaking is key to the organization of space: it determines who belongs and does not belong. White settler societies' disavowal, erasure, and enslavement of labor are necessary to the project of the state and rely on the mapping of bodies into abstract national terrains. Bodies are organized, categorized, surveilled, and made readable to the state by mapping national and non-national spaces and appointing the appropriate bodies in those spaces. In the case of many Native people, this has supported genocide, containment on the reservation, or imprisonment in controlled spaces such as boarding schools or prisons. This colonial spatial construction is not unidirectional, and Native people have mediated these spatial constructions with the best tools at their disposal—storytelling, writing, and sense of place. When passing the Kmart that now stands on top of "storage pits," the poem is recalled, Native presence remembered, and experiences shared.

In simplifying the relationship to land as purely political or as evidence of governmental control, stories are understood in particular ways and bound into court cases and territorial claiming, tending to lose the sets of social relations regularly laid out in their structures. Stories keep us together—not court systems—and it is time we listen, as Schenandoah reasons, to answer our questions "why." Why do the dissolution, erasure, and denial of Native spaces continue even though there is recognition of a violent and torrid past? How are we caring for land and each other? What are the moral geographies we have come to in the twenty-first century? How do the stories that bear witness in many forms and map our intimate and social geographies guide us in the past, present, and toward a healthier future? These are question that guide me throughout as I examine gendered patterns of twentieth-century spatial production in settler states.

My project attempts to move away from concepts of pure and unconnected Native spaces and acknowledges colonialism in its past, present, and even contradictory forms. The process of spatial restructuring is continual and substantiated through a variety of mechanisms such as force, laws, and ideology, and often these are not in agreement with one another, but nonetheless support domination and settlement. In (re)mapping Native lands and bodies in the twentieth century, my main goal is to ask the "why" so that Native nations will rethink spatializing and organizing our communities around the heteropatriarchal structure of the nation-state model. By replicating abstract space in Native nation-building, Native communities move away from imagining new possibilities beyond that mapped out for Native people in settler societies. Like Schenandoah, I want us to understand what is at stake, so that we can make the best decisions in our communities.

From a young age, many Native people are taught where revered points in the landscape are located, some are taught the stories that accompany the landscape, and many forge sets of relationship entwined in the responsibilities that come with this knowledge that belongs to past, present, and future generations. Unfortunately, the spatial violence inflicted on generations of Native peoples has also led to a disruption of this grounding knowledge, whether it occurs through environmental destruction, incorporation into capitalism, language eradication, displacement from lands, and a myriad of other disciplining geographic structures. Native stories speak to a storied land and storied peoples, connecting generations to particular locales and in a web of relationships. By exploring the narrative mapping of land, nation, community, and bodies in the works of twentieth-century Native women authors, I link the reconceptualization of Native land from the beginning of North American nation-building to current struggles with the settler state that continues to undermine the power of Native nations, Native women, and community relationships.

The pitfalls of simplifying Native peoples' relationship to land into romanticized and mystical or merely political categories are that these studies too often overlook the gendered and violent nature of colonizing Native lands, and in this book it is my intention to complicate the narrative maps constructed in the twentieth century and to intervene in the harsh realities of spatial violence that continue to produce colonial logics. These chapters bring into focus the importance of literature in enabling a (re)conceptualization of static assumptions of "Indian," borders, and gender. How do these women actively engage in the movement for representational, intellectual, and political sovereignty? "Sovereignty, community, and the vitality and power of a tradition that is constantly *evolving* are fundamental categories for the Laguna author,"[75] says Weaver, but I would also apply this statement to Belin, Harjo, and Johnson. In their fictional work, these women not only reflect at times their lived realities but they also conceptualize race and gender as evolving, and this is the key to understanding their power to disentangle Western geographical power/knowledge regimes.

As more Native people become mobile, reserve/ation land bases become overcrowded, and the state seeks to enforce means of containment, it is imperative to refocus Native nation–building efforts beyond settler models of territory, jurisdiction, borders, and race. Recent attempts at land acquisition by the Oneida, Narragansett, and Pequot are instances of the reversal of the colonial project of spatial dominance, but these have been met with much resistance by the state and its citizens who fear dispossession of "individual property." Other nations, such as the Cherokee and Menominee, hold elections in urban areas where large portions of their population reside off-reservation. Still, even others are creating maps in their own languages and with knowledge from the elders as a tool for land claims, environmental activism, fighting large corporations, and teaching the next generations. The Nunavut mapping project is exemplary of a decolonial project with immense potential.[76] This reimagining of what constitutes Native space is important to antiviolence projects. As I document and explore Native women's writing and challenge Western forms of "narratives and maps [which] become violent when literalised, [and] mapped directly onto real people and places,"[77] I continually ask how rigid spatial categories, such as nations, borders, reservations, and urban areas, are formed by settler nation-states structuring of space.

While I study contemporary Native American literature and not stories from time immemorial (which is the case with many scholars who have looked in depth at the relationship of Native people and land), its tendency in a single breath or word to recall hundreds, even thousands of years back by employing community, personal, and historical stories in intertextual moments allows us to see these sets of relationships outside the mapping of the state. It allows us to see that the map is an open one and the ideological and material relationships it produces are still in process.[78] The breadth of scale in terms of time, geography, and worldviews provokes a deep reflection on the landscape, and its meanings to Native people beyond the mere political or assumed corollary of Indian is to nature or land is to territory or resource. It comes down to power. In (re)mapping, we as Native people hold the power to rethink the way we engage with territory, with our relationships to one another, and with other Native nations and settler nations. And it is our stories that will lead the way as they have for generations. Native stories extend beyond a beautiful aesthetic and simple moral or fable. These connections are powerful in the struggle against colonialism and empire building—yet they are fragile and need tending. I venture that these stories in their contemporary forms are that tending and will continue to map our future. Mark my words, these imaginative geographies will open up new possibilities and inaugurate new and vital meanings.

1

"Remember What You Are": Gendering Citizenship, the Indian Act, and (Re)mapping the Settler Nation-State

EARLY DEBATES AROUND THE STATUTES OF THE CANADIAN CON-federation's Indian Act coincide with the height of Mohawk writer E. Pauline Johnson's (1861–1913) literary career. Johnson was born into an intricate matrix of emerging borders. Along racial lines, she was born into her father's aristocratic Mohawk family and her mother's well-to-do upper-class English background; she was born between an era of developing Canadian colonies and a Canada that was forming a commonwealth ruled by those of English background; she was born a woman of the Iroquois Confederacy that for centuries recognized a woman's power of autonomy and women's central-ity to its government, culture, and future. At the same time, she was pressured to conform to European concepts of a fragile, weak woman, no more than the property of her husband or father (and even these European gender norms were beginning to change). The geopolitics and biopolitics of Northeast Canada, the seat of the burgeoning Nation itself, were in flux. The colonial powers of England, France, and the United States sought to empty the spaces inhabited and governed over for centuries by the Haudenosaunee (Iroquois) Confederacy and carve out colonial spaces in the place of Native histories and bodies. The matrix that composed Johnson's world and identity was compli-cated, unstable, and filled with possibilities.

The fighting during Johnson's time turned from military wars to a war of words in the form of legislation filtered through the newly formed bureau-cracy of the rising nation-state. The state's force through this legislation con-tinued to perform brute material force in the lives of Native peoples. The

Indian Act reflects the contradictions and paradoxes of colonialism as the settler state tries to solidify itself as a nation and mold a particular citizenship in which a "person [is] an individual other than an Indian"[1] and Indian is defined as a decidedly male-centric category. Throughout Johnson's life the Indian Act would be amended many times, recoding settler colonial and Native relationships into specific spatialized power relations. Simultaneous with the erosion of women's rights in their Native communities, particularly after an 1876 amendment, Indian status and the rights that attended such status would be based on patrilineality. The Canadian settler government was processing the incorporation of those areas not yet "Indian Lands" (or land under the Crown) long before the commissioning of surveys and long before any Native relinquishment of land.[2] Haudenosaunee opposition to the "denaturalizing" of women community members did not pass without public objection. In 1872 Grand River Mohawk Oronhyatekha (Peter Martian) petitioned to strike this section from the Indian Act,[3] and even though he was a powerful figure in Victorian Canada, he was not successful. Johnson's awareness of Haudenosaunee disagreement with the act, particularly the unjust gendered element, provides the backdrop for many aspects of her stories. The amending of this act throughout this period and subsequent generations would increasingly limit definitions of who was Indian, and thus limit access to land and other rights negotiated in the coerced settlement of Canada. Other major amendments to the act would constantly redefine Indian land and its boundaries, commission or authorize surveys on land "not surrendered to the Crown," and define the perimeters of settling and governing Native lands and peoples.

The increasing interpretation and reinterpretation of colonial law pivoted around gendered heteronormative relationships in which the raced, colonized, and gendered body of the Native woman would become a dangerous battleground. In "The Empire of Love," Elizabeth Povinelli states, "If you want to locate the hegemonic home of liberal logics and aspirations, look to love in settler colonies."[4] This is certainly true in Canada, where much of the governing of Native people centered on redefining traditional kinship customs to that of marriage and defining "good moral character" of Native women.[5] As the juxtaposition of the law and Johnson's literary imagining of the betrayed Native women attests, settler colonialism presented many obstacles to maintaining personhood, intersecting identities, kinship relations, and land.

The liberal logics and aspirations of settler colonies in the early moments of the Canadian Confederacy, specifically as they are expressed in the Indian

Act and foment in two late-1800s short "tragic" love stories, are a fruitful ground to expose the contours of settler maps and Native bodies. Christie and Esther, the women protagonists who fall in love with the "new" men of Canada, present a historical lens into Native women's positions at a time when Canada was formulating itself as a nation-state. The Indian Act produces discourses, ones taken up and explored by Johnson, around love, marriage, and belonging, that continue to have material consequences that have lasted for generations. In many ways, it is the limiting of possibilities for Native women through the intersections of structural, political, and representational social fields that founded and continue to support the settler state of Canada. In the state's early geographical imaginings of the Canadian nation-state, the politics and governance of love, marriage, and Native women's bodies set up normative spaces of the Nation and sought to naturalize the dispossession of Native people.

The legal discourse, wrapped in intimate relationships, was both produced and productive of the gendered processes of settler colonialism that would be in the place for years to come. Johnson's work provides a platform for questioning colonial discourses of race and gender and the liberal logics of heteronormative coupling at its foundation. It is necessary as the ongoing mapping of the nation-state depicted in Johnson's stories continues. Johnson's work very much foreshadows the consequences of legal acts on Native women's dispossession through the institution of marriage and processes of racialization, while seeking to mediate the impact of colonial settlement. Johnson's Esther ends her confessional story with: "They account for it by the fact that I am a Redskin. They seem to have forgotten I am a woman," and in doing so the protagonist reminds us all to consider the strength of the personhood of Native women and the contradictions upon which the settlement of Canada rests.[6]

As an avid reader, popular figure, and intrepid traveler, Johnson's prolific writings and mass exposure give us a glimpse into the intricate negotiations of race, gender, and nation at the turn of the century. Native people were no longer needed for trade, access to resources, or survival of the settlers—instead the question turned to figuring out Native people's position and dispossession in the newly forming nation. This figuring and mapping of land and bodies into the nation-state took a particularly gendered form. Writing across the turn of the century, a time noted for its "inevitable" dispelling of the "savage" Indian at the frontier through forced assimilation and genocide, Johnson took up the pen to advocate for Native/women's rights in their newly founded Canadian dominion. I in no way mean to imply that there is a time when race and gender constructions are not in flux and changing; rather, I emphasize that in Johnson's historical moment, the incorporation of race and gender into the nation was forthright and foundational work. At a time when instituted European government policies were attempting to construct Native women in the image of European contemporaries or exile and expunge them from the nation's "proper" territory, Johnson advocated for what was commonly understood as women's rights or women's autonomy and sovereignty and often invoked sentimental discourses to rationalize the inclusion of Native women as part of the nation. In this constantly shifting context, it is not surprising that Johnson often fluctuates in terms of her politics and beliefs, but what she provides us are complicated glimpses into what is too often disciplined into neat "historic" packages.

Johnson's sentimental rhetoric, filled with affect, fit well into the discourses of liberalism that center around the individual and property. Johnson's fiction doesn't directly refer to the Indian Act, but it certainly haunts the political and social landscape of her stories, just as it continues to haunt Canada's continued First Nation and aboriginal policies. Christie and Esther were not forced to marry or to attend school, which would effectively remove them from their communities; their fathers did not force the situation and both possessed autonomy as individuals. They chose their paths as individual, "free" liberal subjects. Yet, what Johnson's work provides is a glimpse into the structures that question the liberal logics around these "choices." What becomes apparent in Johnson's stories are the shortcomings of liberal discourses in terms of achieving gender equity and rights for Native nations and people.

By basing many of her platforms on her experiences as a Native woman, Johnson craftily argues for women's rights and racial justice in her formal and fictional appeals to the newly forming state. In her stories, Johnson often embraces the liberal nation-state, and her characters struggle in the transformation from colonized to racialized subjects seeking the same rights as white male settlers. Six Nations literary scholar Rick Monture rightly criticizes Johnson's rights-based arguments as antithetical to Haudenosaunee understanding of sovereignty and relationship to land and Canada.[7] Johnson is an incredibly complex character in terms of her stance on politics—British loyalist, Canadian feminist, or Mohawk nationalist. Johnson's political agenda is less of my concern and may never be known; instead, I find she presents an interesting foray into a moment of defining bodies, territories, and nations. Joanne Barker clarifies in her work the ongoing conflict between a gender politics of rights-based activism and Native political rights, even in the contemporary reform of the Indian Act's patrilineal amendments: "The forced absorption of Indian women's experiences, perspectives, and agendas into the interests of Status Indian men is exactly why the discourses of rights mobilized by Indian women, band governments, and Indian organizations during the 1983 and 1985 amendments articulated such conflicting notions of gender and sovereignty."[8] This was also true years earlier. As Johnson ventured into the new terrain of a geopolitical system based on the spatialized practices of gender, race, and class inequities, she argues for Native peoples to be included into the national terrain and for women to be taken seriously in public life.

The following readings of Johnson's two stories, "A Red Girl's Reasoning" (1893) and "As It Was in the Beginning" (1899), provide a text from which to contend with the formation of settler space. This approach to Johnson's fictional work is discursive; her literary work provides historical and literary documents that enable us not only to look at the representation of a context of spatial relations, but also to provide an analytical mode to examine what meanings and possibilities were on the table during her time. These literary works lay bare the organization of space through institutional practices, particularly those naturalized and claimed as individual choices—such as love and marriage. The Canadian and U.S. nation-states' obligation to respect the Six Nations in Canada and the United States as separate and autonomous nations would be eroded though the autological (a belief in individual rights) and genealogical (biological determinacy) discourses that inform the many phases of the Indian Act. In her literature, Johnson proposes an alternative to erosion of Native nations and peoples. Both love and marriage are discourses that partake in the ideology of "freedom producing subjects and institutions" in the late nineteenth and early twentieth centuries.[9] Johnson's use of coupling tropes, however, also provides us a way to think through the way colonial relationships are mapped onto bodies through legal constructs that are both produced and productive of spatial and social relations within the state. Ideological worldviews are exposed and engaged by (re)mapping the foundation of settler-colonies' relationships with Native people through a careful examination of the liberal logics in the romantic coupling. As Povinelli questions, "If the intimate couple is a key transfer point within liberalism," which operates around the autonomous subject and supports settler colonialism, "this couple is already conditioned by liberalism's emergence and dispersion in empire."[10] A reading of the Canadian Indian Act as it structures the politics of inheritance in interracial coupling against the imaginative realms in Johnson's fiction exposes the spatial philosophies that lay at the core of settler logics and unveils its implementation of a politics of scale that range from the body to the larger nation-state.

Johnson's work continually takes up the intimate couple, the removal and dispossession of Native people, the mapping of the Canadian Confederation into a settler "we" population under settler rule, and the foundations of imperial expansion. By interrogating the foundation of these intimate discourses, we are able to displace the logics of the geopolitical empire embedded and compelled through legal policies such as the Indian Act. As such, I will continue with a brief discussion of this act, its relationship to the construction of citizenship, and the patriarchal foundations of the nation-state at its core.

Gender, Dispossession, and the Indian Act

The Enfranchisement Act of 1869 and the Indian Act of 1868 were written when E. Pauline Johnson was coming of age—a time when love and romance were to lead to marriage. The codification of marriage at the time of the budding nation-state was fused with citizenship and race. Feminists have long argued that marriage is a form of property acquisition and essential to establishing the state, but rarely have they taken up its relationship to settler colonialism.[11] Marriage during the early years of the Canadian Confederation was instrumental in implementing a citizenship already envisioned as stemming from the stock of northern Europeans. The early stages of the Indian Act were devoted to defining who was a Status Indian and who was a Non-Status Indian, land surveys, and colonial governance of Native territories. In other words, legislation in the act was mainly devoted to defining property, especially if we conclude that whiteness is a form of property.[12]

The Indian Act was to apply to all Indians under the Crown, and the act was later transferred to the state of Canada. It contained many harmful elements that would restrict Native peoples' autonomy over their lands, political systems, communities, and individual actions. Nevertheless, it is important to note that at no time during the hammering out of the Canadian Confederate Constitution were Native people included in the discussion to determine Indian identity or the organization of their communities. The language of the Indian Act read as follows:

"'person' means an individual other than an Indian" and "'Indian' means (*i*) any male person of Indian blood reputed to belong to a particular band;

(*ii*) any child of such person; (*iii*) any woman who is or was lawfully married to such a person."[13]

The gender norms portrayed through the language were based on Euro-American Victorian concepts of the intimate and public/private split. As a Mohawk woman from an aristocratic family, on both her First Nations and European settler sides, Johnson could not help but understand the material effects of land loss and dispossession in the Indian Act and what it meant for her future, the future of Canada, and the future of Indigenous nations.

Christian settler states ignored Native nations' status and racialized Native populations. Defining "Indian" in a settler colonial society is pivotal to marking and naturalizing settler citizenship. Bonita Lawrence contends, "The object of the brutal 'science' of classification and control must not be lost in the details of the horror it enacted. Nor should we separate the brutality of how identity legislation was implemented in the United States with how centrally it has shaped colonization process in Canada."[14] Identity, based on scientific racism, arose in the wake of settler colonialism as a method of denying individuals' access to their nation. "Through such classification," continues Lawrence, "the citizens of subordinated Indigenous nations were not only legally dismembered from their identities and recast as 'Indians,' as part of the process of taking their lands, but in the process they were to be dismembered from their pasts and therefore their futures."[15] Marriage as an apparatus to define one's status, but not to reconfigure one's race, becomes pivotal in the discussion of settler mapping of space. This politically intimate formation upheld the concept of "Indian Lands" and the confederation's control of it.

While the colonial empires started keeping track of band memberships in the 1850s, it was the Constitution Act that coincided with land transfer from the Crown to Canada that Status and Non-Status Indians were registered and under the control and distinct scrutiny of the superintendent general of Indian Affairs. Indian agents, as an arm of the state, were also given the power to declare who had access as Status Indians and who didn't as Non-Status Indians. In 1876, the Indian Act introduced the provision that "any Indian woman marrying any other than an Indian or a non-treaty-Indian shall cease to be an Indian in any respect within the meaning of this Act." Within this act, Native women's bodies and sexual practices and Crown lands become literally mapped through edicts of scrutinizing marriages, designating children as "illegitimate," and declaring the lack of morality of Native women, and through issuing surveys based on Lockean fantasies. The Indian Act states:

The Superintendent General may authorize surveys, plans, and reports to be made of any reserve for Indians, showing and distinguishing the improved lands, the forests and lands fit for settlement, and such other information as may be required; and may authorize that the whole or any portion of a reserve be subdivided into lots. . . .

The Superintendent General shall be the sole and final judge as to the moral character of the widow of any intestate Indian.[16]

Although Native women through marriage with a white man were declared Non-Status Indians, they were still subjected to the laws of the Indian Act and often found themselves in racist, exploitive, and violent social spaces.[17] Gender classification as demarcated in the Indian Act provides a base to examine Johnson's Native heroines who were seeking agency as subjects of empire.

The Indian Act, according to colonial logics, was largely put in place to "protect" Native people from corruption and theft by encroaching settlers. Native women who married white men, according to the logics of the state and the logics of property, did not need Indian status as they were understood to be protected by state-sanctioned marriage and "would acquire property rights under Canadian law through their non-Indian spouse."[18] The presumptuous *guarantee* of property through whiteness was common in nineteenth-century settler nations and led state legislation to codify settlers' heightened race consciousness around whiteness as property.[19] Native women could not possess whiteness, however, as "only whites possessed whiteness, a highly valued and exclusive form of property."[20] The act did not maintain that "any Indian women marrying any other than an Indian or a non-treaty Indian" would become white, but rather that she would "cease to be an Indian in any respect within the meaning of the Act."[21] She would not have the rights to band memberships, which were First Nation rights, but would instead remain an abject citizen of the state. Male ownership and restrictive inheritance laws further hindered and promulgated Native women's dispossession. The Indian Act and its many amendments were continually changed throughout the time Johnson was writing, but the intent remained the same: a Native woman was "to sever her connections wholly with the reserve and the Indian mode of life," according to Deputy Superintendent General Duncan Campbell Scott, "in the interest of the Department [of Indian Affairs]."[22]

Furthermore, Native women were also immediately enfranchised and made citizens of the state of Canada. Attaining the right to vote or full citizenship was to be divested of one's Indigenous rights, community, and status. If married to a Native man who was voluntarily or involuntarily enfranchised (men who attained an education, for example, were enfranchised unwillingly), a Native woman would follow the citizenship status of her husband. A Native woman's rights to land and community were increasingly jeopardized, as these rights were in effect tied to the contract of marriage. Lawrence relates how these legal methods of control worked on the reserves in Canada: "On a daily basis, enfranchisement proved a formidable opportunity for Indian agents to control resistance in Native communities, by pushing for enfranchisement (and thereby removal from their communities) of anybody empowered by education or a secure income."[23] Under the purview of the man of the household, Native women lost all Status Indian rights by seemingly becoming full citizens of the state. These colonial gender logics were meant, as stated by the first prime minister of Canada, Sir John Macdonald, "to do away with the tribal system and assimilate the Indian people in all respects with the inhabitants of the domain."[24] Kinship and community ties were legally dismissed in these patriarchal laws, and there were no provisions made for land ownership for those women stripped of their community status. Gender, citizenship, and marriage were triangulated to unravel complex Native communities, and in doing so, deplete their land bases as their membership rolls were reduced; in its place, the map of Canada and its "Northern" citizens would spread from coast to coast, mirroring and mutually supporting U.S. manifest destiny.

In these moments of defining Status and Non-Status Indians, legislators used the Indian Act in its numerous reiterations to map imagined Native space, reserves, and non-Native space, and the rest of the land. These settling geographies mapped Native bodies into and out of the land. Through the process of mapping Canada, the government assumed a "knowledge" that was objective and pictured its version of truth. The map of Canada (and many settler states) is a cultural text purporting only certain symbolic knowledge that depends upon the exclusion of Native "others." As I have discussed elsewhere, the abstraction of land into jurisdictionally controlled polities disrupted relations to the land and community.[25] The cultural and literal space of the nation was defined through legislative acts and assigned identities ordered in racial hierarchies. The civilized spaces, or those represented as inhabited by white populations and under settler law, were the "proper" spaces of the Canadian nation inhabited by "proper" bodies. First Nation and aboriginal reserves were to be extinguished in time and made property of individual citizens whose allegiance was to the state and not to their kinspeople and communities. In fact, inheritance laws and property coalesced around the

authority of the superintendent general, who had authority over classifications of land and deterioration of Indians' status. The intercontinental map of
Canada was to expand and devour Native lands and bodies.

Johnson foresaw the mapping of Canada from coast to coast, and indeed,
she often looked at it as a remarkable time in Canadian history. Yet she also
emphasized that Canada must acknowledge Native presence on the land.
Through the settings in her short stories and poems, Johnson delineates
these proper spaces of church, city, and domestic "white" homes as separate
from the outskirts, prairies, teepees, lumber towns, crude log structures, and
traders' stores. Johnson's plots are driven by the conflict created when the des-
ignation of spaces unravels in the presence of a respectful and self-possessed
Native woman who refuses to acquiesce to settler law—or to her husband.

Johnson profoundly ties up her geographical imagining of Canada with
recognition of negotiations of power that Canada entered into from the start
of its origins. In one of her most famous poems, which she writes for the
purpose of celebrating Brantford's erection of the statue of the British loyalist
Joseph Brant, she tries to alleviate the building tensions between Six Nations
and Brantford's white citizens who looked longingly at Haudenosaunee land.[26]

> So Canada, thy plumes were hardly won
> Without allegiance from thy Indian Son,
> Thy glories, like the cloud enhance their charm
> With red reflections from the Mohawk's arm.[27]

Phrasing the bond between Canada and Native people as a brotherhood
directly implicates a political and deeply bound relationship. At a time when
the rhetoric of contractualism was deeply rooted in an idea of the nuclear
family and formation of Nations among the "brotherhood" of colonies, Johnson utilizes the language of the state to create a terrain whereby the presence
of the Native is necessary to its conception of self. Brotherhood establishes a
specific relationship of nation to nation in the Canadian Confederation's relationship to Native people, particularly in its obligation to the Haudenosaunee
Confederacy as laid out in the Guswenta (Two-Row wampum), a pact made
in 1613 that forms the basis for all subsequent relationships with European
and North American states. Johnson's writings and stances were often problematic, as Monture points out, because unlike "the majority of Iroquois during her time [who] preferred to uphold the Two-Row wampum philosophy
that maintained the idea of an autonomous nation, Johnson clearly attempted

to promote a new kind of relationship with Canada in her work."[28] Perhaps her push toward inclusion and mutual respect as equal citizens was the only possible outcome she felt she could influence.

Johnson was deeply concerned with the haunting of the Native if the Canadian Confederation did not recognize the territory defined by "her Indian graves and Indian memories" and focused her literary mapping on "her larger project of attempting to incorporate the Iroquois into a national, and physical, space."[29] She aimed to educate settlers by articulating a Canadian national landscape that was infused with the deep cultural history of both Natives and the English—a landscape of liberal possibilities. For Johnson, the connection between a national Canada and its colonial past must be reconciled geographically and temporally. Liberal thought espoused diversity and celebrated a coming together of European differences to create settler subjectivity. In many ways, despite her experience, Johnson believed that liberalism would or could be accompanied by respect for Native nations.

Years later, we see that Johnson's dreams of respect for Native peoples and their political rights are deferred; the failure of a liberal government to treat Native people as equal citizens and uphold its nation-to-nation obligations has had devastating consequences. One need only look at the shocking statistics on reserves and of those Non-Status Indians who live in urban areas to understand how past policies continue to affect Native people in the present. One needs only to trace the origins of wealth in Canada and the United States to understand the material losses for Native peoples and the gains of settlers. Even in this failure, however, Johnson's vision of social and geopolitical space as it engaged contemporary politics raises provocative questions. Johnson's short stories unsettle the presumptuous settler mapping of national spaces at the very moment when the incorporation of the Native into these national liberal discourses fail. By forming heroines who upset the liberal rationale and settler claiming of land and bodies, Johnson provides an avenue to examine the gendered elements of conquest.

Fantasized and State-Implemented Native Spaces

"A Red Girl's Reasoning," first published in *The Domain Illustrated* in 1893, and "As It Was in the Beginning," first published in *Saturday Night* (1899), start the (re)mapping of space by situating their stories and the beginnings of their relationships in places conceived of as uncivilized or Native. Our initial meeting of the characters in Johnson's stories occurs in the Native women's communities or those places that are deemed "lawless," "uncivilized" frontier posts. In a majority of her short stories, it is the love interest, or settler colonial suitor of some sort, who first enters foreign territory to remove the girl to "civilization." In "A Red Girl's Reasoning" we first meet our Mohawk heroine Christie at the edge of her community, at her father's trading post. Christie is to marry Charlie McDonald, a young white archeologist from a wealthy family in the city. The romantic coupling is also set up as a foreshadowing of the conflict that will occur in the metropole as Christie tries to adapt to "civilized" life and the uncivilized behavior of colonial elites. Similarly, in "As It Was in the Beginning," Esther is the young Cree protagonist whom we first meet in her father's tipi. Rather than a romantic interest, however, Father Paul comes to the village and wrests away Esther, who is lured by adventure. Eventually, after growing into a young lady at the mission, Esther falls in love. It is in the romantic coupling between Esther and Laurence, Father Paul's nephew, that conflict ensues. While the couple was allowed plenty of interaction in their childhood, it is through the very act of marriage proposal that the conflict again occurs in this short story. Assimilation of Indians into a national polity was deemed a natural progression, even as the newly anointed political leaders of Canada went to work making legislation to ensure that their vision of a white Canada would come to fruition. Johnson's stories demonstrate the rough terrains of assimilation ideologies. For Father Paul, assimilation of Esther and subsequently her family was inevitable, but her marriage to the colonial elite or an attainment of equal status to his white progeny was never to be. Johnson's narrative mapping of space tells much of the story of the misrecognition of settlers in this moment. Unable to see past European conceptions, the colonial elites portrayed as Charlie McDonald, Father Paul, and Laurence do not quite understand the autonomy of the Native woman with whom he is entering into a relationship—nor does he need to. It is this misrecognition and abuse of power that Johnson addresses in her narratives.

The starting point of the coupled relationship is indispensable to the "imagined rugged independence and self-reliance of the European settlers" understood in national mythologies "to give birth to a greater commitment to liberty and democracy."[30] Johnson plays with the national memory by evoking her primary Anglo audiences' own imagined and projected geographies. The opening of "A Red Girl's Reasoning" addresses this specifically by not beginning with Christie, the mixed-race female protagonist, as the title of the story might imply. I contend here that Johnson's delineation of this first conversation is a parody meant to directly engage the arrogance of white men who presume to "know" Indians. When Native people are left out of the conversation, as they were in the development of the Indian Act, no matter how intimate the relationship between Native and settler, misunderstandings and tragedy prevail.

Johnson foregrounds the historical structuring of race, settler–Native interactions, and gender relations in a third-person parody of a conversation between Christie's French father Jimmy Robinson, the old Hudson Bay trader, and Charlie McDonald, who arrives in the Mohawk territory as part of an assignment for the Department of Agriculture. The familiar depiction of this "outpost" surfaces, yet soon deteriorates as Native perceptions of space appear. The scene takes place on the outskirts of "civilization," in the "remote" area of the trading post. The trading post, or companies such as the Hudson Bay, were pivotal to "civilizing" spaces of the frontier and were known for rugged individualism and making way for "a new man." Through capitalism, the settler progresses and claims settler-nativism through these earlier sets of relationships exemplified in the coupling of Old Robinson and Christie's mother. These "country marriages" were pivotal in ensuring allegiances, trade, and wealth accumulation. Missionaries' visits of the sort that open the second story I discuss were instrumental in civilizing Native space and claiming it for the Christian nation. Native women's voices have been subsumed in settler discourse even though it is often recognized that the relationships between early settler men and Native women were pivotal to negotiations between the Crown and Indigenous nations. Canada's turn toward becoming a settler colonial nation-state, however, changed these early relationships: "Clearly, if a white settler society modeled on British values was to be established, white women had to take the place of Native women, and Native women had to be driven out of the place they had occupied in fur trade society, a process that would continue through successive waves of settlement, from the Great Lakes westward across the continent."[31] Johnson's unions or potential unions reflect the complexities of this changing society. The intimate couple Christie and Charlie (or Esther and Laurence discussed later) stands not only as a foreshadowing of this problematic change embodied in the patriarchal Indian Act, but this intimate event also reflects the direction exemplified in the new and very gendered relationships forming between Canada as a nation-state and Native nations burgeoning as reconstituted entities.

By opening the story with a conversation between men in aboriginal space—a space whose control is being passed down to the younger generation—Johnson cleverly engages with presumptions of Indian women and

Indian relationships at the time. In the opening lines, Robinson warns Charlie about mistreating Christie or "she'll balk sure as shooting."[32] This creates a tinge of irony, as the subtext implies that Charlie will have no sure control over Christie, just as Robinson, an older man of the generation in which negotiation with Native nations was necessary, is still unable to subjugate Native women or nations. These lines foreshadow the eventual upheaval the marriage faces when the couple moves to the "civilized" city and out of a frontier space that is made lawless by Native proximity. Charlie and Robinson are prime examples of a settler masculinity defined by a relationship to "othered" space, dependent on exclusion of "othered" identities. Old Robinson warns Charlie, "'Don't forget, there's a good bit of her mother in her, and,' closing his left eye significantly, 'you don't understand these Indians as I do'" (102). The absence of the two women as speaking subjects is common in depictions of the frontier as primarily masculine space, controlled by European men, yet it is also indicative of the absence of Native people in determining polices developed in the Indian Act. Johnson purposefully creates this connection by using familiar language of possession, such as an assertion of knowledge about *his* Indians, *his* wife—a language that finds its way into the various stages of the Indian Act and legal conceptions of marriage. Robinson explains why he is skeptical of this "town boy": "When you have lived forty years among these people, as I have done; when you have had your wife as long as I have had mine—for there's no getting over it, Christine's disposition is as native as her mother's, every bit—and perhaps when you've owned for eighteen years a daughter as dutiful, as loving, as fearless, and, alas!, as obstinate as that little piece you are stealing away from me to-day—I tell you, youngster, you'll know more than you know now" (102). Robinson lives *among* not *with* the Native people—even after forty years—and he, like the superintendent general or the Indian agent, holds the title and ownership in this moment through the contract of marriage and inheritance laws that follow suit.

The opening of the story serves two purposes: first, it presents a well-known and accepted portrayal of gender and race relations; second, the subtext undermines the "naturalness" and "stability" of these relationships through devices of foreshadowing and irony framed in a conversation between two male settlers. In a provocative essay entitled "A Strong Race Opinion: On the Indian Girl in Modern Fiction," written in 1892, Johnson writes specifically about "the majority of English speaking people" as imagining "an Indian is an Indian, an inadequate sort of person possessing a red brown skin, nomadic habits, and an inability for public affairs" especially as written about in fiction.[33] Johnson critiques authors for presenting Indian women as Robinson and Charles are doing in this scene, stating: "Let the Indian girl of fiction develop from the 'doglike,' 'fawnlike,' 'deer-footed,' 'fire-eyed,' 'crouching,' 'submissive' book heroine."[34] Johnson uses this prologue to disrupt this normative romanticized language of the noble savage, in its tongue-in-cheek conversation between father-in-law and new son.

This short prologue sets up the colonial space of masculinity, but Johnson (re)maps it as an assuming, fantasized space. The Anglo men's objectification of the Native women is clarified further in the next section, which delves into a character description of Charlie. The settler's very portrayal is embedded in his desire and fantasy that brings him to Robinson's trading post: "As a boy [Charlie] had had the Indian relic-hunting craze, as a youth he had studied Indian archaeology and folk-lore, as a man he consummated his predilections for Indianology by loving, winning and marrying the quiet little daughter of the English trader, who himself had married a native woman some twenty years ago" (103). Johnson not only maps out this rejuvenating space of the frontier or aboriginality where the men fulfill their colonial fantasies, the older as conqueror and seeker of fortune and the newer as savior, but she also sets up the absence of Native voices in *their social imaginings* of this space. Charlie's "winning" of Christie is part of the adventure of a young adolescent becoming a man through stepping outside the known, accumulating his wealth, until adulthood affirms his autonomy through marriage. "Superficially, at least, the geography of adventure is unambiguously realistic," contends Richard Phillips, it is "an uncomplicated world of social, moral and political certainty . . . [it] is solid ground, on which adventurous imaginations and colonial adventurers are free to move."[35] We can imagine that this tousled-haired man grew up reading tales of great explorers and wild lands, waiting to be mapped and categorized by new heroes of the nation. The romanticism of "Indian archeology," "folk-lore," and "relics"—embodied in Christie—mobilizes a "geography of adventure" for Charlie, who moves easily between spaces "in which constructions of home and away are temporarily disrupted, before being reinscribed or reordered, in either case reconstituted."[36] Johnson's narrative, however, intervenes in the romantic adventurers' map from the moment the "Red Girl" speaks and reasons.

The characterizations of Jimmy Robinson, Mrs. Robinson, Charlie, and Christie further articulate the racial dynamics of this imagined frontier space, masking it with the common sentimental theme of romantic love.

This sentimentality, however, rests on alterity and difference. In intermarriage and through formal education, Christie and her mother could be lifted from a state of absolute paganism, both ideologically and legally, representing an evolution of the Native in their absorption into the nation's body politic.[37] Johnson refers to the supposed progression of Mrs. Robinson from savage to saved: "Like all her race, observant, intuitive, having a horror of ridicule, consequently quick at acquirement and teachable in mental and social habits, she had developed from absolute pagan indifference into a sweet, elderly Christian woman, whose broken English, quiet manner, and still handsome copper-colored face, were the joy of old Robinson's declining years" (103). Both Native women are presented in the men's narrative as well as by the third-person omniscient as "utterly uncivilized and uncultured, but had withal that marvelously innate refinement" (103). In these moments of coming to know the characters, Johnson presents the stereotyped point of view of Native women ascending into white womanhood through time and intergenerational marriages. Neither woman is presented as exceptional; in fact, the narrator unmasks Charlie McDonald's fantasy of his betrothed: "Personally she looked much the same as her sisters, all Canada through, who are the offspring of red and white parentage" (104). The egocentric fallacies of Robinson and Charlie—respectively representations of a colonial past and a nation-building future—are eventually exposed in the story as the young couple make their way to a "civilized" space where both Christie and her mother become speaking subjects.

The trading post provides Charlie with an escape from the stuffy traditions of Victorian society and fulfills a romantic colonial fantasy of escape from complications and societal bounding. It is a space where boys become men, masculinities are mapped, and settler nations form. Marrying Christie marks the point of his return to "proper" manhood. After the simple marriage ceremony of Christie and Charlie, which takes place at the trading post away from his "swell city friends" and the "flower-pelting, white gloves, rice-throwing, and ponderous stupidity of a breakfast, and indeed all the regulation gimcracks of the usual marriage celebrations" (105), Charlie is now a man and he and Christie are whisked away from the freedom of the pastoral frontier to the awaiting progressive, dynamic space of the city. Rather than endure the effeminate trappings of the domestic space of the city, Charlie moves outside bourgeois space, namely to the reserve, in order to come to know his own place in the world.[38] By entering into the space deemed other, the settler asserts his dominion over both the domesticated space of the city and those

Native spaces yet to be mapped. Most importantly, it is Charlie who has the power to move about at will, unlike Status Indians, who were restricted to the reserve and bound to certain spaces unless they married white men or became enfranchised through education.

In the next story, our Native protagonist is well on her way to being a Non-Status Indian, first through education and second through marriage. As we see, however, the transition to Non-Status Indian does not necessarily mean a freedom from being a racialized subject. Unlike "A Red Girl's Reasoning," Johnson's short story "As It Was in the Beginning" is told as a first-person confessional narrative, yet both stories begin in the "frontier," "uncivilized" spaces of the nation. The stories are similar, as both present the hypocrisy and conflicts inherent in the new liberal map of the nation that rests, as the title reference to the hymn "Glory Be" suggests, on the normative gendered relations established in Christianity as the Holy Trinity: the Father, the Son, and the Holy Spirit. "They account for it by the fact that I am a Redskin," the opening line of this short story, is quickly followed by, "but I am something else too—I am a woman" (144). Johnson asserts the humanity of her protagonist in the lines, "I am a woman."[39] What proceeds is the unfolding of a confessional tale that climaxes in the murder of a young man by the protagonist, implied in the dramatic "it" in the first line. This story illuminates the tensions between the autological subject, or "free" subject who supposedly has the right of choice in personal freedoms through participation in a liberal democracy, and that of a genealogical society whose concepts of race and inheritance are mapped onto geographical spaces. Whereas some subjects, such as Father Paul, are able to move freely, *others,* such as Esther, our narrator, are not allowed such mobility without a threat to their personhood.

From the start, Johnson provides an alternative map of the nation. The plot begins in Esther's Native village, as she tells the reader of the Blackcoat's frequent visits to her father's lodge. Through Esther's confessional, the reader is presented with an alternative perspective of the priest's relatively insignificant presence to the Native people who go about their daily activities, especially the women. Esther's mother ignores the priest completely, and sits quietly engaged in quillwork, waiting for him to leave. After his departure she would scornfully utter, "If the white man made this Blackcoat hell, let him go to it. It is for the man who found it first. No hell for Indians, just Happy Hunting Grounds. Blackcoat can't scare me" (145). The juxtaposition of Hell and Happy Hunting Grounds lays out two divergent conceptions not only of religion, but also metaphysical space. In a sardonic twist, the mother employs the right of discovery to send the white man to hell and reasserts Native claiming of the territory they occupy in the present and beyond through the very same right. The priest is treated as a guest in this marked space of Cree territory.

Esther's father would listen, however, as it was his responsibility to know about the world around him, outside the village. Unlike the priest, he is willing to consider other socialities. Curious Esther was impressed by his stories as well, just as she was curious about what "lay beyond" the "thin, distant line of sky and prairie" (144). After a series of visits, Father Paul asks to take Esther and raise her in the proper ways of middle-class turn-of-the-century Anglo culture. Her mother, however, vehemently disagrees, "'No,' she said. It was the first word she ever spoke to the 'Blackcoat'" (145). Just as Christie's words in "A Red Girl's Reasoning" were a warning, the first words that a Native woman speaks again foreshadow the coming events and disrupt colonial depictions of the passive Native woman. While the priest's stories were used as a "whip to lash us into new religion," the mother "must have known, for each time he left the teepee she would watch him going slowly away across the prairie" (145). However, the Blackcoat convinces her father. Though he "shall not leave the God of my fathers" and doesn't like "his two new places," (146) the pull of the possibilities in the stories and Esther's desire to see a new place overwhelm him. He lets the Blackcoat take Esther so that she can escape the hell impressed on him through many violent biblical stories—the very stories that were used to lay claim to Native land and justify violence to Native bodies. The Cree village and that of the priest are demarcated as two separate worlds in the settler imagination; they collide only when Esther leaves the "uncivilized" village and refuses to become domesticated in the new terrain that is the seat of colonial expansion.

Johnson puts forth alternative conceptions of the nation by bringing the settler into Native territories and imaginings, thus redrawing those spaces as filled with potential for reconfiguring the conceptual maps of the early Canadian Confederation. The place of the trading post and of the Cree village are not bloodthirsty, lawless places, but rather are imbued with traditions carried forth through the young female protagonists. The conflicts arise when the protagonists move into "domesticated" settler spaces and the settler refuses to forego their conceptual maps. Maria Cotera, in her engagement with Dakota writer Ella Deloria's famed novel *Waterlily*, reminds us of the importance of a female-centered protagonist in storytelling as necessary to the process of decolonization. Dakota kinship structures are at the heart of survival for

Deloria, and she writes as a means not only to represent Native women during a shifting time period, but also to imagine what will be necessary to maintain a Dakota identity in the future. Speaking to Deloria, Cotera's focus on the importance of Native women's writing also speaks to Johnson's fiction as well:

> In their novels they reshaped ethnographic data into fictional representations of social reality that not only exposed ethnographic discourse itself as a product of the colonizing imagination but also rejected the mimetic limitations of this colonizing discourse. Fiction writing offered . . . the freedom to explore alternative resolutions to the hegemonic narratives that had written colonized communities, and especially women in those communities, into the margins of history. Their storytelling . . . engaged with this fictive discourse at the level of form, contesting the dominant logics (of authorship and authority) that naturalize asymmetrical relations of rule.[40]

In a time when the Indian Act was rewriting the relationships between families, clans, and First Nations and that of the Canadian Confederacy and racialized others, Johnson also debunks "the dominant logics" at play in the construction of settler liberal democracies.

DOMESTICATED SPACE, DOMESTICATING FLESH

Upon their seeming ascension into white womanhood and removal to "proper" settler society, each of the Native women in Johnson's stories is treated as a romantic other, as a representative of unsettled spaces. Yet, they also represent the hope that Native people will be subsumed into the fabric of the nation, as per the intention of the Indian Act. The connection between domesticating the bodies of Native women, namely those of Christie and Esther, and that of domesticating space is clear in the romantic liaisons of these very different stories as well as in the outlines of the Indian Act. The words "domestic dependent," fashioned in relation to marriage or progeny, or "domestic space of the nation," formed through territorial incorporation, expose the gendered roots of nation-building in settler nations when correlated with the history of settler colonialism and treatment of Native women. Encouraged to form white and Native relationships, the wife of the racialized white settler would then lose her Indian status, as would her children. Many Native women were removed from their communities under these auspices, deemed no longer threatening to the national project and better off than their reserve counterparts. As Indigenous subjects of empire, however, it was Native women who were socially, historically, and spatially criminalized as "improper" subjects of the state.

The intended domestication of Esther takes place over the course of years, through education and religion and the process of storytelling exemplified in biblical stories, yet she is never a "naturalized" citizen but always part of nature that must be civilized as an Indian. Both of Johnson's heroines, Christie and Esther, are referred to in the manner of exotic wild "magnificence" awaiting further domestication; Esther is still consistently referred to as a "pet" and eventually as a "snake," and Christie is commonly known among the elite as "just the sweetest wildflower." The contradictory functions of the domestic—and its connotations of intimacy and control—are exposed as Esther and Christie transgress the boundaries set up in settler imaginings. The unnatural processes of domesticating Native lands and bodies arises as both heroines refute their admission into a racially constructed symbolic ordering of the nation, one in which their ticket for admittance is servitude and obedience to men and foreign law. In this section, the autological subject in domesticated space conflicts with the rising social status of the Native woman who cannot and will not escape her particular genealogy. The settler nation-state relies on the subservience of Native peoples rather than the acknowledgment of their full personhood and rights.

Johnson drives this home by shifting her stories from the outskirts of white settlement to the center of white settlement, and in doing so, the relationship between body, power, and space is apparent. After they leave Native territories, Charlie and Christie's advancement in the city goes well, as they become "favorites socially" and "went everywhere" in the circles of government and in high society. Unlike at home where she is the same as any girl, Christie's difference is seemingly accepted and actively celebrated, as she becomes the exotic object of the colonial gaze: "She was 'all the rage that winter' at the provincial capital. The men called her a 'deuced fine little woman.' The ladies said she was 'just the sweetest wildflower.' Whereas she was really but an ordinary, pale, dark girl who spoke slowly and with a strong accent, who danced fairly well, sang acceptably and never stirred outside the door without her husband" (105). Again, Johnson repeats Christie's ordinariness by exposing the exotic overtures found in the simile of "wildflower." "There are not two of a kind," Charlie tells the diplomats and their wives, though the narrator has already verified that "the pale and ordinary" Mohawk girl in this moment is not unique for her "race." Johnson's recurring gaze on Christie's flesh—her skin, complexion, and expressions—mark the Native body. The popularity of this Native woman stems from the geographies of race rather than any inherent quality. She is "new" to those government officials who dared not venture beyond the "safe" domestic space of drawing rooms, formal state dinners, and grand balls. Under these social-spatial governmentalities, Christie could be easily contained as an exception—or so the settler narrative naively and arrogantly assumes.

During the time in which the story is set, there was clear codification of geographies of race. After the Riel Rebellion led by Métis Louis Riel against the encroachment of the English on French and Métis land, new legislation was introduced into the Indian Act, which invested authority to the Indian agent to institute a pass system as a means to control Indians through containment. This significantly limited contact with whites so that collaborative actions against the state would be much more difficult to plan.[41] Christie's presence in town and in the life of Charlie, whom we can gather comes from a well-recognized and wealthy founding family, is made extraordinary or exceptional through geography. Her presence in the city and in these circles places her in the motif of the "exception." Not all Natives had the unfettered mobility of movement between geopolitical and social spaces. As subjects of empire, Native peoples' mobility was severely limited by legal codes. Glenda Laws makes clear that "both the conceptualization and material constructions of bodies *make a difference to our experience of places.*"[42] The space of the city becomes attached to spaces of the body; in particular, non-reserve spaces are naturalized as white settler spaces. These normative geographies are determined not just through violent conquest and law, but also through imagined and forgotten geographies. Toronto, Quebec City, and Montreal—the seat of European expansion of the settler state—are imagined as "civilized," non-Indian spaces, eliding a history of these meeting centers. During Johnson's era, Natives, as abject subjects of the state, were to be expelled from the cities of Canada; the cities themselves became beacons of liberal democracy monumentalizing the advancement of colonial rule.

While the cities indicate the large-scale conquest of Native land in colonial spatialities, the smaller-scale conquest of Native bodies is often signified through clothing and dress. Victorian and "exotic" Native clothing and the Native body provide spatial-social-historical meanings throughout Johnson's short stories. Depictions of Charlie and Christie's entrance into society include a discussion of Christie's favorite choice of fabric—velvet and silk. It is in this small detail that Johnson (re)maps the colonial fantasy and recalls the history of Native–Canadian relations. Since the exchange of fabrics often solidified early trade agreements, the emphasis on apparel articulates a history of Indian–European trade relations—which were often based on the coupling of fur traders and Native women. No matter how "cultured" (read: assimilated) Christie seems to become, early nation-to-nation treaty agreements are referenced and spatialized in this form of dress: "No woman of Canada, has she but the faintest dash of native blood in her veins, but loves velvet and silks. As beef to the Englishman, wine to the Frenchman, fads to the Yankee, so are velvet and silk to the Indian girl, be she wild as prairie grass, be she on the borders of civilization, or, having stepped within its boundary, mounted the steps of culture even under its superficial heights" (106). Neither Christie, her mother, nor Native women are subsumed subjects of empire no matter where they reside. Johnson takes up this form of dress in nationalistic terms, but also to point out that accepting the concept of the settler as superior is "superficial." Native women through sexual conquest and the early creation of normative geographies and through symbolism such as dress are formulated as abject subjects in these colonized spaces. Johnson remaps Native bodies and politics through the performative act of dress.[43] The pointed remark regarding dress and "superficial" normative culture in this New Canada is heightened when the historical symbolism of Christie's velvet dress is considered. She makes clear that Christie's dress choice in bourgeois society should not be read as a shallow personal choice or racially deterministic, but rather it suggests cultural markers—just "as beef to the Englishman, wine to the Frenchman." The cultural attributes of Native women will not be erased, nor will their inherent rights as First Nations. Johnson's critique of Native women's progression into white womanhood or absorption into the state continues to build as Native bodies move through the space of the city.

While Christie is a romanticized soon-to-be improper subject, Joe and Charlie are Canada's future manifesting its settler instincts. In the city, the couple moves in with Charlie's brother Joe, a surveyor. Joe's and Charlie's occupations are significant to the romantic plot, as both will take part in defining and creating discourses of the boundaries of the nation. Charlie collects census statistics for the state, while Joe the surveyor demarcates the physical space of the nation through imagining physical boundaries and claiming land.[44] Accumulation of land and bodies in this process of mapping are significant technologies of rule. The brothers' imagined geographies are manifested through the data and lines they create and the force they carry as "proper" subjects of the state. Yet their colonial geographies will be tested by their close proximity to Christie. Joe asks the newly intimate couple if they would "prefer keeping house alone"—in private space. The domestic drama of the nation unfolds in the dialogue between the brothers. The too-easy and forced distinction between public and private space is not that simple for Christie, who presents us with Mohawk reasoning.

Charlie assures Joe that the couple does not need to set up a house of their own, for his bachelor brother will be sure to have his own "wild" adventures: "After a while when they want you and your old surveying chains, and spindle-legged tripod telescope kickshaws, farther west, I venture to say the little woman will cry her eyes out—won't you Christie?" (107). The foregone conclusion of expansion into Native territory, expressed by Joe's inevitable departure to survey land to the West, is subtly questioned in this humorous quip. In a taunting response, Christie immediately corrects both men's assumptions for the first time in the text. In doing so, the relationship between collecting specimens and mapping space arises. "'Oh, no, I would not cry; I never do cry," says the Mohawk woman in a playful tone which sets her apart from many sentimental heroines, "but I would be heart-sore to lose you, Joe, and apart from that . . . you may come in handy for an exchange someday, as Charlie does always say when he hoards up duplicate relics" (107). This rhetorical strategy by Johnson recalls the beginning of the story where Christie is positioned as an object without the traits of an individual and no more than one of Charlie's "relics." Besides clearly presenting a Native subject who speaks rather than is acted upon, this passage demonstrates how the collector and the surveyor of land become intricately bound in claiming authority over the West; as one of them categorized and collected specimens, thus evacuating Natives' presence, the other defined the new parameters of space and the nation. This is Christie's first line in the short story, which immediately disrupts the earlier assumptions laid out in the opening and intervenes in a narrative of a destined future between husband and wife and nation and Native.

Johnson further punctuates the instability of the future with Christie's remark that she will keep Joe around "in the event of Charlie's failing me" (108). She employs Charlie's professional language in regard to relics so that she can turn him into one, thus figuring herself in a position of power to collect. The presumption that Christie will cry at Joe's westward movement is dismissed, along with the presumed absorption of the West. When her husband asks if the brothers are one and the same, Christie responds, "Well—not exactly." Her undomesticated body, addressed by her refusal to give up an attachment to velvet, to expunge her in-law from the heteronormative home, or to be a relic in someone else's imagination, implodes the forced demarcation between public and private spheres as she traverses various geo-political landscapes as a Non-Status Indian under the supposed "protection" of her white husband. While Christie is legally domesticated as a citizen of the liberal nation-state under the Indian Act for having married a white man, this does not reduce her to object status. This legal dressing is as easy to take off as Christie's velvet dress and demeanor as an adoring and obedient wife— for no man "can make a slave of a red girl" (124). The public/private spheres that are "cultural classifications and rhetorical labels" that maintain settler state hegemony lose relevancy when the Indian Act, marriage, and the log-ics of liberal love in the settler state are closely examined through female-centered narratives.[45] Gender and race articulated through coupling and codified in the Indian Act become clear settler spatial practices.

In much of her writing and in her own stage performances, Johnson's similar use of dress performs Native women in various spaces and degrees of acculturation. In "As It Was," Esther is presented as a very different central character than Christie. Whereas Christie willingly wears the ball gown and other forms of Euro-settler dress, Esther begins the story as a young woman who has rejected these forms of dress imposed on her by those in the mission town. Esther's "first grief" in life was the removal of her buckskin dress upon arriving at the mission. The symbolic stripping of her identity as a Cree girl is depicted as a painful striping away of her relationship to her people. The now older Esther reminisces about this painful imposition of the intersec-tion of race and gender norms: "They took my buckskin dress off saying I was now a little Christian girl and must dress like all the white people at the mission. Oh, how I hated that stiff new calico dress and those leather shoes! But, little as I was, I said nothing, only thought of the time when I should be grown, and do as my mother did, and wear the buckskins and the blanket" (146). Dress becomes a way to engage with the artificial production of race through reconstituting gender. The place of the mission's boarding school is symbolic of Esther's painful race and gender transformation, but we know through the confessional tone in the opening lines that saying she is a Chris-tian girl does not make her acceptable to the church or the state, even if rear-ranging the corporeal maps of dress. She maintains the mental maps that are more than coverings; one day when she is "grown" she will do as her "mother did," regardless of what she is learning to become at school. She uses the cor-poreal map, the gendered colonial map, in order to survive in the particular space of the nation, but in her narrative she pushes forth a mapping that produces a different alternative than absorption into white norms and gendered subservience.

While Johnson tells a familiar, in fact a simplistic, summary of the missionary school experience that will later turn into residential school policies, she complicates it through the interracial/interspatial coupling of her childhood playmate, the nephew of the priest and son of the school matron. Civilizing Esther is indeed a family affair. Years after her arrival at the mission, the girl blossoms in town as a favorite "pet of all from the factor to the poorest trapper in the service" (147). of white colonial society. Esther's domestication is revealed in Johnson's repeated reference to her as a pet, as well as her lack of ability to become an autological subject in colonial schema. Because she is restrained by her genealogy or perceived inherited racial qualities, she is unable to progress as a full-fledged, self-grounded subject. The narrative of Native land and resource dispossession and cultural genocide "presents the story of the familial progress of humanity from degenerative native child to adult white father."[46] The colonial metaphor of family, especially as it intersected and was codified through the act of marriage, had drastic consequences in defining sovereignty and citizenship for Native peoples, as this emphasis on the autological subject of enlightenment presented an unequal relationship from its origin. The conviction behind this relationship of rule and domination was that the father needed to correct his child in order to help the youngster's growth. As Anne McClintock asserts, "imperial intervention could thus be figured as a linear, nonrevolutionary progression that naturally contained hierarchy within unity: paternal fathers ruling benignly over immature children."[47] Claiming authority over a majority of Native land prompted a response by the settler state to have a strict hand in matters of the intimate, so that its Native ward could achieve the status of man (understood legally as citizenship). The legislation and control over Native women's bodies was an important instrument in this conquest, and like the Blackcoat in Johnson's story, colonial authorities set out to determine who was moral and who deserved rights based on gender conceptions.[48]

Who better to send than a priest, one misconstrued as Father, to accomplish the work of paternal claiming of land into settler property? Esther "mistakenly" refers to Saint Paul as "Father Paul," along with those in town who view him as a saint "because they told me, of his self-sacrificing life, his kindly deeds, his rarely beautiful old face . . . though he never liked the latter title, for he was a Protestant" (147). Rather than this simply representing a correction of Esther's rudimentary religious knowledge, Johnson intentionally misnames and imbues the misnomer with much irony; the naming of "Father Paul" is an intricate strategy to dislocate the hierarchical "logic" of nation-building, the cult of domesticity, and settler discourse. The spatial and temporal schism embodied in the presentation of Natives as savage, infant, and immoral augments the right to expansion, while their inability to become full citizens ensures their social deaths. Esther's confession to the murder of Laurence is a testimonial to her social death in white settler society as well—but one we know from the beginning has grave consequences. Johnson adamantly resisted this hierarchical familial positioning in presenting the "Father" figure of St. Paul as hypocritical, unfair, and not leading "the nation" in the right direction.

Esther confesses that, though she learns to live within strict social rules, she never legitimizes their superiority, but as a child she follows them anyway. She longs for home throughout her years at school, and takes long walks and reminisces about her family and people, but Father Paul refuses to let her go home, because all the "progress" they have made will degenerate back into paganism if she leaves the domestic space of the mission town. In this assertion of geopolitics, the forced schism between past (the history) and present (the social) links with the clear division of frontier and civilized border (the spatial): "I heard the talk amongst themselves of keeping me away from pagan influences; they told each other that if I returned to the prairies, the teepees, I would degenerate, slip back to paganism, as other girls had done; *marry, perhaps, with a pagan*—and all their years of labour and teaching would be lost" (147–48, emphasis mine). The assertion of colonial control over Native women's sexual and legal choices is socially, historically, and spatially constructed. The Cree village stands for an imagined degenerative Native space *as it is still contemporarily conceived by the nation-state*. The Indian Act gendered Native villages to set up masculinized Native spaces that supported a masculinized settler state. Marrying another Native person, which inherently rejects assimilation into colonial ordering, or marrying a white woman or man, did not only have sociopolitical outcomes, but was also highly spatialized. Joanne Barker contends:

> As with all assimilation policies, it was based on an inherently racist and sexist assumption that Indian governance, epistemologies and beliefs, and gender roles were irrelevant and invalid, even dangerous impediments to progress. But in the process of undermining Indian law, land tenure, economics, cultural

beliefs, and social relationships in the name of integration, the Indian Act and assimilation policies more generally ended up reproducing the social conditions of subordination and dependence that they promised to end since Indians were quite unwelcome in areas off-reserve.[49]

This "othered" space correlates to the "othered" bodies—and othering is always gendered. The other, in this case the Native, not only must come to pass as time and the nation progress and liberal society develops, but Native spaces and bodies that reside and make meaning in and with them must be ingested by the settler state and reconstituted as a noble past. The logics of settler colonialism deem the new men of liberal democracy, such as Charlie and Laurence, as inheritors of the newly forming nation-state.

It is in the assertion of liberal democracy based on the autological subject that paradoxes of settler colonialism form in the intimacy of social relations, and colonial spatialities are reconfigured. In "As It Was," racial longing and cultural homesickness are attributed to a passing girlhood. "What mattered it to me now that they had taught me all their ways?—their tricks of dress, their reading, their writing, their books" (148), asks Esther of the colonial enterprise of assimilating Natives. Esther is a woman now, as well as a "redskin," and the juxtaposition of race and gender is repeated at a crucial and decisive moment of rejecting the colonial performativity of gender and white assimilation: "I longed. Oh, god, how I longed for the old wild life! It came with my womanhood, with my years" (147). In the story, there is a reworking of the concepts of progress, time, and domesticated space; Esther longs for "freedom" and reminds the reader to whom she is confessing that Natives may have varying ideas of what constitutes "freedom" apart from the ideals of a budding liberal democracy. If we think about Esther's maturing body and its connection to wild spaces and the position of Native women in settler society as always already genealogically gendered and sexualized, we understand that Esther's freedom does not reside in the liberal state. In this reconfiguration of land and body, she is not restrained from achieving her subjectivity by her racial attributes, but rather it is in belonging to the land she is looking out on and in gazing toward her community that freedom becomes a possibility.

The pace of the narrative increases in urgency as the confession continues. In the in-between space of the trading post, Esther is confronted with her longings for home "when an Indian came in from the north with a large pack of buckskin" (148). The separation between conceived settler and Native space is interdependent in this moment, and the binary breaks down in the space and this moment of economic transactions. Esther's sense of touch and smell, and the sight of the buckskins "devoured" Esther where she immediately went "in a strange, calm frenzy" and "demanded to be allowed to go 'home,' if only for a day" (148). Her demands are not met, however, even though "this time the desire, the smoke-tan, the heart-ache, never lessened"; the fear of Esther's "desire" and freedom she may experience at home, produce "the same refusal and gentle sigh that I had been so often greeted with." She is seized by "the wild wonder of that smoked tan, the subtilty [*sic*] of it, the untamed smell of it!" (148). The story raises questions of settler power over Native bodies in this scene where senses and memory are stained and inassimilable. If Native land is to be incorporated through the control of Native bodies, as the Indian Act sets out to do, then Johnson's storytelling calls for a fundamental rethinking of the workings of the settler state.

In the trading post passage there is a link between Esther's domestication and the experience of lived bodies in different spaces. The mission town in the story forms a complement to other spatial tropes—namely the exterior spaces of the frontier, wilderness, and nature—as it is an interior space that is to be the platform of fulfilling the further domestication of national spaces. The subtext implies that in order for Esther to become part of the national body, she must strip her past and childhood away—there is no true "progress" without this step. This narrative is rewritten in this female-centered short story. Whereas Esther as a young child looked away from the place of her home village out of curiosity, she now looks to the place of her village to help her rise not just to a Victorian sense of womanhood but to personhood. As in Esther's childhood, we find an imagining of what is beyond the confining mission space. Esther is not daunted, and she steals away "to the border of the village to watch the sun set in the foothills, to gaze at the far line of sky and prairie, to long and long for my father's lodge" (148). This time, however, Johnson demarcates the space with the word "bordered," implying exclusion and inclusion. Esther's village is to be excluded from the space of the everexpanding mission village, and Esther is fully aware of the painful process this will incur. The settler map, however, is rewritten by Esther's gaze as she looks toward her village and all the Native land beyond the border of the small mission town, not in wistful remembrance, but as a point that provides hope and continuance.

After positioning this longing for home, the plot becomes complicated through the introduction of a love interest. The symbolic coupling between Native and European provides a ground for thinking about a (re)mapping not grounded in nostalgic terms, but one of imagined possibilities of new terrains. Esther is joined on the outskirts by her young playmate, who "was a tall, slender young man now, handsome as a young chief, but with laughing blue eyes, and always those yellow curls about his temples. He was my solace in my half-exile, my comrade, my brother, until one night it was, 'Esther, Esther, can't *I* make you happy'" (149). Johnson reveals the ambiguity of race in characterizing a subject; not only is Laurence "like an Indian Chief," Esther is "half-exiled"—but from what half is left ambiguous. As Povinelli makes clear in her work, love in liberal logics is the transference point in which the social constraints of race are transcended and the couple recognizes each other as individuals who are full autological subjects. Yet, the repeated use of "my" in his plea for Esther to stay and be his, in fact italicized in one instance ("*my* Esther"), emphasizes the possessive nature of the intimate relationship. The follow-up dialogue's repetition of "no more" intimates the legal action of the intimate contract. From the start of the confessional we know that the story does not end well and are aware that Laurence breaks this intimate contract and the promise of social fulfillment through love. What is certain, and affirmed through the force of the Indian Act, is that Esther's acceptance of Laurence's proposal would mean "no more, no more the teepees; no more the wild stretch of prairie . . . no more the dark faces of my people, the dulcet cadence of the sweet Cree tongue—only this man" (149). Return to her village is impossible in the creation of settler intimate spaces, as the Native woman's social existence is coerced and interpolated through settler logics foundational to the Indian Act. In this spatial schema at the scale of the body and nation, she cannot return home.

The tensions found in Johnson's story are also part and parcel of liberal discourses at the time. The seeming breakaway from "old world" modes of governance that relied on inheritance, social status, and class (the genealogical) in fact only "reorganized how social status was deployed in governmental logics."[50] Through marriage, conceived of in the liberal state as an individual choice, the genealogical forms (mired in racial inheritance) of governance in the Indian Act became an instrument to regulate Native land and bodies. Johnson's characters, set up in the plots as autological subjects, expose the relationship with the genealogical in states that claim a form of liberal subjectivity. In speaking of the moment in which the colonial and colonized meet in an intimate relationship, or the foundational event, Povinelli states: "The foundational event is phantasmagorical in the simple sense that liberal societies are not, in fact, structured in a manner consistent with the ideological fantasy of the intimate event. The very conceptual form of state citizenship, insinuated into the deep tissues of economic, state, and national life, is based on birth from a human body or a territorial body and thus is inflected by the governing metaphors of flesh: race, gender, and sexuality."[51] In so many of Johnson's stories, the young woman is conflicted by memories and allegiances brought on by fabric or dress and by love for a white man; she feels her longing and belonging in the flesh. Her choice, however, is illusory and hindered, as white men do not accept her socially or legally as an equal. Settling territory and expunging Native peoples depends on "the governing metaphors of flesh" and putting women in place and Natives out of it.

UNEASY MARRIAGES, ANXIOUS SETTLER NATIONS

In order to (re)map the nation's imaginative geographies of the metropole and frontier, we must further investigate the substantive content of those spheres in correlation with the presence of Native women's bodies. In the final part of Johnson's stories, the liberal spaces of democratic settler states are volatile and unstable. The Native woman at the heart of each story takes "unpredictable" action as the intimate event of her marriage or potential marriage collapses the public/private, Native/Settler space, and genealogical/autological subject by breaking down the mapping of bodies, land, and geopolitics. When the woman surpasses the role of the domesticated and demands the rights of those now natural citizens, the dramatic event occurs and her exotic and exceptional status declines. Christie demands that her Native rites be respected, and Esther demands to be treated as fully a citizen as a white woman. The potential marriage or marriage between a red girl and Canada's son is an uneasy one, as is the marriage of Native nations and the settler nation. In examining the direct and indirect methods in which Johnson links the nation-to-nation relationships to the coupling of white settlers and Native women, the project of expansion and nation-building is gendered. My analysis of these stories clarifies the liberal logics of love and their complications by examining them as a cautionary tale to the new nation as it mapped its territory and social and cultural terrains. Without recognition of Native women's rights and Canada as Native land, there will always be unrest.

Broken promises and contracts are foreshadowed from the start of the dramatic story "As It Was in the Beginning." Unbeknownst to the men, Esther overhears her benefactor asking his nephew: "You have said nothing of marriage to her?" Laurence responds that surely Esther understood his intentions, recognizing the contract, but is quickly interrupted by Father Paul's renewed emphasis on marriage, that institution that legally binds "civilized." With a "harsh ring," Father Paul proceeds to rationalize the dissolution of the promised union through nineteenth-century "racial logic": "Poor Esther comes from uncertain blood; would it do for you—the missionary's nephew, and adopted son, you might say—to marry the daughter of a pagan Indian? Her mother is hopelessly uncivilized; her father has a dash of French somewhere—half-breed, you know, my boy, half-breed" (152). The hierarchy of the nation's citizenship is laid out in Father Paul's common nineteenth-century racial logic that forms the context of the Indian Act. Esther can mirror the image of a Christian woman in dress and composure, but to Father Paul she will never be a fully realized subject, but always mired by her racialized body and parentage as anticipated by the title reference to the biblical line "As it was in the beginning, is now, and ever shall be, world without end." The liberal logics begin to further deteriorate as Father Paul appeals to less exposed normative settler knowledge:

> The blood is a bad, bad mixture, you know that. . . . I have tried to separate her from her pagan influences; she is a daughter of the church; I want her to have no other parent; but you never can tell what lurks in *a caged animal that has once been wild.* My whole heart is with the Indian people, my son; my whole heart, my whole life, has been devoted to bringing them to Christ, *but it is a different thing to marry with one of them.* (152)

What makes it different from other, say, political and economical, contracts that individuals enter? Esther is not to marry a pagan, nor is she to marry Laurence. The progeny of Native women are not the imagined new citizens of Canada.

Father Paul encourages his nephew to rethink his marriage to Esther and consider a "proper" marriage to the Hudson Bay factor's daughter, since, as he reminds Laurence, "She is *white*"; he pleads with him to go to "Winnipeg, Toronto, and Montreal" (152–53) and break his contract with Esther. Space is mapped in this instance by a set of social productions; Esther's native village is the uncivilized, the mission town on the border presents the boundaries of civilization, and the city to which Laurence flees is the already civilized space of the future. Conversely, Laurence's name stands in for the great St. Lawrence Seaway that serves as a port of entry to new markets, increased trade, and the economic future of Canada. Saint Paul is the man sent to bring the Native into the fold of civilization so that Native peoples will not pose a threat to the burgeoning nation and its imperial interests. The young man in the story embodies a new national identity. In colonial logics, he is a new citizen who has been naturalized by living in this land and removed from exposure to "uncivilized" ways. Significantly, Father Paul stands in for Laurence's father, and as Johnson reminds us, Laurence is the minister's only progeny—besides those Indians he has civilized and paternalistically claims as his children.

Mad with jealousy, betrayal, and pride, Esther kills the young man with poison given to her by her mother, who, foreseeing such troubled events, packed it years ago upon Esther's departure. It is not just the betrayal of romantic love, but the betrayal of her benefactor and kinship and political obligations that prompts the killing. Esther's and Christie's prior Indigenous occupancy strike at the heart of imagining a nation of "equal" liberal subjects. Racial logics become the mechanism for refuting entry as full subjects in the nation and justifying conquest: "Ah there was no mistaking it. My white father, my life-long friend who pretended to love me, to care for my happiness, was urging the man I worshipped to forget me, to marry with the factor's daughter—because of what? Of my red skin; my good, old, honest pagan mother; my confiding French-Indian Father" (153). The more Father Paul calls Esther's womanhood into question based on her genealogies, the more Esther is enraged: "I hated that old mission priest as I hated his white man's hell. I hated his long, white hair; I hated his thin, white hands; I hated his body, his soul, his voice, his black book—oh, how I hated the very atmosphere of him!" (153). The problem of such settler logics creates an "atmosphere" of superiority rooted in race and patriarchy by emphasizing the white body and moral codes of citizenship set up through whiteness. Clearly whiteness and patriarchy is a way to attain and maintain property as demonstrated by Laurence's potential marriage to the rich, white daughter of the factor. Yet Johnson turns the uncle's and nephew's whiteness into disease, degeneration, frailty, weakness, immorality, and hypocrisy.

Laurence concedes to his uncle's *logic,* wistfully replying "thank you for bringing me to *myself*" (154, emphasis mine). Whiteness is strategically deployed by Canada and other settler nations to claim Indigenous land and highly regulate immigrant labor, becoming a form of property itself.[52] Whiteness as property invested in the white body and whiteness as the foundation of settler society is destabilized in Johnson's narrative. Laurence can only be brought to himself by racially ordering Esther as inferior, immoral, and abject body—his rightful place in the nation depends on expunging the Native, or conceiving of her as an "apparition," or by criminalization closely related to gendered norms, "she reminds me sometimes of a strange—snake" (154). In this biblical reference, the snake entices Adam and Eve to eat forbidden fruit in the Garden of Eden. Rather than Esther being of childlike innocence, the priest speaks of her as a carrier of evil and downfall. The dismissal of Esther's personhood gives Laurence his. However, before Laurence can marry the factor's daughter with her "yellow hair," "whitish skin," and "baby face"—and write Esther out of existence—she decides to "kill him first—kill his beautiful body" (155). No matter how Christian and ladylike the young woman becomes, Esther is still a "Redskin," ultimately marking her not only as improper marriage material but also as an improper citizen. The old man's wish is deferred, there will not be "a union of the Church and the Hudson Bay [that] will mean great things, and may ultimately result in my life's ambition, the civilization of this entire tribe, that we have worked so long to bring to God" (153). The refusal of desubjectification or abjection brings Esther to a destruction of whiteness: "Kill him. It will break Father Paul's heart and blight his life. He has killed the heart of you, your womanhood; kill his best, his pride, his hope" (155). While Father Paul's proselytizing of Native people is his supposed legacy, it is revealed in these moments that Laurence, as a symbol of the new nation-state, is his "hope." To kill the body of whiteness or that which legitimizes Laurence's personhood and requires the vanquishing of Esther's personhood is to kill the logics of white inheritance at the heart of the settler state. Esther asserts her Indigenous rights, which are not wedded to capital accumulation.

After the death of the white sovereign, Esther immediately returns home to her Indian village and mother and father who open the story. The new nation has rejected her, and that was a fatal mistake. Her return to the space of aboriginiality further marks her guilt in the eyes of the town. She is suspected as guilty, but without proof, the townspeople can do nothing. However, Johnson again (re)maps race and gender, locating Esther's guilt not in the construction of Cree womanhood, but in a settler universality of womanhood imposed upon her at the mission. She repeats the first lines of her story, "They account for it by the fact that I am a redskin. They seem to have forgotten I am a woman" (156). Esther's ambiguously located womanhood again rises to the surface—she kills Laurence because of his betrayal of their understanding that they would become engaged. For love she is willing to give up her tribal status and, according to the Indian Act, in doing so become enfranchised—that is, legally separated from her community. Intertwining racial injustice with such a wide appeal to gendered emotions presents Esther as an anti-heroine who is struggling with being a woman in a settler nation built on hierarchies of gender subordination and exclusion of Native people, both of which situate white male property ownership.

Embedded in this narrative of love and betrayal is a vision of Native peoples' place in the forming of a new national identity. The young man had the agency to choose Esther, which would have led to her incorporation in the state, but instead he follows the lineage of an old order in which Native people and women do not share equal footing with whites and men, and Native women have no legal recourse at all. The confessor exclaims that the old man had "robbed me of my native faith, of my parents, of my people, of this last, this life of love that would have made a great, good woman of me" (154–55). While this may be interpreted as a spiteful act and not redefining the grounds of the newly forming Canada, the confessional mode of the narrative implies an admittance of something that must be repented, not necessarily the act of murder. Perhaps it is her youthful belief in love's ability to enable her to shed her social skin, or maybe the loss endured through the violence of assimilative practices? In her ambiguity and unsettling through the unsavory, but emotionally understandable, character of Esther, liberal ordering of space is called into question. This story effectively (re)maps meanings of the frontier; her village is the space of vitality, morals, justice, and honesty—all of which is taken away in the nation's expansion, dispossession of Native lands, and abject mapping of Indian bodies. Through the atrocious act of murder, Johnson gives Canada a warning about continuing down the destructive path of exclusion while paying lip service to equal footing in a liberal democracy.

"A Red Girl's Reasoning" also ends in a decoupling of the interracial subject and failed liberal logics of state incorporation. Johnson's foreshadowing of romantic tragedy in "A Red Girl's Reasoning" culminates at the next party Christie, Charlie, and Joe attend. As usual, Christie is at the center of curiosity and attention. Again, the detail of her blue dress and pageantry of "the nobs [who] were in great feather that night" (108), as in so many of Johnson's stories, becomes the mechanism by which the author disrupts colonial space. Christie's casual remark about the factor's choice of blue in her "old home" spurs an uncomfortable conversation around Christie's presence in the provincial capital and the desire for "we fellows [who] so often wish to hear of it all" (109). Christie is not only well aware of racial dynamics and refuses to apologize or be shameful of her home and nationality, but also she understands the complexities of her situation better than those surrounding her: "Perhaps you are, like all other white people, afraid to mention my nationality to me?" (109). She deliberately opens the door for dialogue. Joe quietly encourages from the dance floor, "That's you, Christie, lay 'em out" (109). She associates her identity with her nation, rather than making a claim regarding the equal rights of her racialized identity as a now-Canadian citizen. Like many at Six Nations, she refuses the gender imposition and the laws that would denationalize her identity and make her a racialized subject of empire.[53] While the discomfort shows in the socialites' stuttered speech, their eagerness to *know* more about the *other space* overtakes them, and they continue to press on: "Tell us of yourself and your mother—your father is delightful, I am sure—but then he is only an ordinary Englishman, not half as interesting as a foreigner, or—or, perhaps I should say, a native" (109). The subtexts of Mrs. Stuart's words signify the relationship among race, gender, and nation and pinpoint the proper subject of the settler state—that is, the Anglo citizen subject. The alchemy of normative language employed through a romantic story in this moment makes the settler the Native. By fetishizing and spatializing Native people to the extent that they are now considered foreign or outside the space of the nation, it clears a space that replaces the now othered "foreign" native with the "ordinary Englishman."

Marriage brings Christie into this imagined and material settler state space where the presumptions of settlement are normalized, and it is these conventions in the end that cast her down to the status of a "squaw," an abject subject. Christie's genealogy is called into question, as well as her marriage to Charlie, when it becomes clear that a Catholic priest did not marry her parents. Charlie and Joe are aghast, even though early Canadian colonies depended on these "country" marriages as sources of political and economical allegiances, and it is well known that many surveyors of the West, Joe's occupation, often were involved in similar liaisons as Christie's parents. Marriage, which presumes consent by the individual, is regulated by the church or state and used as a mechanism through which to transfer property—but not equally so. In the case of Native people, these early stages of settlement relied on marriage to regulate property, society, and entrance into citizenship. Native women became dispossessed at the intersections of race, gender, and the intimate event; they lose their "rights" as Status Indians, as they are now understood by the state as under the protection of their white male counterparts. Forced into citizenship in which their genealogical status still regulates their everyday experiences increases vulnerability in the case of separation and abandonment. Many Native women, like Christie, were not able to return home to their families and communities. Johnson was very aware of the use of the Indian Act to assert a bifurcated taxonomy of the "wild" and "civilized" Native women, and by "confounding this boundary Pauline Johnson called into question the logic of the imperial project."[54]

Christie refuses the confines of settler-sanctioned marriage and rising "with the dignity and pride of an empress" declares, "What do you dare to mean? Do you presume to think it would not have been lawful for Charlie to marry me according to my people's rites? Do you for one instant dare to question that my parents were not as legally—" (111). From a wildflower to a sovereign empress, Christie makes it clear that "Indian rites" equally and honorably bind two individuals together regardless of settler state hierarchies. The point is further driven home by Joe's misrecognition. He comforts Christie by telling that neither she nor her parents did anything wrong because "there was no other way" (113). The marital domestic sphere is impinged upon by misrecognition of Native nationhood and, ultimately, the personhood of Christie, who refuses the linearity of the settler project that empties out the political vitality, discourses, and rights of her nation. From its start, liberal discourses of unity fail through the violent policies of the Indian Act.

After being whisked away by the quick-acting Joe, Christie returns home in his care while she awaits her husband. When Charlie does return he is still angered at Christie for having "*disgraced*" herself and both her parents by relating, and more importantly prioritizing, an alternative legal history that preexisted Christianity, the Crown, or Canadian law. He is able to accept neither her nationality nor her personhood, which is embedded in strong traditions. Legal and moral contradictions arise when Native nations occupy the same space and time as the newly forming nation—which they always do—and threaten the liberal settler state. There cannot be a denial of coevalness sought by Charlie and Joe, the practicing anthropologist and the cartographer. Christie is in the present time and in the same geographic terrain demanding that the sovereign laws of her community be recognized.

Christie will not subordinate her nation's rights to the rites of Christianity, to Canada's law on marriage, the Indian Act, or to the cult of domesticity— not even for the sake of love. Christie's rational red girl's reasoning, ensconced in a language that makes a dramatic appeal to emotions, provides an opening in which Johnson confronts the colonizer in his own legal discourses. Here the setting is important; in the private and intimate space of the marital bedroom, Christie reasons through these crises of jurisdiction and law as the couple vehemently argues as if in the public space of the court. At a time when there was a perception of Western law as the necessary condition of civilization, and law was "rational," Christie's only defense is her Native set of reasoning and laws recognized in the Haudenosaunee Confederacy. The argument grows more heated when Christie asserts the equal relationship between Christian rites and Native rites, and Charlie responds in an ever more belligerent tone refusing to recognize and continuing to distance in time and space the presence of Native nations by insisting that they "live in more civilized times"—insisting, as Christie remarks, "beyond all reason" (115). By depicting the dysfunction of the romanticized mixed-race couple, the public space of civilization or the institutions of the settler state are unhinged by exposing the "private" space of love as laden with public dispossession. The Native woman's reasoning capability is asserted and used as a rhetorical mechanism to appeal to her right to not only be an autological subject, but a citizen of her Nation. Johnson challenges the irrational components of the Indian Act and reduces it to settler rhetoric. The autological subject of the liberal state, such as Joe, who ideally stands for the new freedom and democratic subject of Canada, encounters in his formation the genealogical laws of the state and society. The hierarchy of law over that of what is understood as individual feelings of love is linked to inheritance and proper subjects of the state. By conveying her biography, Christie is, in Charlie's eyes, an improper subject, and he deems her "the child of—what shall we call it—love? Certainly not legality" (114). In refuting the colonial discourses of legality, Christie reclaims her personhood. The settler state, in that it relies on constitutive differences between settler and Native, is only able to provide a map that expunges Native women through gendered colonial practices that deem her the property of white men.

This *difference* particularly plays out in the *different history and biographies of the couple from birth.* When Charlie adamantly insists that Christie's parents should have gotten married when the priest arrived, Christie furiously relates her mother's own anger at the priest; the silent and obedient wife pictured in the beginning of the story and mentioned in the first section ascends now as formidable woman who "arose and said 'Never—never—I have never had but this one husband'" (115). Christie clarifies for Charlie her mother's monogamy and that they had already been married five years when she was born—to remarry by "*White* rite" would be "to say to the whole world as that we had never been married before*" (115). The *submission* to this legal reasoning and performative act would be a denial not only of her individual personhood, but also the denial of the legality of "her forefathers, for hundreds of years back." By grounding Christie's and her mother's argument in the reason of the law and backing up the argument with an asterisk that reads "Fact" at the bottom of the page, Johnson clearly is confronting the extension of "*white* rites" over Native rites. Charlie maintains, "beyond reason," that her father "was a fool not to insist on the law, and so was the priest" (116).

While Johnson is talking about a clash between two cultures and their inability to come to an understanding, the use of these cultural wars was at the heart of land dispossession. Johnson was acutely aware of the Six Nations disagreement with the adoption of the Indian Act on the basis that it would disrupt matrilineal descent and the fabric of Haudenosaunee life.[55] Property, as both land and personhood, was deeply tied into the Indian Act and tribal custom laws. Enacting control over Native bodies and space for Charlie, the son of Canada, is about colonial management over bodies, communities, and land through the normalized contract of marriage. The contract of marriage, so often thought of as a choice to love, normalized gendered language and patriarchal control. The expansion of Canadian government is linked to the subjugation of Native women; more importantly, the final subjugation of Native women to settler law and to morality is found in the intimate act. Rather than "progressing" in morality, aptitude, or citizenship, Johnson questions its colonial logic and the imaginative geographies therein. "You go away; *I* do not ask that *your* people be re-married; talk not so to me" (116), Christie declares attempting to force Charlie to recognize his settlement on Native land. Charlie, however, is only bereft with his own prideful arrogance. The italics emphasize the "us" versus "them" dichotomy, but I propose they also emphasize the distinction and location of a politics of recognition. Whereas Charlie invokes power from the state and its normalized theatricalities, Christie is clearly the sovereign "*I.*" "I *am* married, and you or the church cannot do or undo it" (116). Canadian law does not create spaces of consensus, constitute Christie's peoplehood, or solidify permanent maps and jurisdictions. She asserts instead a political understanding in which "purity" and "honor" are foundational and her "nation cringes not to law" (116). In less Victorian terms, the point is that Indigenous peoplehood differs greatly from liberal discourses of the nation-state.[56] Johnson, through the intimacy of a marriage, provides an imaginative mode to examine the Indian Act; the possibilities of "a Red girl's reasoning" to upgrade the current "White man's mockeries" (115) exist in this moment of intimate coupling. By examining Johnson and the currency of the Indian Act at the time, it is possible to delineate the conceptual maps of Canada. I argue that "reasoning" rather than requesting or appealing to the courts becomes a path for unsettling state modes of liberal discourses in which Native women were at a particular nexus of power relations.

Johnson presents us with the possibilities of mapping an alternative Canadian landscape. The couples quarrel, so that the larger "family of the nation" does not have to endure the same struggles. The autonomy of Native women as speaking subjects is transformative not just for Native nations, but for all individuals involved. When Charlie's anger turns toward Christie's father for not telling him of his "illegitimate" marriage and therefore Christie's bastardization, the strength of "love" and brotherly bonds is tested. Even though Christie has been reasoning with Charlie, he is still unable to see Christie's mother—or any Native women—as a viable speaking subject, and thus he does not take seriously the legitimacy of Native nations. Instead, Native laws and customs are relegated to uncivilized spaces and times. When Christie asks if knowing that her parents' marriage was not performed by a *state-sanctioned* priest would have made a difference, Charlie responds, "God knows" (117), and in turn reduces Christie to the status of an illegitimate "squaw"—a term riddled with sexual violence, dispossession, degeneration, and criminalization. In fact, via the Indian Act, Native women's morality and position in this newly mapped territory could mean imprisonment, confinement, exploitation, and community exile—it certainly meant huge reductions of Native-owned land and a reduction of state contractual expenses.

Christie, now denigrated under the unreasonable laws of her husband, makes the only reasonable choice for a woman in this society who needs to maintain her honor and morality. In the most famous passage of Johnson's, Christie forces the gaze of Charlie to "look up" at her as she delivers her closing in "tones quiet, soft and deadly":

> There was never such time as that before our marriage, for *we are not married now.* "Stop," she said, outstretching her palms against him as he sprang to his feet, "I tell you we were not married. Why should I recognize the rites of your nation when you do not acknowledge the rites of mine? According to your own, my parents should have gone through your church ceremony as well as an Indian contract; according to *my* words, we should go through an Indian contract as well as through a church marriage. If their union is illegal, so is ours. If you think my father is living in dishonor with my mother, my people will think I am living in dishonor with you." (117)

Christie physically resists Charlie's rising up from his chair, symbolic of New Canada rising as a nation, and by her words she breaks the marriage contract. The performativity of the legal language is coupled with the performativity of moral systems. Christie's ending the marriage is symbolic of stopping negotiations or reciprocity between Native people and the settler state and acknowledging that she, as a gendered, racialized woman, has the power to do so by invoking her power as a member of a Native nation and the pre-existing contracts that the Indian Act denies.[57] As a Haudenosaunee, Six Nations, Mohawk woman, Johnson was knowledgeable of a woman's right to declare a marriage contract void. Her words carry the same legal weight as the priest and the law—neither god nor abstract laws are above the reasoning of a "Red Girl." Her "purity" and "honor" remain, while the laws of Canada and their application to Native people—Native women in particular—are exposed as "dishonorable."

The destiny of the settler nation-state and its permanence are called into question as Christie forces the acceptance of its imagined geographies. Borders, inheritance, and family ordering are situational and rhetorical acts: "How do I know when another nation will come and conquer you as you white men conquered us? And they will have another marriage rite to perform, and they will tell us another truth, that you are not my husband, that you are but disgracing me, that you are keeping me here not as your wife, but as your—your *squaw*" (117–18). Faced with the undeniable contradictions in his reasoning, Charlie resorts to physical violence by grabbing Christine's wrist. The benevolent, childlike man becomes an enforcer of imagined nation-state boundaries through the only means possible—brute force. Joe, who is in another room, bursts in to "save" Christie, but even these gallant gestures are not without colonial desire of possession. In repeated images of Christie's "bare brown neck and arms," it is possible to read potential violence; Joe might have his own immoral motives: "As for Joe, a demon arose in his soul as he noticed she kept her wrist covered" (119). The sexual conquest of Native women was part and parcel of Native land dispossession. Though Joe does not partake in what is considered the violent past, his future actions of mapping the land are not innocent, nor are his chivalrous actions. Rather, these cartographies of violence create geographies of abject bodies that continue to put Native women at risk. It turns out the need to conquer through force and law does make Joe and Charlie duplicates under the right to possess land and women's bodies through law. The subtlety of the subtext frames colonization as an interconnected system where the collector, the priest, and the law are followed by aggression, making way for those like Joe who will demarcate the boundaries of the nation—through violent mapping.

The Indian Act is subtly and implicitly folded into the plot of the story and haunts the various subjectivities in the text. A colonial utopia, which occupies space from coast to coast, relies on master discourses, mapping of land, and control of bodies. The Canadian nation-state, with British roots, has not only claimed land but asserted colonial rule over all of the map and the Native bodies within its "territorial blank slate." "The land became "civilized," literally, when it became an extension of the European's body," writes Karen Piper.[58] Native women legally were declared extensions of their husbands and unable to return to their communities. Even though Charlie returns and appears before Christie devastated and apologetic for his bad behavior, he still holds a belief in his nation's dominion over the law and rites of all those within the space of Canada and the spaces that *might* become part of the nation through expansion. He does not question his "authority" and "rule" over Christie, for she "was simple-minded and awfully ignorant to pitch those old Indian Laws at him in her fury, but he could not blame her" (120). The mapping of Indigenous people into or out of empire first took the form of fanciful imaginings from British rule, to Canada as rising nation-state, to its ongoing presence as a global force.[59] Yet as Bruce McLeod makes clear, from the first imagined "spatial designs"—a "time when imperialism had more to do with far-fetched dreams than with far-flung territories"—the geographies have had to reinvent, recode, and produce new material territories from their encounters:

> The process of culturally framing or coordinating resistant populations for specific economic purposes was however undermined by colonialism itself. As it produces itself, colonial society threatens to unravel because its "natural order" is constantly questioned by the proximity of and interchange with other societies. It's inevitable cross-cultural and territorially uncertain character means that the colonizers' social order is in constant jeopardy. The constructedness of colonial society, hence its flaws and failings, are exposed as it attempts to conceal them in the interests of presenting natural, coherent, and controlled society fit for rulership.[60]

Charlie, arrogantly assured by love and the contract of marriage, assumes that Christie will be in her place—the domestic chambers of their room. All he finds, however, is a note that only addresses Joe but refuses to name Charlie. *She refuses to recognize him.* The "mockery of her ball dress" now lies on the floor where he had thrown it in anger, along with dead daffodils, a symbol of cultivated English flowers.

These images haunt Charlie "long afterwards," as he spends months trying to find Christie. Johnson paints a pathetic picture of a lovesick and suffering man who "took to petting dogs" (121). Discouraged, but not without hope, he discovers a St. Bernard near death, which he names Hudson and nurses back to health. The "savior" again finds solace in this step of helping an inferior, so much so that Joe says, "I really believe that big lumbering brute saved [Charlie]" (122). Without a loyal and devoted subject, Charlie becomes a pitiable and lost soul, a narrative device that unveils the frailty of white settler space and its reliance on a subjugated other.

Unable to return to her community, in accordance with the Indian Act, which highly surveilled reserve populations, Christie has vanished. In fact, under the various stages of the Indian Act, an incalculable number of Native women and their children vanished as Non-Status Indians and were expunged from Native spaces. Removed from ancestral land and relegated to degenerate subjects still raced and spatialized by the law, many chose assimilation into a white settler society. When Charlie finally tracks down Christie, she is in a small town boarding in an unkempt cottage, recognizably thrust to a lower class, yet employed in the womanly, respectable art of sewing and embroidery. In most cases, when white husbands left their now-Non-Status Indian wives, they did not fare so well and allegedly became "degenerate," individual subjects. In Johnson's story, the reunion of the couple does not end romantically, the usual end in much fiction where the interracial couple is Indian and white—nor does Christie lose her autonomy or personhood through criminalization. No matter how vehemently Charlie begs her to return to him, pleading with her that she "*must* come" because, "you are mine—*mine*—we are husband and wife!" Christie remains cold and like stone (124). Charlie still does not understand the problem of possession and an unequal relationship of marriage or nation-to-nation rights; he is unable to understand and thus does not accept Christie's divorce decree, just as he does not accept the marriage rites of her people. Her belief in her autonomy as a woman and her Nation's autonomy overcome her emotions and wants. Christie desubjectifies her status, "'You cannot *make* me come . . . neither church, nor law, nor even'—and the voice softened—'nor even love can make a slave of a red girl'" (124). Slavery to the laws of an imposed state as instigated in the intimacy of marriage is the denial of personhood; the Indian Act was a denial of Native women's subjectivity, place, and right to land.

In order to assert his superior citizenship rights and territorial claims as an Anglo man, Charlie repudiates a preexisting system of social relations and politics and continues to conceal the power relations in the production of knowledge and production of space. Just as in the case of the dog he names Hudson, a reference again to the Hudson Bay Company, the Native will always be an object for Charlie to capitalize on through discovery tropes, cataloguing, and fashioning from his own desires and imagination. Eventually, Charlie acquiesces, understanding that inasmuch as he "forfeited" Christie when he insisted that "God knows": "he turned from her, but she had looked once into his face as the Law Giver must have looked at the land of Canaan outspread at his feet" (124). The biblical reference to the land of Canaan symbolizes the configuration of Native people as Canaanites, which led to justification of conquering land on moral grounds. Johnson rewrites the process of discovery and the figuring of Natives as Canaanites in this moment, forever disrupting Charlie's colonial imaginings. She may still be in love with Charlie, noted in "vengeful lie in her soul," but she sends him to "a bare, hotelish room" (126).

This moment effectively questions many facets of the newly forming state, based on morality and superiority over the original inhabitants. State values based on genealogical superiority and asserted through autological government apparatus will not bear fruit or a promised land. The couplings in these stories do not affirm the logics of the cult of domesticity based on gendered progress narratives, of racial hierarchies conceived as inherent, but provide a nexus of dissent where the dissolution of Natives' legal rights and the arrogance of the supreme legitimacy of the Canadian government are exposed. Settler spatialities are set up to deny Native peoples' concepts of territory and replace their experiences, or socio-spatialities. However, Christie rejects Charlie as "the law giver" and overrules the absorption of "the land. . . at his feet" (125) by rejecting the absorption of her personhood into the settler state. Johnson ends the story with Charlie in a hotel room, a symbolic space that is rented out over and over without the permanency of settlement. It is a transitive space that is never occupied, comfortable, or, most importantly, settled. It and "his whole life, desolate as a desert, loomed up before him with appalling distinctness . . . [on] the outstretched . . . white counterpane, he sobbed" (126).

Conclusions: Indeterminate Futures

Each of Johnson's stories provides a (re)mapping of abject space from the scale of the Native body to nations by reconceiving the liberal logics bounded in intimate relationships. Lauren Berlant's questioning of the normal narratives of intimacy applies in this instance: "Rethinking intimacy calls out not only for redescription but for transformative analyses of the rhetorical and material conditions that enable hegemonic fantasies to thrive in the minds and on the bodies of subjects while, at the same time, attachments are developing that might redirect the different routes taken by history and biography. To rethink intimacy is to appraise how we have been and how we live and how we might imagine lives that make more sense than the ones so many are living."[61] The subtext in these two short stories provides alternative possibilities to the discourses of the Indian Act and citizenship. Marrying white men does not provide the two women protection, nor does assimilation. In fact, it only makes them more vulnerable as they find themselves under settler legal jurisdiction. Thus, the clarity of Christie's allegiance to her nation is rational and well reasoned, and not based on mere sentiment. She (re)maps the imagined geographies of settler colonialism, reminding her Canadian audience that "my nation cringes not to law" (116). Personhood is not realized in citizenship or the allegiance to an abstract space of the state represented by the church and school or through marriage to a white man, but only through ties to family, kinship, land, and history.

Johnson takes a stand against domesticating Indian policies, and often her sentimental rhetoric radically reminds readers of Native history, land, and rights and how acknowledgment of these would make a stronger nation. Christie's and Esther's intimate couplings were and still are a public affair routed and mired in sexist acts constituted through spatial discourses of morality, citizenship, and nationhood. Each woman handles her abjection differently—one through murder and the other through a divorce decree— but they still end in the same spaces as outside the conceptual maps of the settler state and literally dispossessed in the land of their ancestors. The logics of settler colonialism are exposed when presented with an intimate couple whose intimate choices are constrained by the liberal logics of empire.

During this time, Native women felt "the stings of civilization" at a disproportionate rate. The Indian Act left them on the fringe of society, disposed from tight family networks and dislocated from their communities. Even when bill C-31, which reinstated Indian women previously ripped from their

Indian status, came into effect in 1985, gender inequities remained. The Native population grew by 19 percent alone as a result of the bill's passage, and with natural growth it rose to 33 percent. Yet this number belies the ongoing impact of the liberal logics used to discern Indian status through the politics of marriage.[62] Again, state documents and legal marriages arose as the main point of proof to declare one's status. Those born out of wedlock or into marriages not sanctioned by the Indian Act or the Indian agent at the time had a very difficult process of reinstatement.[63] Though marriage laws that applied to all of Canada would change over the years, just as more amendments were added to the Indian Act, the notion of the public/private and its relationships to "private" property remains consistent. The asymmetrical relationship to power in terms of gender and aboriginality is maintained.[64] Johnson, who herself never married and died in debt and poverty, exposes the logics of marriage. A reexamination of these stories enables us to engage in the geographies of imperialism rooted in and routed through the Indian Act.

In (re)mapping the space of the economic, political, and social through the short stories, I contend that spatial production is not only formed at the moment of colonization, but that it continues to form in its imperial expansion through intimate relationships. While we may empirically never know the impact of Johnson's writings on Canada's policies, we do know that throughout the twentieth century, Johnson provoked much needed discussion of race, gender, and nation, and an examination of her work leads us to consider the possibilities of rethinking spatial restructuring. While many have examined Johnson's work in terms of its loyalist or feminist tendencies as well as to look at her critique of the Indian in popular culture, I believe it is important to examine her work to look at the foundations of the intimate to the settler state.[65] We have the responsibility to excavate her from the mire of racial trappings and approach her work in a new light—one that (re)maps colonial geographies by examining the intimate couple and its relation to the processes of mapping our nations. Most importantly, I propose here that Johnson's controversial commitment to Canada is a commitment to what Canada could be, rather than what it already was—and what it could be was part of what it already was—that is Native land.

2 (Re)routing Native Mobility, Uprooting Settler Spaces in the Poetry of Esther Belin

THE POLITICS OF PLACE FOR NATIVE PEOPLES IS VERY TRICKY BOTH socially and politically. While conceptions of Native identity are legislated differently depending on governing nation-states, tribal government systems, histories, and cultural differences, they share in common spatialized tendencies; identity, social relations, and politics are often conceived, represented, and determined as geographically and historically situated and bound to a particular community. As Philip Deloria reminds us, "fixity, control, visibility, productivity, and, most importantly, docility" were the main objectives in reservation containment and part and parcel of supporting the "colonial dream" of the settler state.[1] Even though set aside as a space separate from "civilization," as I discussed in the previous chapter, and a space of surveillance and control, Native people made the space of the reservation their home and place from which to ground community and the tribal self. This grounding, even while considered abject space by the settler state, is of utmost importance to the imaginative geographies that create the material consequences of everyday existence for Native people, even while the historical onslaught of legislation continues to rip that grounding out from under them. In contemporary politics—and over the last two hundred years—Native communities are depicted and conceived as transitory, dying communities, despite the reality of vitality and strength of Native people who refuse to relinquish land and self to the forces of settler colonialism. Yet, in order not to cede the ground, we must also begin to scrutinize the impact of spatial policies in our cognitive mapping of Native lands and bodies. Beyond examining the discursive frameworks located in specific historical, political, and cultural moments, it is important to think critically about "sets of choices, omissions, uncertainties, and intentions" that are "critical to, yet obscured within," the mapping of the body polity and nation-state.[2] How do we uproot settler-colonial social and material maps that inform our everyday experiences?

In this chapter, I focus on the material practices at work in the termination and relocation era (1952–60), as it is an example of the way Native people mentally and unconsciously react and negotiate with imposed colonial spatial ideology, such as that found in the American Indian Relocation Act of 1955. Esther Belin's (Diné) book of poetry *From the Belly of My Beauty* not only enables us to see the legacy of this era from the perspective of a Native woman, but also provides a glimpse into other possible ways to map these experiences. In this collection, Belin, "blues-ing on the brown vibe" of the urban landscape of Los Angeles and Oakland, California, collects snapshots of the urban Indian community in these major relocation centers, memories of Dinétah, and instances of the routes that take her back and forth both physically and mentally. Her poetry is a potential site for a critique of dominant spatial norms of fixity of Native people in time and space, and it allows for a potential spatial restructuring. Physical boundaries drawn through legislation, social policy, and public narration support the logics of settler colonialism. These imposed spatialities construct Indians' "place" in the settler state. Through a reading of Belin's poetry, it is possible to address these statist visions of place. Donna Landry and Gerald MacLean make clear that material feminism "takes the critical investigation, or reading, in the strong sense, of the artifacts of culture and social history, including literary and artistic texts, archival documents, and works of theory, to be a potential site of political contestation through critique."[3] Belin's poetry is an example of Native women writers presenting geopolitics as a matter of narrated relationships embedded in Native epistemologies and narrations that envision the future. In these poetics, there is a critique of colonial orderings that exposes power relations in the settler map, points out the intentions of the state, and relishes in the uncertainties. Belin's work provides us with a meaningful opportunity to focus on the gendered material practices involved in the process of a federal program that once again sought to restructure land and vanquish bodies.

Through the reinterpretation of Diné stories and philosophies and Belin's poetry, it is possible to achieve alternative understandings of Native spatial relationships to each other and our communities. This chapter is a spatial practice addressing bounded space and immobile bodies structured in U.S.

settler colonial logic that coincides and is integral to the rise of the nation-state to global power. By understanding that space is produced and productive, we unbury the generative roots of spatial colonization and lay bare its concealed systems. Belin's poetry demonstrates the effect of the children born off-reservation and into this spatial upheaval marked by post–World War II Indian politics that pushed for incorporation into American culture and economics at the expense of tribal cultures and treaty-made land bases. More importantly, her poetry mediates the material conditions that these migration policies produced. The reorganizing and ordering of space in the forms of nation-state, reservations, ghettos, barrios, counties, and other geopolitical organizing are necessary to the inner workings of colonialism. This era is vital to understanding the generative roots of the rez/off-rez dichotomy, its impact on Native communities, and its replications in ongoing federal Indian policy in the United States. Most importantly, a spatial examination of legislative policies enables us to engage how imagining spatialized bodies and lands materializes in everyday life.

Gendering Relocation

During the post–World War II era, a heightened sense of nationalism seized the geopolitical imagination of American citizens, resulting in federal Indian policy based on creating a unified political citizenry that required a geopolitical imagining of the space of the nation. Western masculine progress, rooted in the patriarchy of legal, military, and imperial conquest, defined state practices. "Progress" became the mantra for a budding U.S. nation-state and a term evoking American rugged individualism abroad, exemplified by a raw masculinity, reckless bravery, "rational" ingenuity, domination, and ambition.[4] The United States, as a space of patriarchal control through military conquest, formed in this moment as a global power (the effect of which will be taken up again in the last two chapters). Its counterpart of feminine progress, derived from Christian morality, came to define national cultural practices symbolically entrenched in the domesticated space of the home. The white bourgeois American nuclear family became the pivot on which a national imagining rested, and such a family came to be a social formation Native people within the domesticated space of the nation were expected to embrace as part of national unity. Native tribalism during this time was deemed degenerate and passé and akin to communism. As the nation of the United States progressed into a world power, Native people were to again assimilate into the fabric of this particular kind of American sociality. To ensure this, the federal relocation program began unofficially shortly after World War II and officially in 1952. BIA approved the support of programs to "help" tribal citizens move to the city to become part of the cadre of wage-earning U.S. citizens whose individual "freedoms" allowed them to succeed in a forward-moving nation. In 1953, Congress also passed House Resolution 108, known as termination legislation. This legislation led to the termination of five Native nations—the Flathead, Klamath, Menominee, Pottawatomie, and Turtle Mountain Chippewa—and by the end of the era there were 109 termination cases.[5] The relocation of Indian people, however, resulted in consequences to almost all Native communities and families. Underpinning federal Indian policy were cold war ideologies of national and cultural homogeneity. For Native people, this meant the absorption of 1,369,000 acres of land into the U.S. nation-state and a reduction of health, education, and other services that were part of long-established treaty rights. Narratives of progress provide the underpinnings for these simultaneous settler and imperial policies. Rather than Native people being isolated from global expansion, they unwillingly became integral to its development.

The conception in scholarship about U.S. imperialism, that the U.S. eye was aimed outward from its borders, belies the mass spatial reconfiguring taking place internally within Native nations. Jodi Kim's important work on the cold war, *Ends of Empire,* argues for the importance of examining the cold war as "not only a historical period, but also an epistemology and production of knowledge, and as such it exceeds and outlives its historical eventness."[6] Kim's critique of the cold war as a form of analysis rather than an event corresponds with Wolfe's assertions regarding settler colonialism. In this chapter, I entangle both as important to understanding the gendered and settler motivations at work in termination that correspond to what Kim names the "protracted life of the Cold War." The relationship between colonial restructuring of Native lands and bodies—and its continued assumptions in the rez/off-rez dichotomy—has its own protracted afterlife, in that like the cold war, it is a "geopolitical, cultural, and epistemological project of gendered racial formation and imperialism undergirding U.S. global hegemony."[7] With land rich in resources needed for capital expansion, Native nations experienced the threat of termination polices and relocation programs. Kim problematizes the event structure of many scholars contending that the end of the cold war marks the beginning of the new trade war, such as the moment of NAFTA, which I will discuss at length in relation to Leslie Marmon Silko's

Almanac of the Dead. Rather, Kim suggests that "the Cold War itself [was] a trade war," and that to question this premise begins an investigation into the motives behind this periodization.[8] In charting the colonial restructuring of land and bodies, Kim's analysis is useful to think of the way that the rhetoric around Indian policy was formed at both these local and global levels. I suggest that we think beyond termination legislation and relocation policies as a teleological endpoint of assimilated lands and bodies. The solidified coast-to-coast rhetoric used to justify treatment of interior Native nations also demarcated those within U.S. boundaries as citizens with industrial obligations, while those who resided or emigrated from its exterior territories were marked as foreign and disposable entities controlled by American capital interests.[9] Native people and their territories were administered as somewhere in between the domesticated and the foreign, but this ambivalence was only in the political language manipulated to usurp Native resources. Rather, Native bodies and land were considered potential sites of absorption into the nation mobilized through the ideologies of the melting pot and Lockean equations of private property as the foreground for freedom and equality.

The discourse of American democracy rooted in liberal capitalism was also part of the rhetoric found in arguments to terminate tribal Nations. Native rights to self-determination as defined in the Indian Reorganization Act (IRA) of 1934 were suddenly coded as paternalizing, inhibiting freedom of individuals, and promoting inequalities for a targeted group. John Collier's intention in drafting the IRA was to stem the loss of Native lands and allow them to recover in some parts the estimated 90 million acres of land lost between the Dawes Act of 1887 and 1934. In the wake of the cold war, however, communal tribal lands were designated as communist, anti-capital, and un-American. Because of his support for tribal sovereignty, the Senate Committee on Indian Affairs campaigned to have Collier ousted from office as a communist.[10] In this era, tribal kinship and concepts of nation, identity, and relationships to the land were deeply suspect. Men and women were to act according to American patriotic principles with an investment in private property. The liberal ideologies of freedom of the individual (as discussed in chapter 1) manifested yet again in settler logics to dismantle tribal nations and the structures of their community. What remained consistent between the period of allotment, the Indian Reorganization Act, and termination was the implementation of structures of patriarchy in tribal communities as men took the position of head of household, tribal chairman, and wage earner, respectively.[11] Disinvesting Native women from political representation, traditional structures, and land rights served the interests of commercial developers and the settler state as well as imperial interests.

Yet, as Kevin Bruyneel rightly contends in *The Third Space of Sovereignty,* "the federal policy of termination did not subdue and minimize the expression of indigenous political identity and autonomy in the American context, as was its intention."[12] Native communities fought the disruption of Indigenous self-determination and cultural systems. The first goal proposed in the American Indian Chicago Conference was to end the termination policies that were profoundly affecting Native people, but, according to Bruyneel, these policies also provided an organizing moment in which Native people were forming their own language: "They saw the development and articulation of an expressly political *new Indianess* as the proper path for securing and advancing the cause of tribal sovereignty in the modern context."[13] Termination and relocation were not new in their goals or conceptions, but rather an extension of earlier gendered colonial policies of assimilation. But, as Bruyneel's research on the AICC demonstrates, what does become commonly practiced is the articulation of innovative forms of arguing for rights, not as civil rights, but in terms of small Nations, not world powers such as the United States and Canada, but ones with every bit as much legitimacy.[14] This legacy has had a profound impact on Native political thought and concepts of belonging.

Consequences of imposed legislation and settler ideologies reverberate for generations and produce a myriad of ongoing spatial relations, many of which remain underscored in ongoing and newly constructed policies. Questions of place, identity, and community relationships are the by-products of the federal Indian legislation of termination and the policy of relocation, which yet again sought to fashion American Indians as individual property-owning subjects with an allegiance to the settler state. U.S. relocation policies moved Native people off the reservations and into cities such as Chicago, Detroit, Minneapolis, Los Angeles, and Oakland. Newspapers, pamphlets, and statements from the Bureau of Indian Affairs used the common rhetoric of "progress," "modernizing," and helping Indians to become "part of American society" to convince Native and non-Natives that this was the key to their survival. Poor reservation economics had already prompted many men and some families to leave their communities and become wage earners in order to provide for their families. This legislation encouraged even more participation as relocation was made official and bolstered with resources. Indians who migrated were to become part of the American "melting pot" rather than maintain a tribal identity founded in a relationship to land that differed greatly from Lockean notions of property and development. Although Native people were always mobile, this era began a particular form of large migration back and forth from cities to reservations and reservations to cities. According to the 2010 census, we find 78 percent of the Native population living in urban centers.[15]

In an autobiographical essay, Belin articulates these goals while pinpointing her individual story of parents who first attended the Sherman Institute in Riverside, California, and then were relocated to the Los Angeles area: "Goal: annihilation of savage tendencies characteristic of indigenous people. New language. New clothes. New food. New identity. Learn to use a washing machine. Learn to silence your native tongue, voice, being. Learn to use condiments without getting sick. Learn a trade and domestic servitude. Learn new ways to survive."[16] Although migration to Los Angeles began in the early 1920s, the population of American Indians was estimated to increase from 6,000 in 1955 to 12,405 five years later.[17] Like many of those relocating to Los Angeles and other cities, Belin's parents' education worked in tandem with the policies of job placement in the city. She rightly connects the assimilation policies of boarding schools and relocation; these civilization policies were both intended to integrate Native people into American society and create a workforce for the nation. Boarding schools attempted to educate and discipline the body, while relocation attempted to separate those bodies from place.[18] Within the process of respatializing the Native body, men and women underwent a gendering process, which also pulled them away from culturally significant ways of relating to the land and community.

The material practices at work in the process of this federal program were aimed at spatial separation from tribal communities and incorporation into the nation-state in the form of nuclear working-class families. Successful removal from remote reservation communities seemed more likely given the numbers of Native men participating in World War II. The United States envisioned itself as a growing urban industrial nation during this time, and this was reflected in the many phases of the federal relocation program, whose main goal remained consistent: relocation was to integrate American Indians into "normal" American communities, which would aid in transforming them into industrious, wage-earning citizens.[19] Men were especially susceptible to the program, as years in boarding school enforced the American ideal of the head of the household as a male wage earner. The Bureau of Indian Affairs (BIA) provided a small amount of money for transportation and subsistence and arranged some employment placement. Later, in 1956, vocational training would also be added to the program. Officially, termination was to end what was seen as Indian welfare, and by 1969 the BIA was spending over 20 million dollars a year to ensure movement of a large mass of Natives into the cities.[20] Architects of the program, Utah senator Arthur V. Watkins and BIA commissioner Dillon Meyer, used liberal rationales and moral rhetoric in rights-based language to appeal to the American public: "Whereas it is the policy of Congress, as rapidly as possible, to make the Indians within the territorial limits of the United States subject to the same laws, and entitled to the same privileges and responsibilities as are applicable to other citizens of the United States, and to grant them all of the rights and prerogatives pertaining to American Citizenship."[21] This extension of assimilation policies rooted in liberal rationale had significant consequences for Native people. While the United States attempted to impose patriarchal forms of Americanness onto Native people many times before by separating them from their land and communities, the policies of these eras brought more Native people into the flow of the economy and labor force.

One of the most detrimental aspects, and the one I address here, is the spatial dichotomy between rez and off-rez that begins to develop at this time as a marker for "Indian" identity and as a barrier between community members. Cities were chosen based on diverse developing industries and growing populations. In many ways, the aspirations for this program were based on material needs and visions of a monoculture society, or to apply Soja's terms, they were "the real-and-imagined geographies of everyday life," respectively.[22] BIA officials believed Indians would fit in better and have more of a chance to integrate into American society than in the small towns that bordered reservations. Spatial distance in this case was not just the physical distance from the reservation, but was also a distancing between other tribal members. Part of the perceived success of these policies was to ensure that those who practiced similar languages, rituals, and customs were separated. The relocation offices often denied access to and information about family members (conceived of as extended kinship relations by Native people) regarding where their relatives were located in their arrival city. In fact, many of the bureaucrats administering the program made sure to spread people out across cities based on their tribal memberships. This policy is often only examined in terms of the physical distancing of space (the rez and the city), but here my concern is the distancing of bodies (kin-to-kin, tribal member-to-tribal member) and continued distancing of shared lived spaces once in the urban area (location of reservation to location of tribal residences in the city) that were to result in the cultural distancing from practices that maintain the strength of Native people. As will be revealed in the discussion of Belin's poetry below, this did not occur, as Native people marked their own spaces in the city.

Los Angeles was a burgeoning city with a frenzied pace of growth in industrial jobs. This resulted in the increase of an Indian population through relocation and even more, a large contingent who unofficially relocated.[23] Many of the jobs that "unskilled" and "uneducated" Indian men were placed into demanded hard physical labor. BIA 1948 commissioner Glen L. Emmons, who began the relocation program, wrote, "The policy of congress is to make the Indians of the United States, as rapidly as possible, subject to the same laws and entitled to the same privileges and responsibilities as other citizens."[24] Native people were to become law-abiding American citizens and part of a masculine working class. Embedded in these "laws," "privileges," and "responsibilities" are prescribed Western roles and gender hierarchies that undergird the nation-state.

In this social project, single men were often the ones solicited for the program, but after a while, whole families began to relocate to major cities as federal aid was denied those reservations on the termination list. Meyer's disdain for reservation life led him to continue to advocate for a version of Indian "progress" and "normalcy" that reflected a European-rooted racial superiority.[25] Decreases in agricultural land use and an emphasis on resource extraction on the reservation also led to changes in responsibilities between men and women.[26] Those who still maintained a land base found subsistence living without the shared work of men and women very difficult. As time progressed and reservation economics declined, women migrated, and even more families and extended families followed the paths of migration. When Native women found themselves in urban areas in the 1950s and 1960s, domestic labor was a needed source of income and much undervalued in this capital economic system. According to the BIA relocation records, "by 1953 placements had reached 2,600, and they peaked in 1957 with 6,964. By 1960 a total of 33,466 Indians had been relocated."[27] This, however, only accounts for those who formally went through the program. Many followed later and informally. This was to be a catalyst for urban migration that continues today, albeit in different flows back and forth from reservations to a variety of cities.

While less attention will be given here to the passing of Public Law 280 in 1953, which furthered the domestication of Native lands, I believe that it is important to discuss as it was also part of the legislation that reshaped geopolitics at the time, albeit, as Carole Goldberg-Ambrose frames it, as an "afterthought in a measure aimed primarily at bringing law and order to the reservations, added because it comported with the pro-assimilationist drift of federal policy."[28] This particular law turned over "criminal/prohibitory" juridical procedures to states, "but does not extend state jurisdiction to 'civil/regulatory' matters."[29] Domestication of Native lands, and subsequently those tribal Nation members who reside there, created fissures in the justice system. Public Law 280 increased the threat against Native women by giving some of the states the option, and others, such as California, the responsibility, of regulating judicial systems over Native nations while decreasing federal Indian programs.[30] This was coupled with defunding of resources for Indian nations to police their own reservations. States, however, were not provided extra resources to take on the policing of these sometimes large areas, often resulting in the lack of addressing injurious crimes.[31] This law was to have devastating consequences on the ability of Indian nations to regulate resource exploitations and criminal acts. Geographer Nicholas Blomely connects the relationship between law, violence, and the making of property in the liberal state: "Violence and law appear antithetical. Liberalism tends to locate violence *outside* the law, positing state regulation as that which contains and prevents anarchy. The rule of law is deemed superior, given its ability to regulate violence in a civilized and humane way."[32] Rather than regulate violence, Public Law 280 was indicative of the move to erase the political status of Indian nations and incorporate tribal lands under the surveillance of the United States. Again, the argument that Indian nations deserved the same rights as other citizens, in this case protection under the law, continues to be used to erode and undermine Native sovereignty and self-determination. States were to be part of the apparatus of erasing Indian nations from the national landscape, and these laws would exert a physical and cultural violence through spatial control.

"Talking That Talk": Deconstructing the Public/Private

Once forcibly confined to reservations or eradicated completely from their land, Native peoples were now being coerced into controlled migrating movements. Men were to become hourly workers in urban spaces, or "WORKING, MEN / IN PROGRESS," as Belin illuminates in her poem "On Relocation" (11). In this poem, she closely links relocation to earlier notions of manifest destiny and the legacy of narrating imperial space by visually capitalizing, as if in a road sign, the above words and depicting the idea of progress and movement through italicization. Like a road sign, relocation policy was meant to direct and regulate Native existence. Belin confronts Western notions of gendered labor and land through capitalization. "WORKING, MEN" implies ongoing construction that has a tangible result. Within this signage, which also serves as a warning, Belin explores the gender dimensions of a "progressive" labor force American-style. Women, whose roles as farmers and herders were eroded by federal Indian policy, could gain employment in the city as domestic workers and, more rarely, as low-paid factory workers. In Belin's poetry, the reoccurring juxtaposition of strong Diné women who provide strength to their communities and white women who enact power and privilege in detrimental ways illuminates the racial and gender hierarchies at the foundation of assimilation policies. In fact, the poems that focus on the relationship of gendered and racialized labor in white households are tinged with a bitter tone of betrayal and anger. Relocation was not only about a movement of bodies off reservation, but also was about respatializing a consciousness and relationship to land. Mapping space as settler places required the assimilation of Native consciousness, but as others have noted, this did not occur, as Native people, like Belin, held onto their political and cultural identifications.[33]

Women's roles as caregivers put more pressure on them to become more like white women or "to cook roast beef and not mutton / to eat white bread and not fry bread / to start a family and not an education / to be happy servants to doctors' families in Sierra Madre / and then to their own" (20). The economic impossibility of enjoying the position of white women in addition to racial inequities in the workplace resulted in Native women taking on roles as domestic servants and caregivers to others' children, not their own. The placement of women in the "private" sector of the home obscured Native women's political, economic, and social contributions. Feminist geographers challenge the dichotomy of public/private and assert that the public space often constructs the politics found in the private sphere of the home as the intersections of class, religion, and identity come into play.[34] Doreen Massey's innovative work seeks to put forth a notion of the domestic and home that is not separate from public life, but rather informed by it. Indeed, she stipulates that the spatial notion of home is overdetermined by the masculine colonial experience, where men "setting out to discover and change the world" fix the place of home in their imagination as static or as "a place which did not change."[35] Yet, as feminists argue, the space of home is in constant motion and constant change for those who labor in it, whether in informal economies or wage labor. In many ways, I extend this analysis to the reservation—for those who live, work, pray, and enact community on a daily basis, the reservation is not a place of the past, but a place of the present filled with possibilities for growth; nor does this growth end at the imposed legal boundaries of the nation-state.

In domestic worker categories, Native women were placed into this false private/public split or colonial map comprising exterior gender and racial norms. Federal Indian policy attempted to create domestic laborers and exploit labor as well as restructure male/female relations through its promotion of the public/private divide. Restructuring gendered practices of the home in Native contexts is all too often the focus of policy and law, evidenced by their basis in constructing the dichotomy of male/public/production/world and feminine/private/reproduction/home. In these policies, the extension of home to nation and the need for the nation-state to control all within its boundaries is made clear through the familial metaphors of "great white father" or "childlike Native."

The policy of boarding schools and relocation and its effect on Native women and their communities supported the imposition of the public/private and limitation of extended family relationships. Motherhood and home became sites of angst in the face of many responsibilities outside the home, in the community, and with extended family (which is a summarization of the various roles Native women are still often responsible to fulfill). Engendering men and women in the image of the imperial family was of utmost importance in claiming and reordering Native spaces that become stagnant not only in time, but in space. Belin's injunction against this reordering resonates throughout her poems. Women were to "mimic the rituals of Euro-American women" "who never really became women because they / were taken off the Rez before they could go through a womanhood / ceremony" (20). "Mimic" is a carefully chosen word that withstands the socialization of Native women into the image of "Euro-American Womanhood"; it implies imitation of this form of womanhood and not assimilation. She begins the poem by pointing out the intersectionality of the gendered experience of men and women: "Some say the boarding school experience wasn't that bad / because they learned a trade / at least the men did" (20). She reinforces the discrepancies between these experiences and women's coping mechanisms by emphasizing the mimicking and incorporation of Diné-specific cultural and gendered imagery that is rich in meanings of body and place. Specifically, in later poems, she makes reference to participation in the Diné womanhood ceremony, the Kinaaldá, which brings a Navajo woman into the status of a fully realized woman in the community.

Even though Belin "stumble[s] at [her] shadow raised by Los Angeles sky-scrapers," she still has not been erased and recognizes the "ironic immigration" of the multitude of Native people living in Los Angeles. In her opening poem, she not only recognizes her own tribal specificity but extends it to incorporate many others who find themselves in the space of the city through capital forces:

> And Coyote struts down East 14th
> feeling good
> looking good
> feeling brown
> melting into the brown that loiters
> rapping with the brown in front of the Native American Health
>   talking that talk
> of relocation from tribal nation
> of recent immigration to the place some call the United States
> home to many dislocated funky brown (3)

Coyote is on the move, marked by the use of verbs; he is making connections with others rather than being distanced from tribal relationships and the "modern world." The Indigenous "center" for Coyote, indicated by the indent in the lines above, does not bind him but keeps him in constant conversations signified in the "rapping" and "talking." In this poem, Coyote the trickster does not assimilate into a white landscape of the U.S. melting pot, which requires a loss of an Indigenous center and Indigenous land; rather, the "funky brown" is the desirable alliance, further recognized in the lines, "ironic immigration / more accurate tribal nation to tribal nation" (3). The alliteration here makes us pause and question the colonial structuring of tribal lands as distance whose effect leads us to question the notion of the borders of the settler state. "Coyote sprinkles corn Pollen in the four directions" (3) as an offering to the tribal lands that are erased in the settler spatial imaginary that claims the land and expunges the "funky brown." She (re)maps the land in these powerful enactments of recognition, and by thanking the Indigenous people of Los Angeles "for allowing the use of their land," she recognizes the history of spatial restructuring by refusing "to perpetuate the myth" (4). Throughout the trickster Coyote's travels, there is engagement with other Indigenous people, an everyday experience for many Native people, recognizing all land in the United States and other settler states as belonging to Native nations. Movement doesn't reflect dislocation or loss but "more accurate[ly] tribal nation to tribal nation" (1, 3). The loss that occurs in this poem is narrated when an engagement with capitalist modes of production, "Reservation discrimination," occurs, and the effects of colonialism that structure the bodies of "the mythic Indian they create" make Indian bodies and land ready for the taking. Coyote's encounter with a Navajo woman in Winslow, Arizona, makes this incredibly clear. The ease of "talking that talk" between the Coyote and the Navajo woman is natural and only interrupted when a "bilaganna," or white woman, "snaps a photo." The Navajo woman has long learned this colonial song and dance and asks for cash "requesting some of her soul back / instead / she replaces her soul with a worn picture of George Washington on a / dollar bill." (4). Coyote leaves her at this stop "still squatting," as if ready to give birth to new possibilities; she "waits there for the return of all her pieces" (4). Movement does not relate to the foreclosing or death of Native peoples, but Native people "travel together" meeting "in and out of existence" even though this travel can be "rusty at times / worn bitter from relocation" (6). The conceptual fixity of immigration, settler status, and the spatial split between Natives on- and off-reservation implemented through the discursive practices of relocation, termination, and Public Law 280 are exposed as a lexicon of continued empire building.

Important to the lexicon of empire building is a restructuring of space in terms of humanistic geography. Gillian Rose argues that the humanistic geography has long produced a masculine notion of home as a prediscursive place, or an ultimate sense of place, configured in the conquest of the female body as conquest of places, such as the home, nation, and diasporic lands. Relocation of Indian women to the cities carries a particular weight as the female body comes to be ingested in a private/public split that Rose references in the use of the white female body.[36] Rather than as a traditional symbol of strength found in Native relationships between body and space, Native women are domesticated by the too-simple associations of woman, nation, home, private, and tradition that act as symbols to support patriarchy—whether it is asserted through colonial governmentality or through tribal politics. As the pressures to resist assimilation into the U.S. body politic heightened, policing of Native women—as symbols of nation and home—increased on and off the rez.[37] The significance held by Native women on the ground in their communities has more teeth than the private/public stands for. This power is often manifested through a power that stretches beyond the social, cultural, and reproductive, but also into the very political and economic life of communities both in urban areas and on the reservation. In the context of Fort Berthold reservation community, Tressa Berman contends that during the welfare reform era of 1996, many women in this matrifocal community recalled termination legislation and juxtaposed it with the devastating cuts to welfare rolls and shortened time limits as well as the repeated rescinding of federal trust responsibilities to the policies. Both had similar effects on the reservation communities. Women's economic roles, which are too often unaddressed as women become empty signifiers of home or nation, have a profound impact on Native nations:

> Precisely how reservation communities intend to cope with deep cuts to their economies forces a critical examination into the ways in which community members—especially women who receive the bulk of welfare payments for dependent children—strategize to make ends meet. In particular, American Indian women continue to shoulder the responsibilities of balancing work and family life due to the structural effects of increases in female-headed households and interhousehold exchange cycles that radiate out from women-centered kin networks.[38]

This disrupts a stagnant and static sense of home created through masculinist ideologies. Crucial to this analysis, Massey states that "a large component of the identity of that place called home derived from precisely the fact that it had always in one way or another been open, constructed out of movement, communication, social relations which always stretched beyond it."[39] Massey's notion is useful to consider in a situated Native experience, such as Coyote's above, where home is the place that holds traditions, especially those related to land, but whose relationships to other Natives, nations, clans, and families "stretched beyond." While Berman relates to both the physical and social colonial restructuring through the Garrison Dam and welfare reform, respectively, in a reservation community, it is fair to state that even in the urban centers women maintained their matrifocal traditions that thwarted the eradication of tribal relationships. Belin's poem "Indian Mom" speaks to the strength involved in maintaining a "home" as "she cuts beading thread with her teeth" and her "tears are stitched into her beadwork / tight in rows / mending her own hoop" (19). The gendered dynamic of public/private split so often taken up in mainstream feminism elides the position of Native women, who are constantly being displaced, economically disadvantaged, and forced to accept imposed gender norms as their lands become domesticated into the private space of the nation. As "Indian Moms" and "squatting" Navajo women fight in an economically disadvantaged world, selling their beadwork and jewelry, struggling to feed their kids and "mend" family tribal life, Native women are not contained in the public/private dichotomy, as settler colonialism makes Native lands and bodies readily available for consumption.

Termination, relocation, and Public Law 280 presented a tough challenge to those who individually and as nations fought to maintain a distinct cultural and sovereign identity. Whether on the reservation or in the city, times were legally and socially changing for American Indians. Belin's poems recast the power relations at work in these legal maneuverings and move us from teleology of lost members of Indian communities to one of finding new possibilities. Native women play multiple roles in imagining new possibilities in urban environments even as they encounter the violence of changing labor practices. Notice the repetitive use of "and" in the poem, which not only forms a driven rhythm but also emphasizes the pace of this change:

> Instead of fasting and sweating and praying and running
> They set the table and vacuumed and ironed and nursed and fed
> . . .
> They were strong and loved and made love and sobered up
> and organized weekend road trips back to the rez
> Back to the rez where we all came from
> and where we need to return
> to heal our wounds
> from the Euro-American womanhood ceremony. (20)

The split between rez communities that was the aim of relocation did not account for mobility or a community's ability to take care of one another and create their own rhythms. Even though policies have greatly influenced Native women's experiences, Belin also suggests that Native women provide the key to seeming fragmentation, even as they need to experience healing as well. However, healing is not linked to an original, stagnant home, such as that of the masculine notion of the home as discussed earlier, but returning to a specific land and a community that is always in the process of creation. The land and people that strengthen Belin are not stagnant, just as city places are not merely assimilative through ideas of accumulative progress. The debate about authenticity, or who is actually a "real" Indian, is often motivated by the spatial politics I confront in this project. Critical scholars, until the last decade, had divided up American Indians into two categories: traditionalists and progressives. In many ways this split is also spatial, as supposedly progressives leave the rez and traditionalists stay at home.[40] Belin wrestles with the imposed colonial classifications of geographies embedded in the language of "real" Indians, and by doing so she exposes the fluctuation and false premise of the categories in the first place.

Many Native peoples, as a result of relocation, resituated their relationships to their communities and one another in places where lands are not defined or named by the state as "Indian." In the urban centers, however, connections between home and the city changed and new connections formed. Susan Lobo argues in her essay "Urban Clanmothers" that the loss of extended family one would have on the reservation was replaced by an extended network of friends and even distant relatives throughout the relocation site of the Bay Area in northern California; these networks, she argues, are facilitated by women who, in fact, act as clanmothers.[41] Inevitably, Native people gather in what Renya Ramirez refers to as Native hubs, or places "of mobility both in urban and reservation settings, a mechanism to support Native notions of culture, community, identity and belonging as well as a political vision for social change."[42] While speaking to Silicon Valley specifically, Ramirez's work with hubs finds resonance in many relocation areas. Research in this area is expanding to include more in-depth studies of the local. The scale of the local profoundly reframes the discussion of relocation as purely loss. Myla Carpio's examination in *Indigenous Albuquerque,* for instance, reminds us of the twenty-two Native nations that are within a fifty-mile radius of Albuquerque, New Mexico. Furthermore, she reframes the history of relocation not as something that occurred in the event of 1950s and 1960s policy, but as a movement to the city that begins with the railroads and need for money to survive.[43] The structure of settler colonialism worked simultaneously on many fronts, setting up those structures to contain and starve those in the space of the reservation and erase those in wage-earning communities.

Yet Native people have learned to thrive in the city, often returning to the reservation and forming communities, as we will see in Belin's poetry. Often it was necessary for women to practice gendered relations outside the cultural forms learned from their mothers, aunts, and grandmothers. These practices of relating to one another were not "outdated" in the city, however, but instead, the elements of these practices that persisted were and continue to be vital to Native navigations in urban centers. As Carpio, Ramirez, Lobo, and others have contended, Native people creatively enacted spatial practices that kept their connection with their communities, even as they established new ones in the urban areas. I am heartened by the recent work in this area. Uncovering these histories is an important step in countering the narrative of the lost urban Indian so prominent in current imaginations of both Natives and non-Natives. The settler narrative of the rez/off-rez dichotomy is a lie at its very conception—Native death through assimilation eased the consciousness of a nation that relies on the theft of Native land. In many ways, the lack of dominant cultures' understanding of Native peoples' capacity to reach out to others beyond their specific tribal nation was a major flaw in the goals of relocation policy. In fact, the propensity for sharing where one is from and learning to live with one another comes from thousands of years of experience living on this continent together—it is "talking that talk" and as instinctive as breathing.

"We Are Cut Off from Each Other": Breathing Life into Community Relationships

In the decolonization of space, it is necessary to address the gendered sets of spatial practices, such as those created in the era of termination, relocation, and Public Law 280, in order for communities to make changes that will (re)map our "own hoops[s]" (19). The question quickly becomes, how do we find the routes that connect us? When Floria Forcia, a participant in the American Indian Chicago Oral History project, is asked, "Do you go back to the reservation and take part in anything or are you completely cut off from your reservation?" she profoundly replies, "We're completely *cut off from each other.*"[44] Yet at the time of this interview, Forcia had become important to the Chicago community, akin to one of the "urban clanmothers" to which Lobo's work speaks. The connections among Indians in urban communities occur because of spoken connections and the seeking-out of tribal hubs in urban centers. This echoes Belin's reframing of Western notions of physical barriers of dislocation and questioning of the ways that relocation draws boundaries. The detriments of spatial reconstruction embedded in relocation are (re)mapped through imagining new possibilities embedded in much older philosophies. It is not just the individual who feels displacement, but also the community that has lost a connection. It is for this reason that we must critique settler maps and find new ways to (re)map our communities.

Belin's poetry is rich in Diné epistemologies and philosophy that restructure settler colonial maps. The intergenerational philosophy of breath employed in the poem "On Relocation" connects all living entities to one another as relatives. She actively juxtaposes "word" and "air we breathe" in individual lines to emphasize the power of both to reconfigure spatial and gendered relationships through speech and prayer.

> The physical is easier to achieve
> a boundary drawn to separate people
> Navajos say no word exists
> establishing form to the air we breathe. (11)

This act of breath, which is necessary to life, leads to speech. By connecting speech, language, and breath as "a sacred act through which the individual participates in an ongoing relationship with all other living beings,"[45] this speech act defies spatial policies set in place to dislocate Diné relationships to each other, destroy a Diné-gendered sense of place, and dismantle the Diné and urban Indian community. As one scholar writes: "After their emergence onto the earth's surface, wind and inner forms were placed within all living things as a source of life, movement, speech, and behavior. Rather than being an independent spiritual agency that resides within the individual, like the Western notion of the soul, Holy Wind is a single entity that exists everywhere and in which all living beings participate."[46] Remembering the act of breath enables Belin's readers to imagine past the spatial dislocations of urban migration and the individualism foundational to neoliberalism.

In the act of speaking and writing, Belin is articulating a history of connection and mediating the impact of colonial spatial restructuring in order to recuperate vibrant communities that veer from destructive patriarchal colonial patterns of conceiving of space "as a boundary drawn to separate people" on the basis and interstices of race, nation, and gender. The act of breath, inhaling, exhaling, smoking, and speaking reverberate through this collection of urban poems. At times, they occur in particularly difficult moments experienced by urban Indian women. Belin's use of tobacco throughout her poems, for instance, emphasizes connection, prayer, and the making of urban Indian communities. This occurs throughout her poems, such as in the imagery of the newly arrived trickster figure Coyote offering up a smoke to a Ponca and Seminole, or "good thoughts" offered up in admiration in her poem "For Miss Celine Who Smokes." The "bold / and brown / and beautiful" Miss

Celine who "talks a lot while she smokes /one cigarette after another" (54) may not remember the original intent of tobacco so the narrator in a sense of community helps her out. The admiration of Miss Celine, affectuous throughout the poem, compels us to rethink the relationship between breath, smoking, and possibilities. "As she fires up / Miss Celine is signaling the spirits to gather around" (54) through the use of tobacco. Belin then plays with the physical motion of exhaling and inhaling, and it is through this that the physical barriers break down as "they are waiting for her to speak" and as she does so "they hear her words and listen" (54).

Here we can recall the figure of the trickster Coyote or the alter ego of Ruby, who appears in numerous poems in *From the Belly.* These Native women are uncontainable, sassy, and strong, countering the passive image of Indians fading into the past as the "first world" developed. Remembering the spirits and the power of breath is key to creating connections. The capitalization of "As" accentuates the action taken by the author and a specific Diné belief to make connections to other Native people across lines of differences, even in places named by colonialism as non-Native or non-Native acts, like smoking. Even though Miss Celine "forgets about the spirits" who "are waiting for her to speak / As she exhales," the poem's narrator "think[s] good thoughts for her" (54). Belin was brought up in a vibrant Los Angeles Native community solidified as such by crossing these lines of difference.

Belin connects settler colonial history to the policies that have affected her life and works to resituate them by incorporating philosophies of Navajo place-making in her critique of Western spatial practices. In the second stanza of the poem "On Relocation," Belin again personifies the narrative of colonial restructuring as imagined:

This country's stem
relocation
rooted for invasion
imperial in destiny. (11)

The play between "rooted" and "stem" refigures the imperial axiom. Belin establishes the link between displacement of Native people from their lands and America's growth as an imperial force and nation-state in the slippage of the word "relocation," which refers to the first relocation of Europeans to North America as well as the relocation of Native people in the twentieth century.

María Josefina Saldaña-Portillo's work in Latin American development, which may not be self-evident in the context of Native nations in the United States, offers valuable insight into the relocation period as she clarifies how "the idiom of development" operated in the 1950s and 1960s as a gendered language of universality whereby the "leaving behind of one's own particularity" was narrated as "leaving behind the feminized ethnos of indigenous, peasant, or urban black cultural identity."[47] The spatiality imagined within the narrative of development relied on this "theory of human perfectibility that was itself a legacy of the various raced and gendered subject formations animating colonialism."[48] Certain populations once considered exterior were now interior, which seemingly justified incorporation of lands necessary to development. Through ideas of civilizing "emerged two new manifest subjects: the modern, fully developed subject and its premodern, underdeveloped counterpart. These subjects are manifest because their level of development appears as self-evident. What needed to be explained was not whether these subjects were developed but rather how the developed subject came to be so, and how the underdeveloped subject might follow in his path."[49]

In her third stanza, Belin reiterates the narrative of progress implicated in the line of "imperial in destiny" to draw out its gendered implications. Through the use of italics, punctuation, capitalization, and placement of words, the eye is drawn toward the center of the poem:

WORKING, MEN
IN PROGRESS (11)

The present tense of the construction "in progress" reminds the reader of the ongoing effects of colonization and imperialism. Concepts of progress, the development of Indian land into urban landscapes, Indian bodies into urban workforces, and the gendered dynamics are drawn together in the very middle of the poem, exposing the continued effect of spatial narrations of nation-state destiny and its larger relationships in the world. Saldaña-Portillo argues that "we cannot simply read revolutionary movements of the period as against colonial and neocolonial production," speaking to the instances of revolutions in Latin America, but that "we must also read them as *within* a racialized and gendered developmentalism."[50] I extend this argument to include a necessary examination of the narrative of development in the spatial imaginary of the United States, especially as it concerns those territories deemed domestic and already conquered even while it was necessary to legislate, relocate, and reconfigure land and bodies belonging to Native peoples.

The net effect of such restructuring of Native communities and gendered practices informs the next stanza, in which relocation produces an ongoing effect. The impact of spatial restructuring on subsequent generations becomes evident in the adjectives that emphasize the body:

Stand and wait for crossblood babies
generic cultures blending new versions of red nations
brain-dead at birth from pollution ingested
umbilical cord of sweet grain alcohol and sticky TV diaries. (11)

It is important to note that Belin chooses the word "crossblood," rather than referring to relocated Native peoples as mixed-bloods or completely alienated. The word "crossblood" originates with Gerald Vizenor, known for his play with language and critique of what he calls "terminal Creeds," or those who have an essentialized notion of an Indian stemming from anthropology or popular culture.[51] I, too, am concerned by these essential constructions, but most importantly I am concerned with the boxes of our own making that occur as we deal with political and legal systems meant to support settler colonialism. "Crossbloods," unlike terminal creeds, are not fixed by representations of the real Indian comprising proper bodies, such as blood quantum, in proper places, such as a rez Indian. Crossbloods are a category that escapes spatial and temporal fixations, and Vizenor makes the reservation a crossblood space.[52] By using Vizenor's language, Belin pointedly marks the way relocation becomes a mechanism to put in place further representations of the "real" in the rez/urban dichotomy, as well as addressing social problems.

The poetry, like the crossblood, is a potential language site rather than an exploration of the tragically dislocated generic Indian or tragic mixed-blood lost in narratives of development. The possibility, indetermination and agency in the construction of crossbloods in Belin's poems link representations of the "real Indian" it produces to spatial constraints and meanings produced by dominant society. The verbs in the above stanza ("stand," "wait," "blending," "ingested"), call for action versus complacency. The poetic language considers the historic process of colonization and contemporary reality of the political situation for Native peoples, rather than relying on simplistic and generic notions of Indianess constructed by dominant society. Belin uses the form of question to reveal the supposition of what it means to be relocated by linking early colonialism to her current status as a Diné "relocated at birth" in her last stanza: "WHO IS TO SAY? / crossblood babies / relocated at birth" (11). Belin's continued moment of dislocation calls into question the inner workings of spatial colonization by creating a visual link in the poem between the center lines and "WHO IS TO SAY?" The bold visual of the capitalized first sentence in the stanza not only defies the authority of the state to name and regulate, but also challenges other Navajos to consider the importance of Navajo philosophies of speech and breath as more powerful than "imperial" "destiny." The connections made through breath once again withstand the imperial project of assimilation; the power of words to define these connections is important to consider in the struggle for decolonization. As Belin demonstrates, the production of space for Native people is greatly affected by expanding capitalism that requires the restructuring of Native lands, relationships, and bodies.

Here I will conclude by returning to "breathe" in the first stanza of the "On Relocation" poem, but will first juxtapose it with Doreen Massey's questioning of contemporary geographies. She asks us to consider why it is that settlement or place is so frequently characterized as bounded, as enclosure, and as directly counterposed to spaces as flows. Belin's poetic words play against Massey's statement on place in meaningful ways. Belin not only answers Massey's question of why place is characterized as bounded, but also elaborates from the perspective of a woman who has experienced reterritorialization: colonial bounding and renaming of land, bodies, and communities. Through imposed spatial ideologies and its narration in popular culture, land and people become seemingly bound and fit into tight containers, in this case, the reservation. The danger of identities fixed in time and space is well known to Native people—what becomes elided in the colonial political bind are the histories of movement and mobility of people and ideas.

While Massey argues for a conception of place as flow, which for her refers to more than the unrestricted global movement of capital through stagnant place, but also to the permeability of place as a "meeting place" of cultures and people, Belin also delicately longs for a nonreactionary place or one not inscribed by the state. She longs for a place that is historically rooted, and that both claims her and connects her to the Diné nation even while she is located in the urban center of Los Angeles or Oakland. Yet, unlike Massey, Belin's geographical affiliations are not an accidental coming together, nor are they wholly voluntary. Her identity as a Native American woman is regulated by the nation-state and produces certain materialities that compose her world. Reconciliations of the history of settler colonialism in discussions of place, migrations, and economies must take place, whether it is on the grazing plains of the Midwest or in the city of New York. Belin stakes out self-definition and its perils, "My expression is a liberation functioning as a contrived reality boxed into *Indian*" (1). The process of "soul wounds" and "Tongue[s] swollen from word arrows" is difficult, but not unimaginable. Belin returns to a Diné sense of place, this time the specific location of the sacred Canyon de Chelly, "to be cleansed with winds" (1). Liberation begins with these place politics that are not made through legal boundaries, but through communal, clan, and individual stories connected through "stories etched on our backs"; the relationship between geography and story confronts narratives of development that would erode Native gender construction or pinpoint it as stagnant. This Native spatial practice is as much about the future as the past.

Finding the Compass, (Re)mapping Landscapes

In this section, I will explicate Belin's poem "Directional Memory," as it addresses relocation from the perspective of a young woman born into the processes that have been in motion since termination and relocation.[53] The language of the poem reflects a (re)mapping of the discursive settler terrain and provides us with a compass to guide us through those imagined, but very real, geographies. "Let's begin with the first thing you remember," Belin writes in her poem "Directional Memory," which is organized in four sections that correlate with the cardinal directions and sacred mountains of the Diné.[54] The structure of the poem in four parts also refers to the sacred wind briefly addressed in the conversation regarding breath; this wind gave life to First Man and First Woman, the breath or wind flowed from the East and the West connecting the mountains that mark the four directions. As Clara Sue Kidwell and Alan Velie write, "Wind is [considered] the breath of the universe."[55] The section in the poem begins in the West, moves to the North, then the South, and ends in the East, each reflecting on a particular memory in Belin's development as a woman. Through poetic articulation, recalling of memories, reference to culturally specific Diné stories, and the correlating four directions, Belin mediates the impact of colonial spatial restructuring that depends on an understanding of space, of place, of Native peoples as bounded entities destined to be forgotten as the nation proceeds. Rather than "place" herself within bounded "state lines," she uses her memory and Diné maps to reposition herself in relation to L.A., the Diné nation, and within the United States.

By arranging the poem in the cardinal directions, Belin also is recalling the four mountains that mark Diné land: Tsisnaajini (Blanca Peak in the East), Tsoodzil (Mount Taylor in the South), Dokʼoslííd (San Francisco Peak in the West), and Dibénitsaa (La Plata in the North).[56] Klara Kelly and Francis Harris articulate the importance of geography to Navajo subjectivity:

> Navajo geography recognizes the same four cardinal directions as do European-derived geographies, but east is the direction Navajos emphasize. . . . Navajo children in their cognitive development thereby become oriented to geographical space as soon as they become aware of the order in all dwellings. The Navajo creation stories describe the entire pre-conquest homeland as a hogan, with a sacred mountain in each of the four directions compared to a pole in the hogan's framework. So ingrained is this sense of geography that Navajos raised in the old ways will organize just about any domain of knowledge, even abstract or non-geographical or non-Navajo things, by associating the various components of the domain in four directions.[57]

The "organization of knowledge" referred to above is employed in the structure of the poem to combat the notion that a relocated Diné is maladjusted as so much research on urban identity proclaims and solidifies through its methodology. The question of individual memories and belonging across distances arises in the poem and provides a (re)mapping of relocation. As the poem moves in all four directions, so does Belin's consciousness about the landscape, place, and self. In the direction of the West, we progress from her inability as a child to speak of a simple loss of a sandal, "Specific memory of wanting to go back and get the shoe and in your / head you even telepathically announce to everyone that you left your / shoe at the old home" (8), to the direction of the North and her ability to speak to the many losses, both personal and those of the "native brothers and sisters of this tropical climate" (9). These are interconnected losses, albeit at various scales, occurring from colonial spatial restructuring. Individual memory and communal memory are tied to place in the poem, and the memories themselves are tied to the four cardinal directions.

Clearly, Belin values and implements Navajo-derived geographies even if she was not raised within the boundaries of the sacred mountains. It is the map handed down through her grandparents, one tying together places, stories and generations, that enables her to incorporate the non-Diné and Diné things that make up her existence. In the "North" stanza she relates these experiences:

> Kissing me with your red lips
> blessing me with your diva-ness
> shiny black hair dances at Mr. Fives
> swinging wet with heat
> steam from the jungle you emerged
> traces my image in blues ultra.
> Our touch moved people off the dance floor and out of recliners. (8)

While the specifically Diné structure of the poem reflects Belin's consciousness as a Diné woman, she is also influenced by her urban memories. "Emerged," "red," "shiny," "blessing," and "wet" are familiar words to the Diné creation stories and associated with sacred geographies: "emergence" is the word used to note the movement into upper worlds; "red" is the color associated with the sun and rainbow, elements that tie down the sacred mountain; "shiny" and "black" refer to "jet beads, night blackness, dark mist, different kinds of plants, and many wild animals."[58] The geographic and visual images within the poem mirror the journey of Changing Woman, associated with the first blessing way ceremony. Yet Belin chooses not to create a nostalgic return, but instead depicts the usefulness of these epistemologies in an urban encounter and in a capitalist system that seeks to transform those relationships. Each of these "directional memories" imparts a sense of balance in an unbalanced world as they, like the sacred mountains, represent a different stage in her life and place her in the world.

While First Man and First Woman used bits of soil from the other worlds to bring the mountains into being, what ties the Diné community to the land and enables a cohesive identity is its relationship to Changing Woman (Asdzáá Nádleehé), the female deity who brought the Diné people into being through the use of corn, water, and her own skin. In the article "Land into Flesh: Images of Intimacy," Susan Scarberry-Garcia speaks about the creation of Navajo people as it relates to corn pollen: "Changing Woman created the ancestors of the Navajo by rubbing balls of epidermal waste, mixed with corn pollen, from her breast, back, and arms."[59] The relationship of land and the maternal body manifests itself in Navajo organizing of citizenship and responsibility. Scarberry continues: "Land and Human beings are one, bound together by the understanding that flesh takes many forms. . . . From birth to death, our bodies, as parts of nature, acquire new contours, reflecting our experience on earth. The earth nurtures us in our becoming."[60] In each section of Belin's poem, a becoming is taking place. The clan system, reflected in the sacred mountains of the Diné, intimately marks Dinétah (or Diné territory) to the body. This embodied geography passes on through the maternal line and the "becoming" does not rely on a division between men and women or progress and civilization, but rather on balance.[61] Both men and women have important roles in the ceremony. The womanhood ceremony of the Diné, the Kinaaldá, is about the ritual reconnecting to Changing Woman, the land, these sacred stories, and ancestral places.

"Directional Memory" uses image to indirectly address this. The North associated with "confidence, assurance, and security" openly comes across toward the end of the poem with the image of levitating associated with the poets:[62]

> Our touch tack-sharp tickled memories
> of Maxine Hong Kingston and Norman Mailer and Gary Snyder
>   trying to levitate
> the Pentagon
> of small children selling Chiclets
> trying to levitate their image to heaven. (8)

Kingston is often associated with feminist writing, Mailer as a male writer with a heavy, aggressive sense of sexuality, and Snyder as a poet concerned with the rhythms of land—all claim a deep connection to land as writers, but Belin questions this through the "tack-sharp tickled memories." Each of these writers' premises may "tickle" us, but the intergenerational memories Belin is evoking throughout the poem help her find direction. The relationship to land for each differs. As Ursula Heise notes in her work regarding transnationalism and masculine writers, an observation that can be applied to Snyder and Mailer, "local inhabitation was centrally envisioned in terms of the experience of single, mostly male individuals encountering wild landscapes or homesteading agricultural ones."[63] The relationship to land evoked through Belin's poem is not the same, nor is the experience of Kingston, who uses narrative processes to formulate her relationship to the Bay Area as a child of immigrant parents. The juxtaposing of these three very different writers interrogates American relationships to land in relation to colonialism and capitalism.

Belin draws this out in the image of children engaged in the labor of "selling Chiclets." The images of children correlate to progeny that result from a balance between people. Furthermore, the juxtaposition between "levitate," associated with church ("heaven") and state ("Pentagon"), bounces off the word "emerges" found in traditional Diné philosophy. They do not get *into* heaven but rather *levitate* to it, recalling the narratives of development and progress used to disconnect Native people from the land from which they emerged. The line "our touch tender as ginger on tongue forks into the two of us" represents the balance between the sexes under attack during the termination and relocation era, in which the "fork-tongued" politicians called for an end to tribalism in the name of progress. She twists "fork-tongue" to "tongue forks" in order to show the possibilities of having both a consciousness as a Diné woman but also the ability to speak from multiple experiences without eroding a sense of self. She maps her urban experience with the meanings of the sacred mountains to bring her female subjectivity into balance with the constantly unfolding world around her.

Belin's last section, "East," ends her poem and poignantly peels away the colonial mapping of lands and bodies and the seeming effects of the relocation process. Unlike the previous sections, where memories are pleasantly recalled in passion or longing, the action of nagging memory is much more present:

East
When the awe of downtown Los Angeles scratches my back
the ghosts of native brothers and sisters of this tropical climate seers
grade school, high school never told of their existence
Indian land was far away in another world, across states lines where
    grandparents plant corn and herd sheep on a brown-eyed/blue-
    eyed horse . . .
I always forget L.A. has sacred mountains. (8–9)

In this section, memory activates her consciousness and situates her in time and space outside a Western linear sense of progress that would dismember her. She ends the poem in the direction of the East and (re)maps the path of relocation. Rather than ending in the West, the direction of setting sun and the location of the city, she ends with the rising of a new day and renewed consciousness. This is further grounded by ending in the direction of the Diné Nation. The East is also the direction of prayer that acknowledges rebirth and Changing Woman and, as mentioned above, is the direction of emphasis for the Diné. The full circle quality of the poem reconnects and creates a Native spatial practice that begins, quite literally, in the place of human emergence for Diné people. She attempts to construct a space that is not bounded in a land "far away in another world." In times of relocation or displacement, we need to consider the importance of "Directional Memory" as a story that can renew connections among people, land, and their communities. Native women authors are not just representing space as a return to an "original" land or an "original" past/nation/being and, thus, erasing the layers of time, geography, and history, but rather they are mediating multiple relationships and, by doing so, navigating ways of being in the world that reflect—and pro-duce—contemporary Native experiences.

This poem, like much of Belin's work, extends beyond a personal (re)map-ping of her Diné identity. She unmaps state discourses in this East stanza, befitting as in Dine education and philosophies the east is linked to *nitsáhá-kees,* or thinking. It is foundational to a child's education and Diné way of life. In recovering from the onslaught of the schoolroom discourse that cre-ates a tabula rasa of space and erases Native people, Belin relies on Diné epis-temologies and crossblood experiences to reconfigure violent cartographies of U.S. nation-building, stating, "I always forget L.A. has sacred mountains." Her own imagining of Diné directional memory refuses to make absent the Tongra "brothers and sisters" in the landscape of L.A., and thereby refuses the geopolitical organization of the U.S. nation-state. She ends her poem (signif-icantly not located on the Diné Reservation) with respect toward others by reminding herself and her readers that colonialism structures "Indian" land as in the distance and removed. By not ignoring the "scratches" on her "back" and attempting to reconcile the historical spatial restructuring that Native people have been continually subjected to since the beginning of coloniza-tion, Belin is narrating new cartographic encounters in her poetry. Further-more, the tool of "directional memory" reconfigures that landscape where the reader has to confront the perceived notion that L.A. is not Native territory, as she refuses to make absent the Native "brothers and sisters" who first resided on these city lands. Since the city is the place of economic growth, by desta-bilizing its geographical power and promise, Belin questions the geopolitical organization of the U.S. nation-state.

Use of specific cultural references, such as the imagery of the sacred moun-tains and the deities who put them in place, are not merely used to mark ter-ritory or survey it in these alternative geographies. These Native maps, which contain a historicity and sociality of their own, form intricate relationships among people and their surroundings. The Diné cartography narrated in Belin's poems marks maternal clan relationships that hold Diné people in a web of reciprocity and respect. This constant production of relationships within figurative (narrated oral stories of clans that inform ways of acting in Diné society) and literal space (the physical mountains) is temporally continuous, but not bounded and static, nor is it the space of masculinity talked about above. While the instruments of technology reproduce the imagined-as-real in the form of Western maps, Marc Warhus, a historian of early Native maps, notes that the physical paper or bark maps are only a small part of Native cartography. In fact, mapping was often an oral process, whereby stories marked much of Natives' understanding of the world around them: "the Native Americans' world had been explored, named, and integrated into their experience long before the first Europeans came to the continent. This indigenous knowledge was passed down in songs, stories and rituals, and the understanding of the landscape it imparted was as sophisticated as that of any western map."[64] While many current maps produced by Native nations use technology to mark places of importance to the well-being of the community, the knowledge they collect to make these maps is often the "directional memory" of elders and people who possess knowledge of the land—but they are not absolute. Each generation will have to find a map to reconcile the vast changes among generations, however, as time and space are not stagnant for Native people, or anyone for that matter. The process of (re)mapping is not final, but always in process. Belin, though resituated in Los Angeles as a result of historical processes, is able to (re)map her place in the city as she remembers her movement from place to place, her experiences of becoming a woman, and the stories handed down through generations. She also is able to use Diné philosophies to respect the land and California Indians' original relationship to it. Uprooting settler geographies will require vigilance and new strategies.

Conclusion

In an interview, Belin speaks to the process of writing as activism and why she continues the long tradition of countering the U.S. government: "Well, as Diné, to not be participatory would risk laziness which is practically taboo. Writers are scouts since many are privileged to have studied in institutions for higher learning. We are writing not only so that others may follow but also to provide guidance of the territory ahead. Revolution is natural, it is the form that needs to be nurtured."[65] It is the necessity of having maps or "guidance," as Belin articulates it, that weaves us into and out of the various terrains that the settler state uses to impose their own spatialities like court cases, geopolitical boundaries, and Western knowledge systems. Nurturing "the form" of "revolution" means rethinking a relationship to colonialism, and this can be emphasized through articulating the relationship among gender, nation, and space, and rearticulating our relationship to one another. We are not outside the structures of capitalism, colonialism, or increasing globalization but profoundly *within them.* Our ability to understand the connections between stories and space means the difference between loss and continuity. The holy winds continue unabated by policies that attempt to separate people and Native nations. The physical landscape grounds her, as the mountains of the Diné have grounded others for generations.

Locating a dialogue that conceives of space not as bounded by geopolitics, but storied, continuous, and developing, is necessary in creating a discourse that allows Native nation-building at its fullest potential and members of nations its fullest protection. Diné scholar Lloyd Lee profoundly pushes for decolonization of space through the philosophies of *hozho* and *sa'ah naaghai bik'eh hozhoon,* stating that the "present day resolutions have not restored the health and prosperity of all the people. Navajo thought states that *all* Navajo people are integral to the continuance of the nation. Navajo people's spiritual, mental, emotional, and physical wellness is dependent on *all* people of society, not just a few."[66] A dialogue that opens up immutable spaces such as the reservation, itself a colonial structure, becomes extremely important in developing a Native sovereign spatial discourse that includes the "all" mentioned in Lee's analysis. In Belin's poems, breath assures an ongoing set of relationships that is open, and its connection to speaking, telling, praying, and witnessing only assures the power of story to decolonize spatial discourses by reminding of the connections people have to one another and the life-giving force at work.

Although I have been addressing Diné philosophies in one author's poems, my analysis extends to other nations that have their own cultural geographies and their own poets who are working to mediate the consequences of spatial restructuring in the era of termination, relocation, and Public Law 280. It is important to look at our social, political, and certainly cultural relationships in a "framework that allows relatedness to a flexible spatial community, one that allows for strong, mobile, symbolic identity that underlies, and perhaps even belies, external influences," as Seneca scholar Faye Lone suggests.[67] These are recreated through symbolic relationships and obligations rather than inherent rights bounded through nation-state models of borders and citizenship. Recalling how breath connects to Changing Woman and clan and community relationships reminds us of the ongoing strength of women that is necessary in destabilizing colonial geographies. Breath connects Belin to community despite being a "crossblood" or a relocated Diné. The alternative—relying on legal or nation-state concepts of citizenship that bind land and bodies and mirror Western forms of governance—does not create a just spatial "framework" for our future.

3

From the Stomp Grounds on Up: Indigenous Movement and the Politics of Globalization

If it's true that "New fictions of factual representation" are
daily being foisted upon us then the case for inserting a social
dimension into modern cartography is especially strong.
Maps are too important to be left to the cartographer alone.

—J. B. HARLEY, "Deconstructing the Map," *Writing Worlds*

WHAT HAPPENS WHEN THE POET TAKES OVER THE CARTOGRAPHER'S tools? More interestingly, what happens when the poet is from a group of people who were categorized, colonized, and subjugated in the wake of the colonial moment and implementation of modern conceptions of space? What might the poet say when she sees the detriments of colonial and imperial mapping—containment, restriction, restructuring, and erasure of cultures—continue and live in the buzz of a city or stream of nightly news in short sound bites ordering the people of the world through language and metaphors, the very tools of poets? In her books and performances, the Muscogee Creek poet Joy Harjo is continuing to counter forms of colonialism and imperialism and their dehumanizing and violent effects. Harjo is an artist with an intuitive ability to move from a specific cultural and personal location to the wider scale of humanity—in both its ugliness and beauty, or in her language, "in the beautiful perfume and stink of the world."[1] Her poetics sweep across and connect social, physical, and metaphysical boundaries. In one brushstroke of a verse or sentence we are at once in the past and the present and beholding the future as Harjo maps her place in the world through memory, instinct, and desire. The rich intertextuality of Harjo's poems and her diverse connections with others and awareness of Native issues—such as sovereignty, racial formation, and social conditions—provide the foundation for unpacking and linking the function of settler colonial structures within newly arranged global spaces. Harjo's creativity is about human connection as a practice that mends the settler condition of isolating Native people as not part of this time or even this world, even while the material conditions produced during this neoliberal movement affect everyday reality. Harjo *is within the world,* not just engaging it from the periphery or margin. Through an attention to poetic language and the geographies in which they arise, Harjo and many other Native women are making worlds and producing geographical knowledges necessary to the survival of Native peoples.

Joy Harjo's use of specific Creek geographies, such as the stomp grounds referred to in the title, and her narratives of a gendered, colonized body on a global scale provide a rich base in which to discuss the strategies that are guiding us toward a discourse that imagines possibilities and influences subjectivity formation and material conditions of Native communities. This chapter demonstrates that the multiple scales of spatialities Native writers use in their work emerge out of broader social contexts that are dynamic, historical, and consistently engaging with the formation of tribal conceptions of human geography. Embodied geographies, whether a thirteenth-floor window, Los Angeles, Chicago, a plane in flight, or the Milky Way, are vital in Harjo's poetry, and an examination of how they relate is necessary to understanding how settler colonialism operates through intersectional gendered spatial logics. The relationship among the individual, community, and other bodies is a driving force that demands we rethink mimetic representations of the map as delineations of closure formed in modernity's propensity toward "objective" science. Remember, bodies are mobile and not fixed identities. How they are perceived, for instance, might often relate to what space one might occupy. As demonstrated in the previous chapters, spatial control was a necessary part of forming the settler state. For Native people whose bodies are highly regulated by the colonial settler state and for whom places are highly relegated by settler discourses of where one belongs, examining embodied geographies is a necessary component to decolonization. In other words, as Linda McDowell clarifies, the body is the most "immediate place": "The body is the place, the location or site, if you like, of the individual, with more or less impermeable boundaries between one body and another. While bodies are undoubtedly material, possessing a range of characteristics such as shape and size and so inevitably taking up space, the ways in which bodies are presented to and seen by others vary according to the spaces and places in which they find themselves."[2] Native people find themselves in the space of the settler state that enacts technologies of power on individual Native people in place, such as we saw in the previous examination of the urban/rez dichotomy. The nation-state as a model became the unquestionable entity through which Indigenous politics are forged, even though implemented to refute the very vital process of changing federal Indian law or stopping its colonial extension or working with the government to retain and sustain the Indian Health Service (IHS) agency or more mainstream feminist goals to equalize pay scales. Yet, how in taking this interior approach to spatial justice are we limiting other alternatives? Harjo's poetry provides insight by dealing with embodied geographies on a multiscalar level. Much of what she writes about, though in more poetic and beautiful narratives, is mired in her lived reality during an economic shift that occurred during the 1980s and 1990s. This shift created deep gaps between rich and poor as well as displaced people around the globe. As neoliberalism grew and shifted economic power to private entities, exploitation of land and labor also grew on a global scale. In order to push forward a (re)mapping that leads to healthier communities, an exploration of embodied geography is a necessary and important step to (re)map our socialities.

Spatial poetics create new contexts of meanings, disrupting taxonomic and contained racial and geopolitical categories that retain nineteenth-century racial logic. By awakening "dead metaphors"—that is, those discourses normalized through habitual use—and placing them within a context that shifts their normative meanings, I demonstrate that focusing on the production of global space in an Indigenous context and its articulation through language is fundamental to understanding the effects of late twentieth-century relationships among Indigenous people and current immigrants, many of whom are themselves Indigenous and have faced massive land loss. Thus, Harjo's spatial metaphors reposition the relationships between and among Creek people, western Americans, and those deemed in the public sphere as "third-world" immigrants. Here, Azfar Hussein rightly cautions us to be aware of situating Harjo in an "imperial hermeneutic," or what I reference in the introduction as a purely ethnographic reading which tends toward "attempts to control, govern, regulate, or discipline text(s) in terms of policing the boundaries of meaning."[3] For Hussein, and in the context of this chapter, Harjo's work is poetic praxis in that it deters from simplicity that depoliticizes and dehistoricizes and instead fetishizes the discursive. In fact, my strategy of placing Native women's writings and (re)mappings in their historical and political moment stems from a Native feminist praxis committed to the material act of spatial justice. "Harjo's words themselves keep producing signs as the sites of ideological battle within historic parameters," suggests Hussein, "while also pointing up a variety of concrete material sites of counter-hegemonic struggles relevant to contemporary Native Americans as well as to the Third World multitudes suffering and struggling within the spaces of local-global or glocal capitalism, global racism, and glocal sexism."[4] In a (re)mapping of settler colonialism, we also come to understand settler colonial spatial logics as undergirded by and producing spatialized violence, territorial property logics, and uneven regimes of capitalist accumulation.

Geographer and linguist Yi-Fu Tuan poignantly relates the relationship between space and language, aptly resonating with Harjo's poetics: "Humans in general know the power of speech in ordinary day-to-day experience. They know that although speech alone cannot materially transform nature, it can direct attention, organize insignificant entities into significant composite wholes, and in so doing, make things formerly overlooked—hence invisible and nonexistent—visible and real."[5] In this chapter's engagement with Harjo's feminist praxis, histories, and geographies in relation to a claiming of space and place through language, particularly metaphor, we see the vitality of imagining maps that unsettle colonial domination. Expanding on this chapter's title, I will begin with an example of the wealth of Creek-centered meanings found in Harjo's language, particularly in reference to the stomp grounds, which are not foreclosed but rather open up new possibilities of interconnection. The use of this discourse to rearticulate the mapping process will chart an understanding of how cultural metaphors can resituate our spatial understandings. Too often the past events of colonialism and immigrant experience put forward as the present are seen as discrete, especially in the context and hangover of notions of multiculturalism from the early 1980s through the 1990s. I then turn to the poem "Letter from the End of the Twentieth Century," from *The Woman Who Fell from the Sky* (1994),[6] to elucidate further how Harjo (re)maps Native politics as important on a larger scale, resisting the dominant narrative that Indigenous politics pertain exclusively to a small minority group within the larger nation-state. By addressing the performance of global intersections in her music and poems, Harjo breaks from the representation of Native and nation-state spaces as homogeneous, closed systems. Joy Harjo's critical insights into the relationship between the local and the global exemplify the importance of focusing on Native women's writing about spatial violence.

Native activists, writers, and scholars have encountered the dilemma of moving from the local to the global many times before, and it is a part of everyday existence and everyday resistances on the part of Native people to maintain cultural specificity while remaining innovative in strategies for cultural survival. Harjo writes in the context of the state's racialization of Native people into a neoliberal state, which often erases a Native presence or subsumes it in multicultural narratives that elide Native political rights or a human rights framework. Unlike in the previous chapter, where the discourses underpinning the legislation of termination and relocation programs were largely about incorporation into the melting pot or body politic, fear and anxiety drive the anti-immigrant discourses that mark the later twentieth century. The geographies the settler state imagines are not the ones Harjo encounters on the ground as she moves about the world. Scrutiny of embodied geographies and the gendered practices of enforcing settler colonial geographies open up new spatial imaginaries. Harjo, for instance, creates a viable glocality by situating Native knowledge structures as engaging with the world as she simultaneously avoids rendering Native people and communities into neoliberal discourses of multiculturalism.[7] In this chapter, I link earlier privatization of Native land to the early 1980s to 1990s neoliberal political and economic policies that deepen asymmetries between various peoples as capital becomes privatized and global. Harjo provides us a grounding that remains significant to local communities, even while it operates at multiple scales of human interconnection.

The Stomp Grounds

Harjo poignantly reminds us of her own position and what it means to be a Muscogee Creek woman through a recalling of the stomp grounds, history of Indian relations, Oklahoma territory, and her relationship to the land. The stomp grounds migrate with the Creeks from the origin myths of emergence and journey to the historical relocation of the Creek Nation and Five Civilized Tribes, named as such for their seeming acculturation to European norms. Often the stomp grounds are in relation to the various constructions of the figure of the "house" that Harjo takes up again and again wherever she goes. The spaces and places created in Harjo's poetry are not fixed or statically inhabited, but rather are formed in their own geographic history and in the geopolitics that are ongoing and connected to spatial forces across the planet. Harjo (re)maps the United States through gendered and cultural metaphors that recall a long history of relocation, occupation, and exploitation.

This chapter is deeply indebted to Craig Womack's insights as a Creek tribal scholar and all-around excellent researcher of literature and the Creek Nation. From the very start of *Red on Red,* Womack debunks the idea of the tainted or disappeared Native—conceptions largely embedded in colonial structuring of lands that rely on these notions in order to narrate and justify colonial occupation. The account of the birth of the Creek (Muscogee) and later the Creek Nation, stories that find themselves again and again in Harjo's poetry, are pivotal to unfixing these notions. Womack recounts the opening of the earth, emergence of the people, and travel from the continental divide to the Atlantic, where they rested near the Chattahoochee River. The profound nature of the story, which Womack relates through the elder Louis Oliver, is a powerful creation story that marks mobility and migration. This story, like Harjo's poetry, is a speech act: "To exist as a nation, the community needs a perception of nationhood, that is, stories (like the migration account) that help them imagine who they are as a people, how they came to be, and what cultural values they wish to preserve."[8] Creek stories of migration are significant to an understanding of Creek construction of place and its constant recreation through imaging new spatialities; these speech acts enable a reworking through tough times. The introduction of federal Indian law and policy would interfere over and over again in tribal governance, land holdings, and social conceptions to produce those tough times, but as I demonstrate later in this essay through an examination of Harjo's grounding and ability to connect to the world, these economic and political practices are connected to larger scales of exploitation. The Creek conception, based in movement and the establishment of familial or clan relationship to all those around them, differs greatly from the imposition of fixed land rights and privatization that are foundational to a liberal democracy and enforced through the imposition of colonial law. Even through mass destruction the creation stories traveled through the generations, as they have in most tribes.

The mapping of Indian land and bodies through the narrative of the law is more than a violent event of the past in which the nation must be forgiven: various colonial policies also structure much Indian law, policy, material reality, and socialities experienced by people today. Spatially removed, relocated, and already existing Native people in place are deeply affected as law attempts to homogenize Native people into categories and elide particular histories. The imagining of Native land and people as domestic dependent nations became incorporated in law through the language of conquest, thus leading to individual settler land titles affirmed through the very same process. Settler spatial imaginaries and their enforcement implemented removal, formed Indian Territory, remapped it as the state of Oklahoma, incorporated it into the settler state, and eventually applied the Dawes Allotment Act, all of which continue to affect Native lands and bodies. What little land legally left under tribal jurisdiction is pivotal to contemporary survivance, even as many must relocate to sustain themselves and their families financially because of economic tyranny exerted through federal Indian law and policy. In knowing historical geographies and temporalities, Harjo's creation of different possibilities is all the more amazing.

Yet the death of tribal lands and people was not all that occurred—many of these unjust spatial policies also culminated in the violent interruption of cultural epistemologies. Throughout her multiple books, Harjo writes of places that converge with multiple temporalities in her poems, and in doing so, she makes numerous connections, forming patterns between the various points in her life. The literal stomp grounds are found in a particular tangible space, Oklahoma, and are a place where Creek dances and ceremonies continue to be held. However, that space is not fixed in time or landscape and has many meanings. Harjo's stomp grounds are present in various moments of global traveling or in examining global restructuring and thus (re)map our nations in significant ways that do not alienate us from the land. Native subjectivity, in this case specifically Creek, is intimately tied to this space of original creation but also to its generative abilities of recreation. Harjo is acutely recalling Creek specifics to help balance human and all life-forms that she finds in other areas of the world—a world increasingly connected through neoliberal politics even while founded in the settler dynamics of colonialism. In fact, much of the landscapes reflected in Harjo's poetry are not fixed, inanimate places to be mapped by grids, surveys, and legalities. In my previous work, I examined the ways that her poetic metaphors based on traditional stories reflect a history that is then passed down to her granddaughter, a necessary step so that the next generation is grounded but not confined.[9] Harjo's work is an example of recreating new possibilities, even new collectivities, which transform the settler state ideal of transforming Indigenous land into individual private property.

Thus, the stomp grounds are a particularly apt vehicle for Harjo's scalar approaches: the local is already in relation to these larger global forces. The stomp grounds are a place of familiarity—a tangible space of ideological dimensions embedded in politics and memory. It is a space she constantly embodies as she moves and experiences other spaces. "The body that navigates the geography of daily life bears a visible mark," attests Mona Domosh and Joni Seager in their examination of the way space is socially constructed around sets of gendered, ethnic, racial, and class norms. "In all societies there is an intertwined reciprocity between space, bodies, and the social construction of both—neither 'space' nor 'bodies' exists independently of a social print."[10] For Native people in place, overt control by the state on the reservation exists, again as discussed previously in terms of access to resources and residency—which again on many reservations is spatially constructed at the level of the body through blood quantum laws conceived of by the state and adopted by various, but not all, Native nations. Native mobility, however, often reflects an ideology of gendered and spatialized erasure. Harjo instead presents us with a different vision of moving through space. She looks to her traditions and a culture that has already withstood the onslaught of spatial reorganization in U.S. nation-building processes to find strategies for dealing with modern reorganizations of the social, political, and economic construction of places. The violent force and oppressive ideology that marked the days of a colonial "civilizing" of space, a process that entailed the extermination, assimilation, and criminalization of Native people pushed to the unruly boundaries of the nation and erased in the cultural imagination, remains embedded in the modern nation-state. In looking at global spaces and global displacement of Indigenous peoples, Harjo reaches into Native traditions and language to guide her through disputed land and buried histories.

Calling a Meeting

Many of Harjo's poems recall the neoliberal shifts of the 1980s and early 1990s and a time when women of color and Indigenous women were organizing around injustices that were occurring at the intersection of race, class, gender, and sexuality. As manufacturing jobs were exported and social services overhauled, and many people were routed into the prison system, traditional communities of color underwent drastic changes, particularly in deindustrialized cities.[11] Reservation communities had a history of and still experience high rates of unemployment, policing, and daily violence despite rich resource holdings on their land. Harjo's poems provide a base where we can reflect on the affinities among communities that increasingly have become surplus populations as neoliberal politics and economics shift to transnational finance capitalism. Federal Indian and military policies have continually categorized Native people from the continental United States to its territories in Pacific Islands as surplus populations. Thus, settler restructuring of Indigenous land is closely linked to the rise of the United States as a settler colonial society to a global settler nation-state superpower. The trope of vanishing continues, despite evidence to the contrary, and the rhetoric of majority need versus small "special interest" populations proliferates as a part of mapping bodies and land. Harjo's poetry provides a narrating witness to the burgeoning collaborative politics that arise in this moment. Many women of color, disillusioned by the disparities between them and their "white sisters" who were benefiting from the focus on private property, sought to intervene in a mainstream feminism based on the experience of the white woman as a property-accumulating liberal subject. Gaining more individual property in the form of civil rights, or individual rights, was of less interest to Native women than was, and still is, a commitment to protect land, community, and kin.

Collaborative and grassroots forms of organizing arising during this time period are still pivotal to collective cultural and political rights. Grace Hong, in her examination of the genealogy of liberal capitalism, national narratives, and women of color writing as an intervention, understands the use of culture not as something that is bounded, pure, individual, and merely about identity expression. Rather, the use of culture, and how I use it within this book, "encompasses a system of meaning-making, a system ordered by relations of power."[12] I find this redefinition important, considering legal policies that seek to rid the system of meaning-making of Native people by its simplifying and narrowing definitions of classification that then trickle down to what constitutes a tribal nation or even at times our own narrow definitions of what should be the aim of sovereignty. Harjo, as part of this group of women writers, produces counternarratives to founding mythologies that Native people are dangerous, primitive, or nonexistent, and in doing so, she creates meaningful knowledges through her positionality as a Creek woman living in a world that too often renders Native people, issues, and land invisible or hypervisible in a temporal past.[13] Furthermore, by putting forth an analysis of the social and spatial as sets of relationships, she provides an intervention into the reduction of sovereignty as merely territorial in terms of dominant geographic knowledge.

In her poem "We Must Call a Meeting," found in her earlier volume *In Mad Love and War* (1990), Harjo calls for social action mirroring the discussions around race, poverty, and gender that were occurring throughout the United States. To this discussion Harjo adds the experience and historic memory of Indigenous women. In situating metaphors of colonization—both internal and external—in a struggle over language and language production, the poem begins with meeting at a place of fragility, a vulnerability that often occurs when people from various positionalities come together, listen, and attempt to make change. Even in a "cross fire of signals" that may occur, a meeting is necessary.[14] The structure of the poem, in its symbolic resemblance to the rising fires in the center of the Creek stomp grounds, reflects the meaning-making definition of culture given above. In a Creek context, the spiral is fluid, dynamic, and unfixed; it is a space of three dimensions connecting the lower world of chaos, the middle world of humans, and the upper world of order. The spiral signifies the moment of disintegration and simultaneity of boundaries, both temporally and geographically. Imagine how useful this might be in working across differences and avoiding collapsing various subjectivities into a universal subject. The form of the words along the page spiral, collapsing space and time as the past speaks to Harjo in traditional images and brings her to "call a meeting," a form of social action. The words of Harjo's poem dance on the page, with more space in between the steps until she gathers strength:

I am fragile, a piece of pottery smoked from fire
                              made of dung,
    the design drawn from nightmares. I am an arrow, painted
                                  with lightning
    to seek the way to the name of the enemy,
                          but the arrow has now created
    its own language. (9)

In this poem, humans are positioned as vulnerable, not just sources of labor or exploitation, but also as products of intense emotion emerging from their material circumstances. The "I" of the poem is "fragile" and made of "dung" and "fire"; she is a product of colonization and its ongoing hold over her imagination, as referenced in "nightmares." The precise instrument of the arrow is a metaphor for the powerful tool of writing; the language of the poem is formed in the context of various power relations. Audre Lorde, in a manner applicable to this moment in Harjo, addresses language as a call to action: "In the forefront of our move toward change, there is only poetry to hint at possibility made real. Our poems formulate the implications of ourselves, what we feel within and dare make real (or bring action into accordance with), our fears, our hopes, our most cherished terrors."[15] Harjo addresses the specificity of her "nightmares," struggling with the creation of a language formed in the intersections produced in the context of settler colonialism.

The first step in gathering strength is finding a language. In a rhythmic call and response form and in their meanings, the placement of words on the page resembles the Creek stomp dance. "We have / begun to hold conversations," Harjo says as the words dance back to the margins, indicative of the spiral in the stomp dance. She further employs this motif by emphasizing the importance of these meetings which are held "long into the night" so that she forgets to eat or work; the language and dance are sustenance, giving her strength "to name the enemy" or what she will later in her work refer to as "reinventing the enemy's language."[16] She declares:

> I begin to draw maps of stars.
> The spirits of old and new ancestors perch on my shoulders.
> I make prayers of clear stone
> > of feathers from birds
> > > who live closest to gods (9)

The language map she designs in this instance is not permanent and unchanging, but one that can adjust according to needs. The words on the page become tighter as the poem progresses, and the direction starts to resemble the counterclockwise motion of the stomp dance. In this structuring of the poem, many elements often conflated as opposites are linked: the past and present (in the "ancestors"); the earth ("birds") and "gods"; and "this thin line between the breathing / and the dead (9)."

By connecting these categories, the narrator grounds herself as she balances "the crossfire of signals" of politics, traditions, history, and language—all aspects of material spatial production. She ends the poem with the following lines, which have raveled themselves in a counterclockwise circle fashioned through the spatial division:

> You are a curled serpent in the pottery of nightmares.
> You are the dreaming animal who paces back and forth in my head.
> We must call a meeting.
> > Give me back my language and build a house
> Inside it.
> > A house of madness.
> > > A house for the dead who are not dead.
> And the spiral of the sky above it.
> And the sun

and the moon.
          And the stars to guide us called promise. (9–10)

The alliteration and repetition of the "and" and "a" produce a rhythm and pattern in the poem. The shortened length of the lines and the capitalization represent quick dance steps in the pattern of the spiral returning to its center. The center, however, is vast and ubiquitous, filled with "promise" and "madness" rather than stability, foreclosure, and limitation. "The design," or colonial reasoning, breaks down into "madness" as the poem spirals into the fertile chaos of the lower world. These spiral metaphors, such as the curled serpent and the spiral of the sky, are recurring mythic images present throughout Harjo's poetry. The spiral of memory, the spiral of creation, the spiral path, the spiral of time, and the spiral of power are all images of Creek epistemologies that bring forth balance as Harjo connects to the world around her, yet other meanings are not narrowed in this moment. Language, culture, and history converge as the meaning of the spiral transcends the root of Harjo's traditions. The spiral becomes an epistemological retooling of spatialities produced in the organization of market economies that increased global migrations in the early 1990s. These cultural geographical elements become foundational in a (re)mapping of the global city built on Indigenous land.

In my discussion of the three worlds of Creek tradition represented in the spiral and in many other such literary insights, as noted earlier, I am indebted to Craig Womack's book *Red on Red*. In speaking of the division between the three worlds, he states:

> These divisions are spiritual as well as geographic and stratospheric. Upper world and lower are opposed to each other, and humans are in the middle, in a fragile balance between the three worlds. Creek medicine often involves playing one side off against another to restore things to a proper scheme when someone is sick or events have gone awry. The upper world is a realm of order and periodicity because of the lunar cycle and planetary orbits. Thus, the "spiral of the sky" actively reaches out to celestial bodies symbolizing order and peace. The lower world is one of chaos, though also of fertility. This world, where humans live, is a less ideal version of the Upper world. Rivers, lakes and caves are entrance points to the underworld.[17]

"The sun," "the moon," and "the stars" are all images of the upper world, "the house" the middle world, and "the snake" the lower. The language of the poem reflects the moment when chaotic thought turns to action and language with a capacity to "build a house." The poem restores balance between the three worlds, symbolized here as a relationship between "the serpent" that occupies her subconscious and the "stars" that hold promise. The "curled serpent," or the narrator of the poem who moves between worlds just as the snake does, waits to break free from an abstraction of colonial space that relies on disconnection through producing difference and a fear of the other. This is symbolized in the form of the pottery vessel as a container that holds our nightmares that are a living subconscious fear. This ordering of space, in the sign of a container or traditional form of pottery or the cage, obfuscates other ways of knowing. The "dreaming animal who paces back and forth in my head" illustrates the danger of a pent-up process of thought and its repression. Aboriginal scholar Irene Watson questions the mobility of Indigenous movement across space and thus theorizes the detriments of containment of bodies in relationship to the theft of land and neoliberal politics that seek to contain through multicultural policies of inclusion. In reflecting on post–Mabo era reconciliation politics, she asks if these politics of the settler state altered "the capacity to roam the land of our ancestors." Like Harjo, she questions neoliberal politics and asks, "or have we witnessed merely the illusion of change?" Ultimately, Watson concludes, "We must be able to imagine alternative spaces in which our thoughts and bodies are free to roam."[18] To me, the work of both of these Indigenous scholars is necessary in investigating the link between the local and the global as it pertains to the material conditions of Indigenous people.

The lines of the house meet in the shape of the poem itself; the continuous lines run without a stanza break, only shifting spatially and rhythmically as they move into the center. The poem uses the cultural material of the spiral to break free from internal and external restraints assembled through the social processes of colonization. This use of traditional spatial images associated with the three dimensions frequently appears as a theme in her poetry, as we see in this meeting. Building houses out of our own material, largely embodied material as Robert Warrior notes, is necessary to decolonization. Warrior, in his examination of the importance of the erotic in Native writing, reminds us of the connection among "the erotic, bodies, and Native survival," claiming that "our bodies—or our skins, which are the parts of us that most immediately touch and relate to the rest of the world around us—are not only the most immediate site of the battle for ourselves, but also the primary guide to where we ought to be headed."[19] Finding freedom in language—and applying it to our politics—becomes the mechanism for producing a space free from subjugation; the act of calling, praying, and "hold[ing] conversations" is the precursor to building a house strong enough to deal with the madness of colonized life.

A new house designed as cyclical and unbounded with possibilities, unlike the house of the nation based on exclusions of citizenship, gendered conceptions of the public and private, and transfer of Native land to private property, is built to create connections. By centering the poem on the house, the domestic realm is emphasized as an interiority that must also be politicized. The importance of theorizing that women's spatial imaginaries materialize as solutions to world issues is sought—issues that are not relegated to the house but are part of the economic and political spheres rendered as masculinized space in settler state discourses. The metaphor of the house is coupled by the exchange of pronouns throughout the poem. In the closing lines, the shifting pronoun usage signals a struggle taking place. "New ancestors" and a broader "we" must partake in this collaborative call to action and as such the poem ends with the celestial images of order and the inclusive pronoun "us." The poetic narrator recognizes that the enemy is also found within her and that it is the past ancestors and spirits as well as the new that have to meet if she is to build a house based on possibility and not foreclosure.

The methods of communicating across difference—devoid of collapsing into neoliberal models of multiculturalism meant to absorb difference into the state without creating any real difference in the structures that dominate— are not easy. Tokenism, omission, and appropriation will not change the structures of the settler state.[20] The necessity of balancing the spatial relationships between the local and global is at the heart of many of Harjo's current poems that are trying to mediate through the reality that difference poses without essentializing the experience. Her poetic ponderings work through the complexities of the human condition. In an interview, Harjo tells us that she sees "memory as not just associated with past history, past events, past stories, but non-linear, as in future and ongoing history, events, stories. And it changes."[21] If space is socially produced through memory, history, and events, as Henri Lefebvre and subsequent human geographers have argued, it stands to reason that we must constantly interrogate the ways in which we approach changes in spatial production. For Harjo, as for Leslie Marmon Silko, who will be discussed in the next chapter, the past is living and calls one to action, so that even changes reflect multiple moments in time.

In other words, conceptions of self in relation to space are not inscribed on a tabula rasa. Some traits of the old are remembered and incorporated into the present, some forgotten, and other socialities may unconsciously reside in our current conceptions of space. Yet, as I will discuss below, our actions are not merely determined by the spatial structures set up by state powers. This is evident in Harjo's uses of traditional images or mythic figures entwined with contemporary images and given everyday qualities. Her belief that "we are part of an old story and involved in it are migrations of winds, of ocean currents, of seeds, songs, and generations of nations" is the backbone of her poems, especially those dealing with (re)mapping the world. Traditions inform a way of knowing, and this epistemological basis produces material conditions as they are acted out in the world. The related concepts of the spiral and the stomp grounds, for instance, prompt Harjo's action to call a meeting. The locality of traditions does not have to be static, fixed, or marked as a moment in time that has passed; rather, traditions migrate through time, ideas, and places. These migrations, however, are not always "easy" or smooth, especially as bodies are relocated in the name of advancement and development.

NATIVE LOCALITIES AND GLOBALIZATION

In her poems, Harjo often connects and relates her individual story to that of the people in the space of "contact zones," understanding the constant creation that takes place among "strangers" who find themselves in the same place through global political and economic forces. In "The Path to the Milky Way Leads through Los Angeles," Harjo reflects her concern with space and the forces that disconnect people from one another:

> There are strangers above me, below me and all around me and we are all strange in this place of recent invention.
> This city named for angels appears naked and stripped of anything resembling the shaking of turtles shells, the songs of human voices on a summer night outside of Okmulgee.[22]

Deeply moved by the forces of globalization on Indigenous people in the world, Harjo writes of a world devoid of the markers of identity evident in the imagery of the turtle shells and reference to the place stomp dances are held. In many ways, we can liken Harjo's words to the critique by many that globalization has flattened the world in the proliferation of consumerism, a point that arises in much of Harjo's work. Through "imagining" she seeks to address this alienation that relates to an abstraction of space and construction of humans as consumers, declaring, "We must matter." Los Angeles is only one such city, Harjo imagines; she also writes poems of Chicago (addressed in the next section), San Juan, Mexico City, Honolulu, Albuquerque, New York, and many more places where people from all over the world meet.

To demonstrate the movement between the local and global, I created the title of this chapter with two metaphors of the ground on up in mind. "From the ground on up," a common expression in global studies, is a metaphor that implies restructuring the way centers are examined and the way the world is structured in terms of identity, culture, and relationships by starting with the local and particular to understand the global. Harjo in the above lines is imagining the stomp grounds in order to make a connection to those she finds in the city, but "we can't easily see that starry road from the perspective of the crossing / of boulevards, can't hear it in the whine of civilization or taste the / minerals of planets in hamburgers" (45). Global restructuring involves processes of communication that have an impact on the way we conceive of space. In these lines, Harjo is using the spatial metaphors of the upper Creek world to seek balance in a world of fast food and "several brands of water." Global restructuring orders and systemizes local communities and nation-states and is historically contingent on previous conceptions and reordering of space. The idea of the ground on up in globalization is a metaphor often used in the media, popular culture, and academia to discuss spatial relationships and the problematic of a world under threat of being consumed by multinational or even transnational corporations. It conveys the idea of starting with specific communities and working out to the larger-scale global community. Usually the meaning conveys economic and political nation-state status—or civilization for those deemed to be on the "periphery."

Harjo uses the metaphor of the stomp grounds and other specific Creek and tribal metaphors to locate herself within a Creek tradition, to note her connections to others, to recenter those normally left out of knowledge production, and to thwart the violence of global designs, a term Walter Mignolo defines as a "hegemonic project for managing the planet."[23] Geographer Derek Gregory tells us that "it is possible to use maps, landscapes, and spaces *and also* images of location, position, and geometry in ways that challenge the Archimedean view of knowledge, in ways that insist the geographies of knowing make a difference. But these are not absolutes and the differences that they make depend on the specific ways in which they are used."[24] Gregory's statement opens up possibilities in mapping, possibilities that are at play in Harjo's use of spatial metaphors that require an understanding of various knowledges too often erased. Harjo's metaphorical use of the stomp grounds, in its various forms, is of utmost importance in examining what happens when the Native of this country confronts an immigrant Native from another continent who has been displaced through similar mechanisms of the privatization of land and detribalization of people that brings Harjo and many Natives to the cities and landscapes she speaks of in her poems. First contact with Europeans set in motion the first stages of globalization as markets were established on Native lands and resources exported to Europe. Mignolo speaks to this moment of contact as engendering the "first global design of the modern/colonial world system and, consequently, the anchor of Occidentalism and the coloniality of power drawing the external borders as the colonial difference."[25] Concerned with knowledge production that is centered in universalism and colonial difference, Mignolo links the aggressive suppression of the Other's local histories and forms of knowledge as an expansion that "has not only been a religious and economic one, but also an expansion of hegemonic forms of knowledge that shaped the very conception of economy and religion."[26] Harjo's poetry, as is true in the theorizing and writing of many women of color, provides important feminist analyses of these masculinist universal global designs. She describes how her common experience of constant Native displacement and positive Native continuity is embodied: "When I am home in Oklahoma at the stomp grounds we may talk about the complexities of meaning, but to comprehend it, to know it intimately, the intricate context of history and family, is to dance it, to be it."[27] Harjo's poem counters forms of knowledge that would erase and deny Native presences.

In reading Harjo's poetry, I address her rethinking of globalization and seek to answer the question of what happens when the Indigenous person acts as an agent of global restructuring. The question that arises from this discussion of the colonial and gender politics of globalization is, where do extremely marginalized peoples, often erased citizens with histories of violent repression within their own state, fit into the analysis and theories of globalization studies?[28] For instance, many of the people who are migrating and creating diasporic communities are displaced Indigenous people, and yet much of the work being done on globalization concentrates on economies, capital mobility, transnational corporations, and labor. In this arena, the Indigenous is replaced by national identities; rather than tribal specificities being named, they become Mexicans or Salvadorans. What is lost, and how is this gendered, in this refusal to identify whose lands continue to be exploited and whose bodies are displaced by ongoing global expansion? Harjo's use of spatial metaphors and world-making helps raise these significant questions, as well as demonstrate how the silenced are living and maintaining their culture while acting as important agents in global restructuring. The way we relate to land and to place changes on a regular basis, though this does not preclude consistencies. In working toward a spatial justice, it is important to continually ask questions of the metaphors we use to describe the literal space, what that space signifies, and the context from which the metaphors emerge.[29]

Global restructuring, the act of producing space, is not accomplished by anonymous global forces, however, nor is the force purely in one direction.[30] Harjo dispels the notion of anonymous force in the poem and again calls us to action:

Everyone knows you can't buy love but you can sell your soul for less
than a song to a stranger who will sell it to someone else for a profit
until you're owned by a company of strangers
in the city of the strange and getting stranger. (45)

The repetition of "strange" in this passage simulates what happens in the city for Harjo. The forces of capitalism would alienate Native subjects from culture, relationship to land, and autonomy. Harjo, however, counters this process, by asking the trickster Crow, "So what are we doing . . . parading on the ledge of / falling that hangs over this precarious city?" (45). The global city does not have to be anonymous or make you a stranger as crows are everywhere "finding gold in the trash of humans" (45). Out of the scraps of consumer waste and displacements, Crows maintain kinship. Harjo's local metaphors (re)map a global restructuring of space. Doreen Massey examines the political space of the local in theorizing concepts of global space arguing against interrogating the small scale as mere descriptive analysis of the impact of globalization on specific communities. Instead, she emphasizes the importance of utilizing locality studies as the starting point, but also understanding that the local is comprised also of complex processes.[31] Harjo's work correlates to Massey's idea that the local is an important starting point and is also heterogeneous. In much Native thought, the local is always connected to multiple stories that move across time and space. In order to disrupt the global designs produced and productive of colonialism, it is necessary to collapse the dichotomy of the global and local and (re)map knowledges that would differentiate them in ironclad theories whose power is hidden behind the word "objective." Harjo contends: "There is no such thing as a one-way land bridge. People, creatures and other life will naturally travel back and forth. Just as we will naturally intermarry, travel up and down rivers, cross oceans, fly from Los Angeles to Oklahoma for a pow-wow" (38). Movement and mobilization are naturalized in Harjo's stories, upsetting a terrain of Western knowledge *about* Native peoples, a colonial knowledge used to control, regulate, and discipline the supposed static space and time colonial subject. Again, Harjo's spatial justice approach to the global city mirrors the words of Soja:

> The urbanization process and along with it what can be called the urbanization of (in)justice are generated primarily in and from dense urban agglomerations, but in the present age of accelerating globalization the urban condition has extended its influence to all areas: rural, suburban, metropolitan, exurban, even wilderness, parkland, desert, tundra and rainforest. In this sense, the whole world has been or is being urbanized to some degree, making the search for social justice relevant at many different geographical scales, from the global to the most local, and everywhere in between.[32]

Deep-well drilling on Native land, coal mining in Dinétah, or the damming of the Colorado River may begin on Native land and in Native places, but those resources are extracted to the urban centers. Meanwhile, Native people are left with the residue. Harjo addresses the intensity of capitalism she finds in the city of Los Angeles, a capitalism that hides "the path to the Milky Way": "But we can buy a map here of the star's homes, dial a tone for dangerous love" (45). The local map linked to capitalism's "illusion of the marketplace" and "someone else['s] profit" obscures the "starry road" bringing the world into imbalance or in many ways makes us all strangers as we are prevented from seeing how "we revolve together in the dark sky on the path to the Milky Way." Local spaces and studies of them or tribal perspectives are not isolated and provincial. They are ever moving and fluid, and it is this vantage point that can provide valuable insight into human interaction and spatial justice.

The debate concerning local tribal studies recurs in the field of Native literature and broadly in Native American studies as well. The need to derive literary theory from tribal culture remains an important approach in Native American studies, yet it is often one that can mire us in pure ethnographic readings devoid of any political context or one that does not acknowledge Native people as part of and influencing a global world. Often the call for an emphasis on cultural centers is a call for an emphasis on place and positioning oneself in a particular community. Harjo's use of the local to theorize the global is critical to Indigenous people whose land and labor are exploited in global finances. In order to substantiate the importance of the local in Native conceptions of the global, Harjo's literary use of the stomp grounds is key, as it details the intersections between the local and global. The local spaces of Harjo's production are more than descriptive—they call for action and a rethinking of space, time, memory, and culture.

The current topic of the relationship between globalization and social violence has permeated many theories of globalization across disciplines. Tyron Woods, for instance, takes globalization scholars to task for the confined emphasis on globalization as an economic and political science construct, asserting that instead there is a need to examine globalization as "referring to certain political strategies to resolve the crisis of the capitalist state," such as immigration and trade policies.[33] His argument is significant for the way I examine it in the next section: "The process of globalization includes a set of spatial rearrangements, and, second, space is reconfigured through race and gender. [Woods's] contention is that far from signaling a diminution of boundaries, globalization more often than not reinforces and fortifies geopolitical and racial borders."[34] Violent ongoing racializing and gendering projects continue to be carried out against Indigenous people in the Americas by nation-state governments. An emphasis on the effects of globalization processes on Indigenous communities is vital to disrupting political and economic discourses of globalization in which Native people are acted upon.

Two general approaches arise when globalization theory rests on the assumptions of Western hierarchies. The homogeneous approach attempts to adhere to nation-state borders and boundaries when studying the consequences of globalization in terms of world systems. The heterogeneous approach concentrates on particulars apart from a larger framework of systems and connection. Both general conceptions are inadequate methods for examining how Indigenous people are positioned politically, culturally, and economically. These approaches to culture found in simplified definitions of globalization obfuscate particular historical practices, such as the subjugating, assimilating, or murdering of Indigenous people. Too often, Indigenous people and their communities are overlooked—perhaps due to "perceiving" a lack of a political and economic body, marginalizing "real" Indians to the borders, creating homogenized subjects from national identities in which the Native is erased in national narratives, or rendering Indigenous people as invisible in the national cultural imagination that represents them as relics of the past.[35] Regardless of the reason, the end result is a violation of legal and human rights and a lack of access to resources.[36]

Fredric Jameson's view of the ideological structure of globalization as "a communicational concept, which alternately masks or transmits cultural or economical meanings," is pertinent to an examination of how global imaginings affect Native people.[37] This corrects the heterogeneous approach referred to above of mapping subjectivities based only on isolating political or economic concepts of the global, which materially and ideologically affect Indigenous people even as they are dismissed from globalization discourse through the ideological apparatus of the nation-state. By this I am referring to the way Indigenous people from Mexico or Guatemala are not recognized as Indigenous people but as immigrants from another nation-state. The erasing of their indigeneity results in a dismissal of the context of their situation. As Young asserts, examining globalization as a purely institutional, abstract space of the state and a network of world systems omits the agents of global restructuring. If the world is left mapped in this way, only a story about continued global imperialism and the splintering of communities is left. Harjo imagines a different story, however, and creates an awareness of Native people in cities and in nation-states, telling us that it is easier to "perceive" beauty and place "when those who remember us here in the illusion of the marketplace / turn toward the changing of the sun and say our names" (45). The force of globalization, as the ideology of manifest destiny, preordains the fate of supposedly vanishing Indigenous people as a consequential geography of capitalist development. Harjo recognizes the tensions of globalization in line with Jameson's position but extends it to recognize our relationships to the nonhuman as well, and interrupts the narrative with an alternative examination of social spaces in a native context. Indigenous peoples' movements begin to burgeon in the 1980s and 1990s, informing the discourses and practices around space.

In a 1996 interview by Greg Sarris (a Miwok/Pomo American Indian writer, political activist, and American Indian studies scholar), Harjo was asked how she believes we can break barriers (later referred to as boundaries) as American Indians. Standing in for abstract margins and the material life of Native Americans, these barriers and boundaries are spatial metaphors both ideological and very tangible for American Indian people. In her response, she extols the power of communication theories, declaring that she strives for a space in which there is no room for lying. Her poetry seeks the truth, as she tells us in an intimate postscript to a poem: "If I am a poet who is charged with speaking the truth (and I believe the word poet is synonymous with truth-teller), what do I have to say about all of this?" (19). Her poetry addresses issues of identity, locality, justice, and politics—all of which are called into question when the Indigenous person of this land encounters another Indigenous person who has been displaced and exploited by global economies. Many of Harjo's pieces begin from the ground up with her personal experiences as an Indigenous woman living in a colonized space; yet in this constant invention of settler colonial space, Harjo finds ways to remember, reminding us that "like the crow I collect the shine of anything beautiful I can find" (45).

Letter from the End of the Twentieth Century

Harjo's poem "Letter from the End of the Twentieth Century" seeks to undo the damage of a Western mapping that homogenizes and defines Natives. By combining global forms of music and poetic verse, she addresses the forms of globalism I spoke to above. Harjo has often said that she sees her poems in music form before the language comes, and in fact she took up the alto saxophone in her early thirties as a result of trying to express language through sound. This performative dimension has truly influenced much of her current poetry, and she continues to create CDs based on her poems.[38] Music, visual arts, and language are deeply connected in Harjo's work, creating multilayered dimensions in the imagery and metaphors of her poetry. The musical form of Harjo's verses emanates from the beat and pace of the poetic words. The sound and the backbeat to the poem not only add an aesthetic dimension to the work, and to my analysis, but also illuminate how Harjo rearticulates space, restructures globalization in terms of Indigenous peoples' movement on the global scale, and collapses time so that history is always present.

Harjo (re)maps the place of the Indigenous in the global through the musical forms of jazz and reggae. These genres of music are an unmistakable mixture of the cultures of Indigenous people and Africans brought to the Americas as slaves. Harjo herself suggests that both runaway slaves and Natives, with whom they often intermingled while hiding from slave catchers, influenced the formation of jazz. In an autobiographical note preceding a poem about the jazz musician Jim Pepper, Harjo confides: "I've always believed us Creeks had something to do with the origins of jazz. After all, when the African peoples were forced here for slavery they were brought to the traditional lands of the Muscogee peoples. Of course there was interaction between Africans and Muscogees!"[39] Aware of musical forms and the historical implications of colonization, Harjo chooses a musical genre that originates in Africa, forms anew from a system of subjugation, and continues to exist and creates a path toward decolonization. The instrumental elements with their political connotations are a constitutive element of the overall meaning of the poem, an aesthetic choice mired in historical, economic, and political materialities. The skank guitar is an instrument that came about through the slave trade. It has African roots and found its current form as a cultural innovation of the Caribbean. It has been important in the foundation of ska music, a combination of jazz and Caribbean rhythms. Cowbells, African indigenous instruments, and the conga drum create meaning together with poetic language and metaphor. The instruments and the musical forms employed by Harjo, too, have migrated and been (re)invented in the wake of the first waves of forced (im)migration during colonization that I discussed in more detail above. The globe was reshaped by the slave trade, and its consequences produced diverse communities and cultures—Africans, people indigenous to the Americas, and the European settlers. Like new music, new socialities were produced and productive, literally shaping the world around us. The cowbell from Africa makes its journey to the Caribbean, where it joins with the innovative skank guitar to produce a new cultural sound. In the song, the travels do not stop there, as the music itself migrates to the Southeast where it joins the beats of the stomp grounds. This restructuring of people's relationship of space through colonial practices, such as Creek removal to Oklahoma to make room for immigrant Europeans, finds itself in this contemporary milieu of jazz, ska, and Indigenous beats that continue to mix with displaced people from multiple and overlapping places. Through the use of various instruments that signify the paths of colonization and original displacement of Indigenous people, the musical form of the poem adds an important pathway to discuss a history of violence, slavery, rape, massacres, and death at the hands of colonizers; more importantly, the music represents a history of cultural survival and beauty still to be found in the world.

The connections between the local and global produced in Harjo's language fortify the "Letter from the End of the Twentieth Century," pushing the language in the poem beyond rhetoric or mere reflection of the economic conditions of the dispossessed. The poem tells the tale of an encounter with a cab driver who picks up the narrator from the transnational space of the airport. They begin a conversation, telling each other stories—particularly stories of their individual histories—in hopes of creating understanding. In sharing both beautiful and violent stories of immigrant men working in the dangerous world of cab drivers and her own stories of colonization, Harjo is able to reckon distances between the abject subjects of immigrants who are deemed as not belonging to the nation, but whose labor is necessary to sustain an exploitative capitalist system. Native people who haunt seemingly from the past but practice the everyday reality of fighting for land and their people are also abject subjects. By articulating these connections in the stories of the terrifying and random murders of individuals, Harjo comes to grips with the violence produced by global restructuring and destruction of communities and our connections with one another.

Mapping and narrative converge in Native intellectual discourse, not just as a way to counter colonial processes, but also as a way to create relationships among land, people, and cultures. Harjo, along with many other Native writers and activists, is not just deconstructing the terms of nation mapping. Nor does Harjo replicate statist maps with the same effects of exclusion from/inclusion into the nation-state. Rather than mimicking Cartesian forms of mapping, Harjo supplants this methodology with Native knowledge that deals with an ever-spiraling world. Black, Caribbean, and Native (specifically Muscogee Creek) converge in Harjo's musical and poetic compositions to fight what Andrea Smith frames as the three pillars of white supremacy; she argues that in order to overthrow the larger structure, we must examine the logics of slavery, colonization, and orientalism in our models of liberation practices.[40] Harjo's poetry is in constant dialogue with these logics, which are key to understanding how we relate to each other and how we hold each other accountable after we hear a story.

By creating relationships through narratives or a sharing of stories and by determining the spatial metaphors used to create a subject position, Harjo builds relationships among community, land, culture, and history—relationships that counter the fragmentation and loss created through colonial exploits. She says in the autobiographical note to this poem, "As an Indian woman in this country I often find much in common with many immigrants from other colonized lands who come here to make a living, often as taxi drivers" (38). Far from being an American Indian closed off from the world, Harjo deeply engages with it from the minute to the vastness of space. As a result of this multiscalar perspective, she is aware of how the movement of people on a global scale is connected to the first wave of immigration by European settlers. Indigenous people face an astonishing rate of displacement as a result of increased globalization and privatization of land through free market principles. Yet this accumulation of land and labor is not new, as you may recall from the above historical content. Harjo in this instance draws another map, created through the sharing of stories, that connects her to the waves of displaced people entering her homeland. Rather than denigrating these forms of music and narrative stories as "other" or not of her nation, Harjo connects histories without losing the particularities of being Muscogee Creek.

The very structure of this poem, in the shape of the spiral, reflects a commitment to connect stories. The composition of the music and the breaks in the poem produce three rhythmic shifts in the song, written in the form of a letter telling us about violence on a global scale. Letter writing is personal, intimate, and directed. Above all else, the form of a letter demands a response. Harjo begins her letter poem by positioning herself ("I spent the morning"), yet moves outward to encompass a global community ("with Rammi, an Igbo man from northern Nigeria"). In the end stanza/rift, the poem spirals back to the personal beginning, as if signing her name at the end of the letter ("It sustains me through these tough distances"). By dividing the letter poem into three parts based on shifts in the rhythm of the music and a correlating shifting subject position, three related times, spaces, and relationships arise: first, the present of Harjo in Chicago; second, the in-between of the murdered man's ghost searching for his killer; and third, the past or memory that is deeply personal to Harjo and many tribal communities. The literary device of the spiral structure serves to layer and converge stories, time, imagination, and reality as it seeks answers, justice, and our response.

The poetic imagining of the Creek idea of the spiral is a powerful tool for (re)mapping our nations. The spiral has many meanings in the cultural context of Creek people; in this particular poem, the spiral correlates to the three worlds of Creek cosmology represented by Harjo in the shifts of the music, lyrics, and voice. As in her poem "A Map to the Next World," Harjo rejects the linear Cartesian model in favor of the Creek structure of the spiral and stomp grounds to draw a new global map. Harjo's map does not imply "real" or "objective" space that categorizes, contains, and isolates humans by representing homogeneity within its border, regions, and nations implementing policies to force their stableness; rather, she creates a space that converges time, space, and human relationships. For example, the instrumental choices discussed above invoke a connection between past times and ongoing forms of music. Rather than categorizing the saxophone as purely an Afro-American instrument, she makes it a historical tool that produces poetry and political theory.

In performing the poem Harjo deploys a variety of poetic strategies to mend from the violence. After establishing a steady jazz beat with the saxophone, the poem opens with the conversation with the driver. The spiral image enters at this point: "Chicago rose up as a mechanical giant with soft insides / buzzing around to keep it going. We were part of the spin" (35). In this postindustrial image of the stomp grounds, Harjo depicts the cityscape as "mechanical" and "buzzing," but not necessarily as alienating. The buzzing insides are reminiscent of the stomp dancers positioned around the fire, dancing in circles and counter-circles. The word "rose" has many important connotations about the use of language as a call to social action. In reference to the phrase "rising up" used by Silko and Harjo throughout their works, Womack suggests, "If one has racial memory, then one of the primary recollections has to be the fact of genocide and land theft, and the ancestors may have more in mind than quick spiritual highs; perhaps a call to action is being elicited."[41] The image of dancing and the act of doing so was so powerful that it elicited the response of being outlawed by the settler state and enforced through sheer brutality. I believe that the point here needs to be elaborated on. The Creek stomp dance, in particular, represents a part of Creek culture and cultural continuity, as well as its innovation. The history of the origins of the Creek dance relates to the displacement and diasporic condition that colonization creates and the history I mentioned above. The loss of loved ones was compounded by what those lives meant for future generations. Creek knowledge and way of life were threatened by the massacres and disruptions of the transmission of culture. In this light, given such a momentous blow, these dances came to sustain the Creek people and the Nation.[42] The practice of outlawing Native expressions—ceremonial, artistic, social, and political—was about the control of land and creating a spatiality that forces Native peoples out of existence.

In Oklahoma, many tribes were thrown together in the process of "civilization" and nation-building, forcing them to interact and find new ways of being in a new space. The displaced Indians pushed to the frontier found dance to be an important communal aspect and kept their traditions despite official policies and U.S. governmental terrorism that took away any rights to religious practice. In Harjo's poems, Indigenous people are displaced into the global cities. While assimilation policies are not as outright brutal and violent as in the days of boarding schools and earlier, they are still an everyday part of Indigenous life in the United States. For Indigenous peoples from the global South, English replaces the previous colonizing language of Spanish, and these Indigenous people face immense pressure to conform to American culture and values. This is all too similar to pressures felt by American Indians—Indigenous communities from both locales are deeply affected by national policies seeking to homogenize a national subject. The continuity of resistant movement in Harjo's poem counters the continued efforts of nation-building to form an "American" citizenship rooted in the ideals of settler whiteness. Using the images of dance ("buzzing" and "spin"), the narrator rises up even in the new landscape of Chicago.

In the first lines, the words are accompanied by a consistent rhythm, until the last line of the stanza when the beat speeds up with the celestial metaphor that brings order, "We were all part of the spin." This line is spoken in double time with the music. In this quickening of pace, which reoccurs in later stanzas, Harjo brings all those in the city of Chicago into her circle. At a stomp dance, the outer ring of dancers moves faster than the smaller inner ring. Where people are placed is determined by many factors, including age, race, and role in the community. Harjo's spoken words mirror this as they extend from the personal, the beginning of the poem that opens in the first-person, "I shared an hour of my life," to the more general "We." Through these particular spatial metaphors, the Creek stomp grounds merge with the bustling city landscape of Chicago; through the trope of dancing, the displaced are brought together. Dance can create a community that resists the practices of the nation-state.[43] In dancing, people refuse to stay still and static in a collaborative politic that becomes a mechanism of resistance. Harjo is simultaneously positioning herself through this image in the stomp grounds, a Creek gathering, and the city of Chicago, a place in which she is making a call to action.

Harjo is telling a narrative of a contemporary Muscogee woman, but within her story, her historical and contemporary encounters direct her to other narratives. The second stanza of the poem is Rammi's story about the murdered friend. The "I" of the poem does not meet the young man in person, yet he becomes a core part of how she perceives the world. Through narrative she makes the connection reminiscent of Silko's words in *Almanac of the Dead:* "One day a story will arrive in your town. There will always be disagreement over the direction—whether the story came from the southwest or the southeast . . . But after you hear the story, you and the others prepare by the new moon to rise up against the slave masters."⁴⁴ The power of story resounds throughout these writings, and in this poem in particular Harjo depicts a woman deeply affected by an African immigrant's tale. By recapping the narrative in Harjo's own language of both words and music, she makes the story a part of her and a part of her larger community, connecting the routes between two seemingly disparate subjects of the state—the immigrant and Native.

The layers of the story are signified further as we learn about the importance of story for the murdered Igbo man as well. His mother's story of the sun performs the function of what Elizabeth Deloughrey refers to as a heliotrope, found in a global collective imaginary. Deloughrey builds on Jacques Derrida's understanding of a heliotrope as "the father of all figures of speech," to speak of the fallout from post–World War II ecological policies that have resulted in mass devastation for Pacific Islander people. She speaks to the ways that the heliotropes are indicative of the ways solar and atomic energy have produced both environmental crisis and at times been presented as their potential solutions. In Deloughrey's analysis of the "complex relationships between Cold War ecology and radiation," she engages the heliotrope "and its byproduct, radiation, as traces for modernity, figures for alterity, and the material legacy of the militarization of the Pacific Islands."⁴⁵ In many ways, Harjo's use of the image of the sun as a heliotrope maps the connections between the global and local; its meaning in a specific Creek context can also have great depth to (re)map relationships between seemingly closed-off (both geographically and temporally) Indigenous populations.

This brings us back to our earlier discussion of difference, displacement, and the abstraction of land into jurisdictional, state-run zones and the naturalization of space and military occupation. The mass devastation of island land from nuclear tests or resource mining results in the land no longer being able in many cases to sustain its original inhabitants. This has led to the displacement of large island populations and other Indigenous populations facing neocolonialism who also find themselves in the urban centers of places such as Los Angeles and Chicago. In the poem, the heliotrope connects the Igbo man's specific story to a larger global scale by the presence of the sun. The sun becomes the focus: "As the sun broke through the grey morning he heard his mother tell / him, the way she had told him when he was a young boy, how the / sun had once been an Igbo and returned every morning to visit / relatives" (35). The repetition of the rising and falling sun and the story sustains him, and gives him a way to cope with poverty, work, and foreign lands. This recollection of the sun's image brings him home. Through myth, memory, and imagining, his homeland is brought to the city of Chicago, preventing the alienation of the global city or the violence of absorption: "These memories were the coat that kept him warm" (35). In the poem's use of solar metaphors, an alternative spatial poetics is conceived. The traveling or movement of the sun, whether held in memory or from the act of looking up, provides an alternative to complete alienation or declension narratives. While the city structures the everyday, it does not determine the practices and relationships forged in the meeting of stories. The sacredness of places and myths enabling a return "home" are constant themes in Indigenous cultural production.[46] Harjo enables a return or memory to create a relationship or map to the land we are standing on, even if it is "in a labyrinth far, far, from home" (35). While many critiques, especially William Bevis's development of the important concept of "homing in," have spoken to Native writers' relationships to home, health, embodiment, and the theme of return and consequent healing, Harjo provides a model for examining Native people always in movement across space.[47] As Bevis states, "Nature is home then to Native Americans . . . Nature is not a secure seclusion one has escaped to, but it is the tipi walls expanded, with more and more people chatting around the fire."[48] I think of this, also, from the Haudenosaunee perspective of extending the rafters, a concept briefly approached in the first chapter. These are concepts that allow us to not mark difference as threatening or dangerous—and I mean this in its spatial differences as well—but as a moment to be incorporated into our knowledge systems. Accepting different knowledges and rethinking them in relation to specific cultural traditions does not necessarily mean replacement, erasure, or assimiliation, but rather it means that Native peoples decide what knowledges are important to their communities' health. As Harjo's poetry suggests, the planet is always in movement, spinning on an axis, and always part of something much larger, as are we.

Just as dance creates connections through the rhythm of the words and music in the first stanza, in this second stanza we are brought into the Creek woman's story and the story of Rammi and his friend by the image of the sun. Harjo doesn't lose the sound of the stomp dance but repeats the sound double time by speeding up the line "And the same sun, the same Igbo look- / ing down on him in the streets of the labyrinth far far from home" (35). Again, an established tempo, and the image of the sun ties to a story that we can only imagine, yet we're imagining the story and its ability to determine the everyday practices of this man as it provides "sustenance," "warmth," and the strength "to keep him going one / more year until he had the money he needed to return" (35). Possibility in the form of the story connects these global participants. The history of colonization and globalization that brings these stories and people together is ever present in Harjo's images, asking us to think about the ways that the terms "Indigenous" and "immigrant" have primarily worked to create disparate identities, supposedly at odds, rather than peoples with specific histories and coalescing reasons to work together in this neoliberal world created by humans.

Harjo sets up the middle world of humans, and as she does so she brings globalization into a local Creek knowledge system through the structure of the poem and use of spatial metaphors. Yet the form is not only nationalist (that is, purely Creek), nor is the content indeterminate cosmopolitanism; rather, the story complicates the often strict categories of positions in the field of Native studies. Her use of Creek metaphors intersects with the global story of a Native Igbo man from Nigeria. The Igbo people were colonized by the British and have a similar, though, of course, not exact, history as Native tribes in the United States. The Igbo, too, have fought for recognition, independence, and the right to act as a nation-state. While representing this history in the context of this chapter would be dense, I believe that it does suggest that thinking of these histories as separate from ours as Indigenous people severs possibilities for rethinking justice. The stories presented in this letter poem take a step toward representing the reality of Native people interacting in the world rather than confining the representation of Native people as existing only in the past or confined to a geographical place located only on the reservation or even solely in U.S. relocation cities. The letter addresses the violence of settler colonialism and imperialism at multiple scales of economic processes and spatialized injustices.

Another shift occurs at Rammi's friend's violent death, marked through the syncopation of the drums and sax. The event of a shooting at the gas station is motivated by poverty, greed, confusion, and alienation; it is a moment of global violence that upsets the balance of the middle world laid out in the conversation between the poetic narrator and Rammi in the first five stanzas. The change of pace in the music and poem is marked by spatial metaphors of the upper and lower worlds of Creek cosmology that are signs of Harjo working through the deaths of Indigenous peoples and their meaning to an Indigenous woman in this century. She struggles to bring the worlds into balance by mapping the path to justice in Creek epistemology:

> As we near the concrete plains of O'Hare, I imagine the spirit of
> Rammi's friend at the door of his mother's house, the bag of dreams
> in his hands dripping with blood. His mother's tears make a river of
> red stars to an empty moon. (36)

Through the water image (particular to the lower world of Creek cosmology that denotes chaos) of "his mother tears," Harjo is able to imagine the beginning of the healing process. As she slips into the lower world through the image of water, she imagines the young man searching for his killer to set things right. From the lower world of tears, she pulls the world into tension in the images of red stars and empty moons, planetary symbols of the upper world of order. The young man rises in an effort to put things in balance again from the chaos and disruption caused by violence. His story does not end with his death.

At every shift in the poem, marked by the sound of the drums and sax, the Indigenous woman places herself physically and in connection with others, even if it is a painful connection that recalls past violences she has witnessed. In this instance, she is in the present, indicated in the "concrete" landscape description of a modern-day city. But rather than feel disconnected to the earth, she modifies her description and imagines O'Hare as "concrete plains," presenting a historical continuity of land. The transnational space of the ever-moving and unstable airport is a global metaphor—it represents moving and transitory space—but it is a Creek metaphor of the upper world as well; the ability of the metaphor to be global and local simultaneously enables Harjo to (re)map her subjectivity. She is not an anachronistic Native woman displaced by the construction of cities, industrial movements, and policies that abstract Native lands and bodies into profit. Stories are key to unpacking these everyday realities and contemporary complexities—they are a matter of sustenance.

Harjo's poem, dated as written at the "end of the twentieth century" as the title and letter form of the poem suggest, is about rising up to advocate for a justice that entails love and forgiveness. This is not easy, however, and requires a long look at historical violence and spatial construction of the city: more importantly it calls for action. At the young man's death,

> The whole village mourns with her. The ritual of tears and drums
> summon the ancestors who carry his spirit to the next world.
> There they can still hear the drums of his relatives as they accompany

him on his journey. He must settle the story of his murder before
joining his ancestors or he will come back as a ghost. (36)

Inner-city violence and death become abstracted in the media, as are the
bodies who feel the everyday violence in the postindustrial city. Domosh and
Seager pinpoint many of our assumptions of the modern city, especially in
its conceived, represented, and produced masculine rationality, as beginning
in the age of "discovery" of the new worlds. They contend that these gendered conceptions of the city—and their correlation to freedom and excitement—are largely contrasted to the countryside or the modern suburbia as a
feminized domestic space. The domestication of reservations, as legally conceived domestic nations, seems to mirror these principles, and in large part
reflects some of the previous chapters' work with the masculinization and
urbanization of Native communities during the relocation and termination
era. After all, many people left the "stifling" space and poverty of the reservation in part to have new experiences and seek new fortunes that the legacy
of spatial restrictions and imposed poverty through economic and political
policies denied. Domosh and Seagar's examination of the global city, defined
as "shar[ing] certain characteristics typical of the postmodern era: declining
industrial and inner-city areas, pockets of gentrification, suburban expansion,
the dominance of consumer economies," aids in our understanding of the
gendered city and our "perception of cities as dangerous, almost pathological,
spaces inhabited by minorities and single mothers, was self-fulfilling—more
and more businesses, jobs, and services left the city."[49] For Native people, however, the city was and is often seen as an escape from violence at home, and
for others, as pointed out last chapter, the city occupies their homelands. Yet
the violence is never over there. As Harjo's witnessing attests, the violence
stems from centuries of exploitation of certain bodies across various spaces
and must be recognized or it will continue to haunt. In deconstructing the
binaries of the violence of the global open city/domestic reservation and
immigrant/Native, we all are held accountable.

Harjo's letter implies that there is a participatory reader and intended audience who must address the subject of urban violence consistently reflected
and produced through media sensationalism in the early 1990s. As spaces
were deemed too dangerous to raise a family in, economies were moved to
the fringes. The city norm in cultural production is too often conceived of
as inherently violent, while the connection to material forces that sets up
violent conditions is too often denied. The death of the man, a man who

"saved every penny because he knew when / he returned he'd be taking care of his family, a family several houses / large," is not inconsequential, forgotten, or isolated. His family understands the loss on a very real material and emotional level, and the poet and the immigrant communities note the death of the man, acknowledging it through rituals and a sharing of culture. Harjo in this poem pays homage to the man and others like him, acknowledging the social violence produced through economic exploitation stemming from the privatization of Indigenous lands. Yet she also acknowledges the effect social violence has on both of these communities. The young man may come back as a ghost, not just in an individual sense, but his ghost will return on a community level, conjured up through memory and the continuity of historic acts of violence. Harjo collapses the "distanced" space of the city and instead connects violence as interconnected at both the global and local "domestic" scale.

As the young Igbo man searches for his killer, or justice, the music shifts in tempo, and the conga drums are incorporated to evoke a stalking effect. The hunt through poverty-stricken areas of the large city inhabited by the displaced furthers the mood, which in turn becomes exacerbated by the description of the cramped jail cell where he is eventually found. In this moment, many scenarios arise:

> The smallest talking drum is an insistent heart, leads his spirit to the killer, a young Jamaican immigrant who was traced to his apartment because his shirt of blood was found by the police, thrown off in the alley with his driver's license still in the pocket.

> He searches for his murderer in the bowels of Chicago and finds him shivering in a cramped jail cell. He could hang him or knife him— and it would be called suicide. It would be the easiest thing.

> But his mother's grief moves his heart. He hears the prayers of the young man's mother. There is always a choice, even after death. (36)

The ability of the ghost avenger to see relationships across space and time gives him agency. While he has agency, however, he is held responsible to his community through familial ties. The choice of how he will reconcile the violence done "even after death" is the ultimate agency to commit (in)justice. The past is brought into the present; the Igbo community is brought to the jail cell in Chicago in the beat of the drum. The ambiguity in "but his mother's

grief moves his heart" focuses the decision on community and family relationships. The personal pronoun does not have a direct referent; "his" could
refer to either man. The grief could signify his own mother's loss or it could
mean his killer's mother's loss—either way, they and their communities lose
in the continued destruction of life. The enactment of the ritual in the poem
engenders the intactness of the community—it becomes a way to heal not
only from an isolated and random act of urban violence, but also a way to
enact justice that will be most beneficial for future communities. Families
and communities have the ability to make choices, and it is this ability that
allows for the tangibility of (re)mappings' healing significance and revolutionary power.

When the murdered man finds his killer, he decides to love him—not to
do "the easiest thing." As in many of Harjo's poems, love becomes the answer,
but not in a trite, over-romanticized way. The Muscogee poet specifies actions
that demonstrate how to love or to begin that process of balance. Though the
men are from Jamaican and Nigerian communities, and Rammi, who tells us
this story, is from India, it is human relationships that overcome the violence
of a global market. Instead of centering on the colonized/oppressed dichotomy, Harjo refocuses her poem on a Creek center, bringing the worlds into
balance through her consistent use of the Creek spatial metaphors of the three
worlds. She does not leave it at that, however, and expands her lyricism to
encompass those of other tribes who have also been displaced by colonial
practices. The Afro-Caribbean beat and drum, as well as the imagery in the
stanzas, resemble a heartbeat. This affective (re)mapping of our relations in
the world in these instances refocuses the discussion of globalization and U.S.
imperialism not on difference, but on connection and practices of healing
and choice. It is a choice that advocates a responsibility to see relationships
between people, places, and times seemingly at odds.

For many centuries people have needed to try to achieve balance and
had the means to do so in traditional medicines and knowledge. The space
Harjo maps in the Creek images is not merely a counterspace to colonization. Rather, it is a space defined by tribal cultural knowledge, relationships,
and experiences. Not only does this knowledge predate Western cartography
and its implications for race, gender, and nation-making, but Harjo's relationships (re)map in a manner that extends beyond territorial claims and
the borders that exert them. This is signified in the rebirth of the young pris-
oner; his enemy's love and forging of a new relationship with him enables
the young man to come to terms with a history of colonialism. Harjo relates

this in the following renaming of the young man, which signifies rebirth. The Igbo man calls him brother and thus binds him in a familial relationship:

> He gives the young man his favorite name and calls him his brother.
> The young killer is then no longer shamed but filled with remorse
> and cries all the cries he has stored for a thousand years. He learns
> to love himself as he never could, because his enemy, who has every
> reason to destroy him, loves him. (36)

In her imaginings, Harjo makes connections between people and at the same time situates these connections in a Muscogee framework. The man haunted by his death brought about through the economic process of displacement is also haunted by the legacy of colonization and imperialism. Harjo dates evil, sorrow, and disruption *before* colonization: "He cries a thousand cries he has stored for a thousand years" (36). She positions the world before Columbus landed and repositions human hierarchies by connecting through the most basic of all relationships—that of the mother/child. Thus, she is not just dealing with colonization, but with human imbalance. The colonizer/colonized dichotomy disintegrates when Native people enact their agency. This maneuvering between local epistemologies and global frameworks strengthens the notion that Indigenous people, though they experience the material realities of globalization, do not necessarily have to be determined by a global world of faceless systems and institutions.

In the last shift, apparent again by an emphasis on the drums and saxophone, we return to Harjo's voice, time, and space. She tells us that this is the story that follows her "everywhere and won't let me sleep" (37). She lists the many places where she resides, travels, and has connections, "from the Tallahassee grounds to Chicago, to my home near the Rio Grande. / It sustains me through these tough distances" (37). In a previous personal note to the poem, Harjo relates the story of a man in Albuquerque killed in circumstances similar to those of Rammi's friend. The exile felt by these subjects may be repaired and does not have to be an unhealed rift resulting from the spatial dichotomies that discipline and control our movements and interactions throughout various spaces. Harjo, through Creek literary symbols and places such as the Tallahassee stomp grounds, is able to connect the story of the young Igbo man, the Jamaican man, the man killed in Albuquerque, and the men and women who have destroyed themselves in trying to cope with displacement and diasporic conditions. By forming a global poetic narrative from tribal cultural contexts, the poet represents diverse narratives that constitute the central tale of the Muscogee author. In this end-of-the-century tale, the diasporic displacement of Indigenous people affected by globalization is highlighted as well as the social violence that results. Yet, imagining possibilities beyond declension narratives is spoken in the power of narrative to help travel "these tough distances" (37).

Through memory and connections created through myth, language, and love, Harjo is able to place and center herself—wherever that may be. At the end of the poem, distances become bearable through acknowledging pain, sharing stories, and performing acts of forgiveness. Thus, in Chicago, the poetic voice still holds the communal event of the stomp ground with her. Though the poem opens with a global conversation, it is still a Creek image she recalls; this is an important convergence of the local and global enabled through metaphor and poetic verse. These literary strategies allow for an expansion of healing to a global level without losing the specificity of individual tribal culture. Although the poem's musical form and voice return to the beginning, Harjo is not in the same place, physically or metaphysically.

CONCLUSION: SOVEREIGNTY AND SPATIAL JUSTICE

While this chapter focuses on Joy Harjo, she is just one example of how Native writers are examining our material socialities and looking for solutions that (re)map our relationships along the lines of our ancestors' paths. This couldn't be more important in the wake of neoliberal global politics and economic policies. Just as Harjo has influenced many lives, many of the poet's greatest influences are other writers, both Indigenous and non-Indigenous. She is able to create vital "spaces" by "reinventing the enemy's language"[50] and looking at traditional story and narrative mapping as ways to map our futurities. The breadth of her influences and her ability to incorporate them into her poetry through the density of language generate an imperative intertextual dialogue.

To become part of the "modern global culture," Harjo does not have to lose her culture or forget her history. The insertion of the local into her poetry allows for a (re)mapping of our nations—both Native nations and nation-states. (Re)mapping is a multiscalar process able to recast the discourse establishing the paradox of being Indian. We can adjust the discourse surrounding immigrant Indigenous identity in the United States into one that culturally fits our communities, many of which used to be based on making connections with others and respecting those differences. Immigrants are not coming and giving up their epistemological bases in favor of becoming "American," but instead are finding the mechanisms to retain and perhaps return to their lands, provided that there are healthy lands to return to. Many Native peoples and Indigenous immigrants from other continents are holding on to their cultures, not out of pure nostalgia or self-discipline, though that undeniably happens, but the epistemologies found in stories often create the maps that guide us to important relationships to land, people, and place. Native people have been remembering and practicing their culture in order to fight colonialism, economic exploitation, and erasure as well. Holly Youngbear-Tibbetts, the dean of outreach and director of the Sustainable Development Institute of the College of the Menominee Nation, writes about the use of spatial metaphors in feminist scholarship to elicit connections among the "metaphormaker," landscape, and culture. By invoking spatial metaphors to talk about the personal or positioning of Native women, Youngbear-Tibbets deconstructs some of the dichotomous relationships that have been set up in the use of spatial metaphors, such as mobility and home. Home, travel, mobility, and immigration are concepts that are particularly important to Native communities. In the closing to Youngbear-Tibbets's essay "Making Sense of the World," she writes of the relationship between spatial metaphors and alliances with immigrants to the United States:

> While the broad outlines of communities in discord with one another regarding their identification with particular metaphors of space and place are undeniable, almost invariably native women would comment that there were women of immigrant ancestry who had proven to be exceptions to the rule, feminists with whom they felt more than a sense of camaraderie, who evinced real solidarity with Indigenous communities, places, and struggles. When native women commentators would talk of these women—and sometimes communities of women—or when I would later have the opportunity to see them interact, it became clear that these women were in no sense displaced. They shared with native women a genuine fidelity to place, a sense of shared living experiences, and a sense of shared destiny that was unmistakable.[51]

In mapping new landscapes through language Native people possess an important means of articulating self, but it is not a closed system of ahistorical referentiality. Harjo can examine the detriments of globalization, such as the economic exploitation and fragmentation evoked in "The Letter from the End of the Twentieth Century," while engaging with her tribally specific relationship to these patterns of destruction. The Indian is not anachronistic—she has always played a part in the mapping of the world. Culture is not an irrelevant tool for fixing world issues. In fact, the ability to see the connections and nodes of comparisons among cultures is vital to understanding the making of the world. Harjo restores balance in both traditional and contemporary narratives by revising the spatial discourses in terms of culture and the migratory spaces of Indigenous people.

Harjo does not view culture as an isolated way of knowing, and in fact she takes into account the multifarious experiences and changes that have affected her own ways of knowing. Harjo takes on the polemical task of trying to create self-determined and community-driven geographies—not a space that is either haphazardly new or nostalgically old. Instead, she highlights the inextricably linked spheres of time, memory, discourse, and Indigenous geographies. By sifting through the memory of her people, the discourses that have created them anew in the Western cultural imagination, and the remnants of a tattered history she fashions a place for Native people that is contained by colonial and imperial ideas of spatiality. "In the dark. In the beautiful perfume and stink of the world" (135), Harjo is moving us toward a spatial sovereignty and a spatial justice. In a global world, we need to find strategies to cope and remain connected. Narrative and telling, as well as the trope of mapping to work out new relationships, allow us to explore many future possibilities that go beyond positioning the Indigenous in colonizer/colonized, modern/premodern, civilized/uncivilized, oppressed/oppressor binaries. Harjo's poetry exemplifies many such sovereign spaces, constructed through metaphors, metonymy, and other aspects of poetic language—in both the English language and, increasingly so, the Muscogee language. Yet these are part of Indigenous peoples' everyday lives as we recreate each day, for "the red dawn now is rearranging the earth / thought by thought" (128). Our thoughts map our world. We engage relationships to the world around us and posit solutions for contemporary issues—whether they are located near the stomp grounds or in the bowels of Chicago, or the superimposition of the two.

"Someday a Story Will Come": Rememorative Futures

> Perhaps empire never ended, that psychic and material will
> to conquer and appropriate.... What we can say for sure is
> that empire makes all innocence impossible.
>
> —JACQUI M. ALEXANDER, *Pedagogies of Crossing: Mediations*
> *on Feminism, Sexual Politics, Memory, and the Sacred*

EXCERPTS FROM HISTORIC ALMANACS, DIARIES, TRAVEL JOURNALS, AND other writings by explorers and men of the frontier are examples of the written colonial world that was and still is instrumental in mapping the often-violent fantasies of American masculinities, frontiers, and borders. These itineraries of violence in their cartographic forms, literature, and almanac writing were tools used to shape the world we have come to know as the United States, Canada, and Mexico. Within these writings that circulate on a global scale, Indigenous peoples hold a particular place in the construction of global economies; they mark the settler colonial narrative as the constant present absence upon which the myth of nation-state dominance depends and expands.[1] By linking fragmented spatialities and their narrations to a past telling of stories from those who are not invested in maintaining the nation-state, Leslie Marmon Silko's novel *Almanac of the Dead* provides us a critique of a faltering present in stories that (re)map the narratives of the past. Accounts of Wounded Knee, Sand Creek, Yaqui slavery, Pueblo revolts, rape, devastation, and cruel missionaries compose a litany of stories that are at once local and global. These are not just unfortunate accounts of a temporal past, but are part and parcel of events that have led to current geopolitical formations not only in the Northern Hemisphere, but globally. The (re)mapping of the violent events that led to the deaths of millions of Native people occurred so that spatial and economic dominance could be maintained in a fantasy of national futurity (the not yet) that was and still informs notions of destiny and destination. Yet, Silko presents accounts where the deed of these manifest acts are never complete or final, rather they are ongoing, and even as they continue to affirm patterns of dominance, they also engender resistance and complicity, thus producing and productive of socialities.

The lost, collected, and created narratives that make up the cryptic, unfixed 763-page novel are at the center of the struggle within the text. The writings from notebooks, diaries, and various almanacs are the narrative mapping tools Silko uses in her project of countering the further theft of land and dispossession of Native peoples in the heightened moment of the late 1980s and early 1990s. Narrative mapping in *Almanac* foregrounds and opens up the process by which marginal peoples—such as women and/or the colonized, and/or people of color—are appropriated as emblems of the liberal tradition of inclusion as a form of progress. The central consciousness behind inclusion and individualism is reflected in the narrative apparatuses that map bodies and lands temporally and spatially, as I have discussed throughout the previous chapters. This particular chapter takes up the challenge by Matthew Sparke to complicate studies of resistance to colonialism, neocolonialism, and globalization. In his work, studies of place must avoid the pitfalls of blaming or pathologizing the dispossessed and certain geographies as a strategy of resistance, but instead provide an investigation of the history of dispossession in an effort to access the power relations involved in geopolitics. Silko does not ignore the violence that stems from living in colonial conditions, and in fact her epic novel confronts the effect of colonial conditions on all of humanity. Rather than romanticize resistance, Silko turns the table and pathologizes forms of extreme capitalism and aggregation of bodies and land into commodities. Sparke calls on us to see how "we can counter pathologization by exploring territorial particularity in terms of extra-territorial globality."[2] In examining a text that lingers on the pathological and that emphasizes the locale (in this case Tucson as borderland or new frontier) and its relational exteriority, we are able to explore a decolonization that necessitates an engagement with a production of space that is naturalized and mythologized through regimes of geographic power/knowledge.

And, as I argue in the introduction, if the spatial is always in process then so too is decolonization. That is, by depicting the brink of decolonization in the form of an always-in-process map and almanac, Silko's text provides a backdrop to think of decolonization not as a spectacular event but one that entails the everyday and constant readjustment of structures. Silko's (re)mapping is one of (re)mapping power relations abused in the global capital system as much as that of undoing a colonial map that was constructed through governmental technologies of power (surveying of Native lands, cartography as realist depictions, regional descriptions that make absent Native histories and colonial violences, statistics that elide sources of capitalist wealth, education that promotes the ideals of freedom and democracy while obscuring the coercive force, and constructions of alterities that confine bodies in spaces). Silko's (re)imagined geographies and attention to place and specific histories call for a cognitive mapping that threatens the worlding of colonial and imperial dominance. Her reclaiming of land also imagines a world rid of exploitive structures—such as nation-states, racial categories, gender hierarchies, world banks, militaries, and governments—that are the tools in the cycles of mass destruction of people and the earth. She imagines an apocalyptic end to such world dominance, but in rendering no one as innocent, she reminds us that dominance comes in many forms and vigilance is always necessary.

Most of the action in *Almanac of the Dead* takes place in present-day Tucson, Arizona, a town situated on a constantly unraveling border. The story begins around a kitchen table with the central characters of twin sisters Lecha and Zeta; Lecha's son, Ferro; his friend and ex–prison mate, Paulie; Sterling, a banished Laguna Pueblo man who takes care of the property; and an ex-stripper named Seese, a strung-out coke addict who has lost her son. With gruesome stories of psychic visions, serial murders, sexual abuse, abandonment, kidnapping, hangings, slavery, torture, and tribal banishment, Silko pulls many other characters and their stories into the web of this motley circle. Each section of the book is labeled after colonized continents and nation-states, starting with the United States, moving south into Mexico, and then over to Africa, and back to the Americas, reassembling the historic and ongoing trade routes of colonization, slavery, capitalism, and imperialism. Silko's novel is difficult to read not just for its immensity of various plotlines in ever-changing geographical locations, but perhaps more so because of the sexual violence and mapping of bodies that takes place within its pages—some of which is fictionalized and others culled from the historical record. The ugliness of placing bodies in hierarchical spatial and social orders and putting bodies in place is reflected in the very language of the novel.[3] It is not a pleasant book and requires a reading practice that jars us into attention.

The aesthetics of the novel in many ways reflect the ugliness of mass consumption and human exploitation. In speaking to the aesthetics of place-making for black Americans, bell hooks reflects on the late 1980s and 1990s, when social programs were under attack as culture shifted from an agenda of civil rights and group equalizing through inclusion to one of individual progress through neoliberal programs. "I grew up thinking about art and beauty as it existed in our lives, the lives of poor black people," writes hooks. "Without knowing the appropriate language, I understood that advanced capitalism was affecting our capacity to see, that consumerism began to take the place of that predicament of heart that called us to yearn for beauty. Now many of us are only yearning for things."[4] The landscapes in *Almanac* are filled with humans obsessed with things or objects, an obsession that has gone awry and wherein very few of her characters are exempt. In her use of language and forms in the text, Silko intervenes into the sanitization of history that too often affects "our capacity to see." The theme of conquest and liberation is related to the extreme objectification of abject bodies, not just in a distant temporal past but in the present day. In fact, the recovery of the twins Lecha and Zeta's notebooks and the twins El Feo and Tacho's revolutions depends on seeing the patterns and reading the signs. Written at the time when the North American Free Trade Agreement (NAFTA) was deeply debated and coming into effect, stories that comprise *Almanac* link present-day border policies to historical pasts. NAFTA is a policy with deep implications for Indigenous people on all sides of the Mexico–U.S.–Canadian border, and thus I argue is similar to other polices that instigate a colonial spatial restructuring of lands and bodies. These patterns in *Almanac* reveal the ongoing disruptions of normative geopolitics and the effort that must be exerted by the state to create an illusion of control. As the story expands from these main characters, a narrative mapping of experience begins. The stories encompassed in the mapped chapters demonstrate the movement of people, capital, and ideas across space and time. From the very beginning of the text, the nation-state fails to hold omnipresent power over the characters in the novel that reflect the dispossessed.

The geopolitical web that begins in Tucson, on the border, reflects not only the impermanency of its construction, but the reality of its force on bodies that move through the violent landscape. For the characters that are aware of geographies of power, the border is not a given, not to be feared, but one that is to be used for profit or more liberating purposes. The stability of the nation-state map and colonial laws are called into question as Silko unfolds the history of the land in this region and exposes the fact that the arms being smuggled across the border go to the Native uprising in Chiapas. This is only one thread of the uprisings and impending revolutions depicted in the text of many woven into this massive almanac. The lines of the stories travel in all directions, but are always brought back to these central characters, just as the strings of a spider web lead back to its center. The text within the text, or rather the almanac in the *Almanac,* reflects the intertextuality at play in the production and imagining of space. The cryptic almanac fragments deciphered by Lecha, the Indian psychic, and Seese, a white woman in search of her missing son, are left for the reader to decode. The reader is on a journey, much like the old grandmother Yoeme who has seen the changing geopolitics throughout her many years, to figure out "the meaning of the lost section and . . . to find a way of replacing it."[5] The recovery of the almanac, its safekeeping, and its translation are essential to the strength, protection, survival, and reclamation of land for Indigenous people.

Almanacs, which will be discussed at length in this chapter as a mapping apparatus, were various in forms and function, yet as such were instrumental in early American production of social spaces. The narrative apparatus of the almanac was found in everyday locations, such as parlors and outhouses; used by politicians and government officials for propaganda and outreach; by women for tips on taking care of families; and by farmers for tips on planting; and carried on surveying expeditions to the West. This form was a large seller, and as American colonies grew, so too did publication numbers and popularity, in fact it is estimated that they printed four thousand copies for each edition of these early almanacs, and that by 1800 there were half a million almanacs printed each year.[6] The almanac printings were enough for each household in the colonies and thus made it the most common form for debating politics and pushing forth ideas, and as a touchstone for common narratives. With such a far-reaching base, almanacs were essential to forming American culture and mapping the Americas from the sale of the body, to regions, to the global. In the early years, almanacs were instrumental in bringing forth enlightenment ideas that materialized in the everyday realities and continue to organize our various spatialities. Silko taking up the form of the almanac underscores the multivocal narratives and genres that constitute community, such as that found in her earlier book *Storyteller.*[7] In this instance, however, there is also a need to speak to the multiscalar component of community.

Right before her death, Yoeme warns the twins that finding the code and translating the notebooks will not be easy: "The woman warned that it should not be just any sort of words." Finding the words to deconstruct colonial spatiality and power structures has rested in protecting tribal stories that center nations and recall the ethics and center of the people, as the old woman states: "I am telling you this because you must understand how carefully the old manuscript and its notebooks must be kept" (129). The rememorative words—that is, words that remind us of a past and its meaning in the present—carry important weight for our futures. The aim to recover the notebook and translate its meaning into the present is also at the heart of Silko's vast text. It drives the characters and plots forward as they each try to recover what has been lost in the wake and processes of mapping the Americas. By constructing the story in a pattern that resembles a web of relations, Silko is (re)assembling seemingly disconnected events, such as the Chiapas uprising, the environmental effects of deep-well drilling, uranium mining in Laguna, or the displacement of the poor to develop or create progress in impoverished parts of Tucson into connected patterns of exploitation of land and human suffering in a local and global context. Most incredibly, the text enables us to examine a complex human resistance to the geopolitical terror of neoliberal capitalism, sexual violence, and ongoing forms of colonization and empire in which no one is left unscathed.

DISLOCATING THE MAP

Silko's resistance and revolution is often depicted by literary analyses as too sweeping in its myriad of revolutions that fight against neoliberal nation-states. Sven Birkerts critiques the novel for its "premise of revolutionary insurrection [that is] tethered to airy nothing" and is "naive to the point of silliness," particularly when Silko imagines a world without jurisdictional, militarized boundaries.[8] Approaches such as Birkerts's miss an assessment of the generative roots of domination tethered to colonialism and foundational to economic exploitation. Native studies critics, however, have incorporated readings of *Almanac* that begin to address its glocalized nature. Eric Cheyfitz, and later Shari Huhndorf, outline the debate between nationalist Elizabeth Cook-Lynn and critic Arnold Krupat regarding the politics within *Almanac*. While Cook-Lynn emphasizes the need to account for specific treaty relations in a tribal/nation sense, Krupat expands this notion and asserts that the book is committed to a cosmopolitan approach or Pan-Indianism on a global scale. Cheyfitz, however, posits that the (post)colonial nature of the text resides in the "dialectic nature of the transnational and national": "The transnational cannot articulate itself except through national situations; the global is grounded in the local because it needs a *place* to give it form—there is no simply global place."[9]

I agree with Cheyfitz and believe that in our approach to examine the scales of spatial injustice, we must avoid literally mapping space in as a form of containment that closes off possibilities for collaborative justice; that is, if we do not position spaces of the nation or globe in an either-or state as the place in which to form our politics, we may be able to address the various scales from the body to land that operate in structures of domination. There simply isn't an unconnected place, as our most likable character, Sterling, finds out when he returns to his village. The reservation, too often positioned as a place of authenticity for the very reason of its isolation, containment, and racialization of Indians, is often used to discipline Indians as well, as discussed in previous chapters. What if we were to (re)write the map? What if we were to see this place of presumed authenticity as such because normative maps are repositories of knowledge, but that knowledge as always already a place that is connected to other conceptions of spaces? What if the importance of this locale is such because it is a place determined and imagined into existence through Native geographic stories? And if we think about these Native places as ones existing through our own geographical desires, doesn't that give us the ability to imagine other spaces as such beyond those demarcated by the state?

The geographies of the West and the rest are intimately linked together and cannot be dismissed and othered. Huhndorf briefly speaks to the interconnection of communities in the text, stating that "although it takes up issues specific to Native communities, *Almanac* emphasizes their interconnections and presents the Americas as a singular entity with a shared colonial past and revolutionary future." In her analysis, it is important to note that she rightly critiques Silko for eliding specific histories, specifically those that deal with various groups that aid or detract from Indigenous autonomy claims and collapse the specificities. Huhndorf suggests that this "exemplifies the inherent paradoxes of contemporary Indigenous politics, which must inevitably negotiate between the distinctiveness of individual tribal communities and the histories and social issues that render them a collective political force."[10]

I believe, if we examine the continental shifting in the divisions of the book's various sections from Africa to the Americas, that it speaks to white possession on a global scale extending beyond the Americas, and in doing so, perhaps, starts a (re)mapping that depends on the specifics while not eliding the connections at a larger scale. After all, as Rachel Adams clarifies in her book, continents themselves are formed in a network of power relations and reflect the desire and power of the United States and European nations. Adams pinpoints the rise of continents as largely a part of military force. This is useful in thinking through the ways that continents are an important geographical scale in *Almanac* that organizes knowledge through entitling large subsections that reflect the early European spatial conception of the land-masses of Europe, Africa, and Asia. The instantiation of continents was not natural or self-evident, according to Adams; rather, "the modern notion that the world could be broken down into continents must thus be seen as a part of these larger planetary shifts [of 'new world' discovery and colonization] and, as such, it is deeply implicated in the hierarchies of power they intro-duced."[11] In her spatial organization of the novel and use of narrative appa-ratuses, Silko presents the spectacle and terror of colonial mapping on lands and bodies. I am interested in the way power manifests itself in the geopol-itics of writing and this past–future that Silko portrays in almanac and car-tographic form—for surely an Indigenous reclaiming of land would shift the entirety of global politics.

The key to dissimulating traditional geographies in the text is instigated with the recognition that borders, while not arbitrary or without material con-sequences, are imagined into being and reinforced through state apparatuses. Borders, like Indians, become common sense. Current conceptions of living Native people as only existing in the past or only "real" in certain geograph-ical regions permeate "commonsense" knowledges about Native peoples and geographies on a global scale. Here, I am riffing on Kara Keeling's work with the presence and absence of the black femme in cinema, particularly in her interpretations of Gramsci's notion of common sense and Fanon in relation to decolonization and possible futurities of the dispossessed. Keeling posits that our present perceptions are shaped by repetitive past images that when seen—or in the case discussed here seen, heard, and read—form the com-mon sense or cliché, thus representing a "truth" that restricts imaginings of other possibilities. With such a long legacy of writing and visual imagining of Indians necessary to a claiming of land there is an immense amount of material to recall when the "memory-image" is projected, thus often obstruct-ing decolonization as the habituated images of maps and Indians are ingested as the norm by both Native and non-Native. The commonsense notions of Natives and borders, used all too often by settler states to dispossess Native people of personhood and land, are quickly complicated in *Almanac* by the introduction of characters who don't care to be "good," "dead," "poor," "deeply spiritual" Indians, nor do Silko's characters possess a spirituality that is peace-ful. They are constant border crossers, literally and figuratively, as the non-commonsensical image of Indians dominates the text. There are no helping, noble, meek, or weak Indians, there is no pretense of redistributive justice that does not include the return of the land, and this process itself is deeply bound to confronting global capitalism. The use of technology and engagement with the economy, as well as the everyday commodification that takes place in the text, depict Indians who are very much a part of modernity. There is no one "Indian Way" that remains unconnected to the world at large—in fact Silko through her narrative depicts this as a false construction in the first place, a fact backed up in numerous tribal stories as well as those documented.[12] The critical thinking and "seeds of good sense" that Keeling advocates exist even as common sense governs become possible as Silko proceeds to imagine one alternative becoming that serves as a warning and (re)maps geographies. Instead of refiguring the Indian or continents in hegemonic or counterhegemonic narratives, she positions the commonsense image of the Indian and regimes of geographical knowledges born out of ideological and physical violence.

In the hardcover edition, the map that provides the key to following the novel is bound directly into the binding, suggesting a reading pattern. This seemingly realist map that literally forms the material of the book comprises a multitude of signs, many of which are unclear till we gain literacy of the text itself. Throughout this chapter, I return to the form of this map and the form of the almanac, its origins, its proliferation in the Americas, and its relation to mapping and literacy in order to engage Silko's novel as a form of (re)-mapping hemispheric relationships that privileges people and the land over global capital. The map guides us through the story and the various entries in *Almanac*. Yet, far from a common map, Silko presents us with "The Five Hundred Year Map," which has no solid borders or conventional symbols and is as dynamic as an almanac; gender, sexuality, race, nations, creativity, destruction, life, death, past, present, and future become uprooted from stable places and moments in history. In the structure of the novel and map, events and details of the past simultaneously occur in the present, prompting a new investigation into categories rigidly defined in mainstream ideology. Silko's "Five Hundred Year Map" is not merely a guide situated in the first two pages in order to help us figure out where the characters are located in the space of the novel; rather, she intends for the map to provide keys to understanding how the upcoming narratives are related to the longer narrative of history and the production of colonial spaces. In this epic novel, Silko creates an unstable terrain and uproots naturalized "truths" in the narratives of settler colonialism. Crucial to opening up new possibilities beyond romantic resistance or pathology of the border and bodies that occupy those spaces is telling the stories of spatial restructuring.

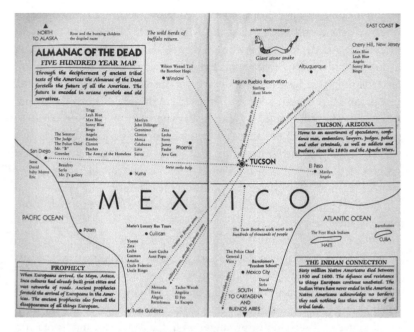

End paper map. Reprinted with the permission of Simon & Schuster, Inc., from *Almanac of the Dead* by Leslie Marmon Silko. Copyright 1991 Leslie Marmon Silko.

Yet, there is caution to be had in recovery processes. I propose that in considering the map as an active apparatus that restructures spatial domination, social relations, and epistemological violence, we move away from romanticized notions of resistance. It is necessary in this move to also reconsider the operation of power in settler societies, especially as they are articulated and enunciated at borders. Sparke critiques those who "observe how the precariousness of life provides some sort of postfoundational foundation for planetary solidarity": "It is quite another to fail to distinguish between different forces that contribute to precariousness in different ways in different places at different times. And sanguine invocations of 'the resistance' only seem to make such failure more likely by rushing so quickly to vindicate the humanity of those involved that they risk ignoring how one community's resistance can become another's violent demise."[13] Clearly, Silko is not vindicating her characters, even while she does often elide the details of local movements in order to address the pattern of the global. The main characters that put into motion the revolution, the members of room 1212 (a reference to the Mayan calendar and widely presumed date of apocalyptic collapse), are not beyond creating "another's violent demise," as we will explore in Bartolomeo's hanging. Silko powerfully refuses the image of romanticized Indigenous warrior— her warriors are flawed, violent, and reckless. The commonsense image, the one recalled when we see the presence of Indian women or their absence, is thwarted by the women warriors that predominate the book. The warriors are working on a global scale often "in different ways in different places."[14] In these representations are possibilities for rearticulating a definition of power-geometries, as Sparke speaks of in his address of theories of globalization and romantic or tragic resistance. I recall Sparke's words, as they are significant in my articulation of a (re)mapping of settler spatial imaginaries and as an attempt not to reproduce the cliché but seriously question it in the context of revolution and NAFTA.

While the almanac and map are often taken as Western conventions, many Native forms of articulating time and space existed before colonization, and these forms were instrumental to colonial mappings in the early years after the arrival of Europeans.[15] Warhus clarifies: "From the earliest encounters through modern anthropological studies, western persons have asked Native Americans for geographic information. This exchange was often made in the form of maps made or related by Native Americans."[16] Native knowledge of the land, hunting grounds, weather cycles, and planting times were essential to tribal survival as well as to settlers' survival. The perceived absence of Native maps not only coincides with the tenets of settler colonialism's eradication of the Native from the present time and interior space of the nation-state, but also is a form of structured epistemic violence in the form of abstracting land. Denis Cosgrove in his introduction to *Mappings* speaks of the historic moment of 1992 in which Columbus's legacy and first voyage provoked new lines of inquiry on an international scale into the relationship among geography, history, colonialism, and modernity.[17] Around this same moment of academic critique of "mapping as a signifying practice across historic time," Silko drew her own map based on the stories of Indigenous peoples and presented a history of countermapping and Indigenous resistance to colonial spatial restructuring. She documents it in the struggles of Indigenous people and the prophecies of tribal imaginations and the story that "someday . . . will come" and change the world. These paths of exploration clearly show, one through fiction and the other through cartographic histories and cultural geography, that "acts of mapping are creative, and sometimes anxious, moments in coming to knowledge of the world, and the map is both the spatial embodiment of knowledge and a stimulus to further cognitive engagements."[18] Silko's "act of mapping," with its accompanied rewriting of manifest destiny and the frontier land, reforms our thinking of the world, our systems of knowledge, and calls for action.

Silko's "Five Hundred Year Map" is a visual representation of this struggle over power and knowledge. Silko uses the Western form of cartography, but in a very multidimensional and autoethnographic manner. Instead of a flat one-dimensional figure that supposedly depicts "objective" space, the handwritten scribbles emphasize the mapmaker. Silko makes visible the false "objectiveness" of colonial cartographic projects and their relationships to constructing modernity. In playing with the form of maps, narratives, and history, her characters traverse time and space, and cross geopolitical borders; people are not bound by static national, racial, and gender identities. Most importantly, these characters do not occupy different maps or planes but exist and converge with each other. Silko's map, which "is encoded in arcane symbols and old narratives" (14), destabilizes borders that are "always already crossed and doubly crossed."[19] Her map actively writes the Native into memories and history, not only by visually representing them on the map and effectively naming them but allowing for the movement of characters that represents the continual, multiple, and shifting connections to space and to each other that have existed since time immemorial.

In *Almanac* the map is not objectively timeless but is embedded in the events of history. The key to this map, and thus the novel, is found in separate textually composed titled legends: "Five Hundred Year Map"; "Tucson, Arizona"; "Prophecy"; "The Indian Connection." These legends are similar to what may be found on a modern map. Silko's representation of this cartographic norm makes visible the "internal power" of mapmaking. Harley makes a clear distinction between the external power of cartography, the map that might be employed by a monarch, state government agency, or a corporation, and an internal mapping that

> is local and decentralized rather than being centralized and concentrated; it suffuses the practices of all cartographic workshops rather than being targeted only at the projects of state patronage. As it acts through the cartographic workshop, internal power is not necessarily consciously exercised; its practice is taken for granted, unlike the deliberate acts of externally applied power. Yet these differences between internal and external power do not obscure the fact that power relations penetrate the interstices of cartographic practice and representation.

Maps may be read as texts of power-knowledge no less than other fabricated systems of signs.[20]

Silko deliberately produces a map that illuminates the geographic struggle of power and upsets our commonsense notions of geography. Instead of an explanatory list of symbols on the map, Silko composes a legend based on the definition of the word that pertains to myth or story, something that may or may not be true. In doing so she defies the colonial cartographer's "tools of normalization" in which he could "reinvent or redescribe reality in the process of making the world."[21]

The "Five Hundred Year Map" alerts the reader to the bloody events that take place or are recorded in the coming chapters—in each legend's box there is a reference to struggle, war, and "disappearance of all things European" (14). Though Silko's legends are primarily composed of narrative rather than symbols, they serve the same function of giving the reader the tools to decode the map. In an interview with Laura Cotelli, Silko contemplates her use of the visceral image and its importance in the way the text is read:

> Maybe the almanac is a map of the past five hundred years—that is, a "map" made out of narratives. But these narratives themselves seem inextricably bound to certain geographical locations, so I drew that map in Almanac as a "glyphic" representation of the narrative. This "glyph" shows how the Americas are "one," not separated by artificial, imaginary "borders." The landscape, the spirits of the places are known by the narratives that originate in these places.[22]

The map is a representation of fierce struggle and stories that will not rest and continue to extend beyond the spatializing of bodies and structures of nation-building. Layers of history are told through these narratives. For instance, by placing the main characters, twins Lecha and Zeta, in Mexico as well as Tucson, she is representing the historic patterns and cycles of migration. The women's movement is represented on the map by a dotted line, open at one end. It is not a one-way movement, but rather a migration back and forth that marks the map and the twins' movement, both Lecha and Zeta as well as their male counterparts El Feo and Tacho.

The use of the graphic symbol of the dotted line is similar to attributes of maps drawn by Native people. One such map is that of Iowa chief Notchininga, who offered a map in 1837 to Washington officials that depicted the lands of the Iowa. The map was written for the express purpose of documenting land that Notchininga and other tribes in the Midwest feared would be further encroached by settlers. As a document, the map combined elements of the Western traditions of cartography, yet its composition is largely derivative of Iowa oral traditions and Native land beliefs.[23] A comparison between the purpose of a dotted land and migration can be drawn between Silko's and Notchininga's maps: "The dotted line that begins at this ancestral village represents the Iowa's movements over time. It connects the ancient settlements where the Iowa began, and ends with the sites they inhabited in the nineteenth century. The map is not simply a picture of territory; it is a map of tribal memory; noting the places and events that made this land part of the Iowas. To Notchininga and his people, this was the land of their ancestors, the land that 'bears our name.'"[24] Silko's map is similar in its intent and purpose, but, as the years have passed, she is also concerned with the recovery of land. Just as in Notchininga's map, the recovery of the stories is of the utmost importance to this process. Yet Silko also must account for a history of colonialism. She cannot return to those ancient forms of mapping but invents a new one as she interprets a history of almanac writing, hero worship, and manifest destiny.

Rather than a new version or a postmodernist map, Silko's mapmaking is always, and if we take seriously her play with reoccurring time will always be, in contestation. In his compilation of vintage Native maps, Warhus points out the oral component of mapping as vital to understanding the visual image. It is the narrative and epistemologies of the local that enable a map to be useful: "The graphic systems used in the maps are often adapted from picture-writing traditions used to visually convey information. Far from primitive, these picture-writing systems used an economy of detail to convey their messages and could be easily read by anyone familiar with the oral geography of the region. To read the maps it is necessary to see how picture writing functioned within the oral traditions of these societies."[25] The "glyphic" representation of the "Five Hundred Year Map" is elaborated on throughout the text. Definitions of border found in the text differ, overlap, and converge depending on the character's relationship to that particular space. The key to the map also comes into focus by the end of reading the novel. Yet, with each step toward the end of the text the map expands and the enormity of the stories grow. By the end of the text, the word "border" no longer means the place at which the United States ends, but rather the power of this geographic imagining is called into question. The symbiotic, complex relationship of narrative and spatial understanding exposes how national narratives actively seek to control and confine traditional knowledge of Native American people.

The state's attempt to disconnect people from the land is at the crux of Native battles across Canada, the United States, and Mexico, though each use a different political apparatus for colonial domination. In *Almanac*, as well as in many of Silko's other works, the land is essential in examinations of power structures and Native peoples obligations to it, each other, and all living things on the earth. Borders map out artificial constructs that limit our sense of self and connection to others, because of the way in which they make meaning by excluding certain relationships. Borders, both material and cognitive, limit the possibilities of Native existence. The power and brutality of colonialism, which Silko maps though the pages of *Almanac*, produced and continues to produce colonized Native subjects and space, and thus, repossession of the land does not guarantee a recovery of Native spaces free from a colonial past or present. The need for a return to stories, exemplified in Sterling's return to Laguna, will always be necessary to balance power relations.

Destabilizing Knowledges

Recalling the marked use of almanacs and other forms of writing as a devices to (re)map the Americas in a settler vision positions us toward an understanding of the narrative function of mapping and maps as a powerful discourse in ordering "normative" spatialities and naturalizing settler ideologies. As Ricardo Padrón makes clear in his exploration of the invention of America in early modern Spain, "Maps—in the invention of America, the Orient, Australia or any other such entity—join history, literature, painting, architecture, and many other kinds of cultural endeavor to create a mutually reinforcing, albeit partially fictional, geography, one that locates and characterizes both self and other."[26] While other scholars, including Padrón, Edward Said, Benedict Anderson, J. B. Harley, and Matthew Sparke, examine the relationship between discourse and power in European mappings of empires and nation-states, I uproot the discourses that obscure the sexual violence necessary to maintain settler and colonial nation-state and global order. Silko's (re)mapping of the violent histories of settler discourses in the form of the map and an almanac provides a point in which we can examine the processes of spatial (in)justice. Edward Soja clarifies that a move toward the spatial does not dismiss other forms of justice, such as the economic, political, or social, but rather it provides an understanding of the ways geographies impact dominant structures, and can affect them negatively and positively. Thus his play with (in)justice combines both words. In particular, I argue that *Almanac* not only elicits the intersectionality of the power dynamics of race, class, and gender, but pushes these intersectionalities to scrutinize the very construction of the structures of settler colonialism itself by examining how "everything that is social (justice included) is simultaneously and inherently spatial, just as everything spatial, at least with regard to the human world, is simultaneously and inherently socialized."[27] Thus, this section turns toward an examination of the social and spatial aspect of the form of the almanac and its relationship to (re)mapping the Americas.

As its title suggests, *Almanac of the Dead* is very much like historic forms of the almanac, which are an apt form to address modernity, knowledge production, and power. The form of the almanac and the book project *Almanac* is intended to encompass a multitude of historic points, knowledge transfer, and call to action. Walter Mignolo's argument about writings of the "new world" during the Renaissance asks more explicitly about the connections among writing, the *organization* of knowledge, and the production of history. He concludes that the effect of organizing discourse in genre formats is pivotal to issues of authority, power, and the colonization of memory. If maps organize knowledge (as they assuredly do) and the literary genre of the almanac also has a stake in this organization, consider Mignolo's comments:

> In the first case [referring to letters written by the colonizer], genres as social practices worked toward the spread of Western literacy and the reconfiguration of the classical tradition. In the second case [letters written by Amerindians], genres as social practices work toward the preservation of Amerindian memories and the discontinuity of the classical tradition. In a colonial situation the conflict of interpretations is played out at the basic level of cultural conversion, on the one hand, and the transformation of cultural traditions that give rise to new and emergent identities.[28]

In *Almanac,* Sterling is indicative of transformative thought throughout the text, particularly as he reconciles the world around him. He is acutely aware of the different understanding of temporalities that occur simultaneously, as noted by the event of the Great Depression that marks a supposed communal event in U.S. history: "Sterling had been a boy during the depression, but it had made little or no impression on people at Laguna. Most, especially old-timers, had said they never knew a depression was going on, because in those days people had no money in banks to lose. Indians never had legal title to any reservation land, so there had never been property to mortgage" (41). Here, our understanding of time and geographies is reconfigured as primarily an organizing of different knowledges. The character of Sterling prompts us to see the relationship between historic events and colonial structures, but most especially an alternative to them: "But winters those years had been mild and wet for the Southwest. Harvests had been plentiful, and the game fat that winter. The Laguna people had heard about 'The Crash.' But they remembered 'The Crash' as a year of bounty and plenty for the people" (41). Silko's almanac, like that of early American almanacs, documents time and place in relation to harvesting rather than capitalism or traditional geographies and temporalities. How we approach and interpret writing is important in understanding not only the way that territories and places emerge, converge, and diverge, but also how they continue to reproduce asymmetrical relationships, producing new identities.

Almanacs and the mapping of the Americas are closely linked, seemingly innocuous genres. Almanacs in Europe dated to at least the thirteenth century and were very popular in the fifteenth century.[29] While the origination of almanacs is not certain, publication in the colonies and on Native land was one of the earliest and most widespread forms of writing. The high volume and easy accessibility of almanacs ensured their reach across class, race, and differences, and thus, in Benedict Anderson's conception of an imagined community, almanacs were a form pivotal to forming allegiances and identities. Alison Chapman makes clear in her essay regarding almanacs that there was a turn to a "mapmindedness" in the sixteenth and seventeenth centuries, and early almanacs quickly became a form in which individuals could make their own entries; where once notes existed in the margins of the almanac, bookmakers began to construct blank pages in-between the published entries. The connection between almanacs and diaries is further elicited here. Chapman argues that a "trend" in these almanacs was "the tendency of these texts to provide complicated and precise descriptions of both place and time."[30] The articulation of history and claiming in the almanac form is geopolitical production. Within the written pages and even the blank ones there has been a glossing over of the spatial and sexual violence of conquest through law and through force. The violence depicted in the stories between Silko's map and in her narrative discourse fills in the blank pages, both in the text and in the reader's capacity to understand just how the violence of conquest continues to exist in the present moment. In her depiction "normative" narratives and maps of the United Sates become incredibly unstable.

Arlen Large in "How Far West Am I?" explores the importance of early almanacs to an assortment of founding figures: European explorers, conquistadors, and government men of the colonial states. Almanacs were instrumental in the expeditions of Christopher Columbus, Lewis and Clark, George Vancouver, and many others that sought to claim Native land titles by writing about contact with non-Christians. Almanacs were extremely important in shaping what we have come to know as the Americas: "Both Columbus and Lewis investigated distant places at a time when astronomy was considered the main scientific way of fixing their positions. . . . These explorers needed almanacs predicting the times of various celestial events to help locate their place on earth. Their travel accounts, however, rarely explained how almanacs contributed to their own measurement of daily progress and to the maps they brought home."[31] The almanacs, while receiving less critical attention than maps, were equally important, and are distinctly tied together in the mapping of the Americas.

The structure of an almanac emphasizes the cyclical, as does Silko's text, and its tie to the local is particular and necessary for future predictions. As Patrick Spero, writing on the form of the almanac and its generative nature for politics and everyday life in colonial America, writes: "At its core, every almanac was a utilitarian text that conveyed such useful information as tidal predictions, lunar calculations, court and market days, and distances between towns. Because the almanac contained such a variety of information, its utility extended to almost everyone: a captain needed to know the tides; a farmer needed to know the rising and setting of the sun; a merchant needed to know market days; a lawyer needed to know when courts met."[32] At the same time, this information was geographically specific: a farmer in Massachusetts needed to know the rising and setting of the sun in Boston, not Philadelphia or London; a circuit lawyer in Philadelphia needed to know when courts were meeting in Pennsylvania and Delaware, not Connecticut and Rhode Island; and people bringing goods to market needed to know the market days in towns near them, not in distant colonies. In his argument, Spero convincingly claims that the local informed the content and position of each almanac, so that instead of a uniform approach to the genre of almanacs, if we look at the differences we can begin to see the history unfold in the local in different ways. He states, "Historians have tended to describe the almanac as relatively monolithic throughout colonial North America and the Atlantic world. Yet the evidence surveyed here suggests that *regional traditions and economies* played large roles in materially forming almanacs and shaping their content.

With this understanding, we can begin to see how local economies and culture were intertwined."[33] I find this significant if related to the context of Silko's usage of the almanac to form her text, as she clearly is presenting a local version of an almanac that also documents history in a "local" economy. Yet this local economy in the height of neoliberal economics, particularly NAFTA, is on the scale of a global magnitude.

The history of the almanac form reflects the ability of it as a genre that collapses the local and global with a potential to shape world outcomes. Under the 1763 proclamation, for instance, the British Crown controlled lands and forbade colonial settlement west. This was coupled with the Stamp Act (1765), which demanded that printed writing material in the colonies be on official stamped—and thus costly—paper. These laws cohered to exert crown discipline and thwart the distribution of knowledge and local collaboration. The assortment of these commands as well as their wide distribution through almanac publications would lead to war, land theft, and what becomes narrated as a heroic American Revolution. Spero speaks to the way that the almanac's form of including events to be commemorated changed after the Stamp Act eroded ties between Briton and its colonies: "The imperial crisis and especially Independence presented a straightforward challenge to this historic calendar, the most explicitly political element in mid-eighteenth-century almanacs. After Independence, printers tried to reshape the calendars in an attempt to express the shared history of the new nation."[34] It is not until after its appeal and after independence however, that writing in the colonies begins to look inward and construct a narrative formulation in the almanacs. "With Independence, almanacs-makers in Boston once again transformed the calendar," writes Spero, "this time to commemorate a new nation free from monarchy." The first writings to shape an American identity were formulated in war as American colonists "based this national identity on the war and Independence by adding military events that occurred in other colonies, thus helping evoke a sense of shared experiences among diverse states."[35] Controlling history and monumentalizing the heroic discovery and development of former "crown" land became the basis for later almanacs, the most popular form of writing in the newly formed nation.

In fact, it wasn't until the late nineteenth century that new technology would replace such almanacs as a means of determining geographical position with new technologies of producing jurisdictional boundaries of European nations. The use of almanacs to document trade with Native peoples extends beyond documentation of stories past—they were political and would have devastating consequences on Native peoples as title passed between European nations. These early documented encounters were used to claim territory; they essentially positioned Native land under the authority of the crown based on the Doctrine of Discovery, an international law that was meant to regulate European nations more than Native peoples who occupied, lived on, and worked the land. Robert J. Miller indicates that "the symbolic possession" of lands did not mean that European nations discarded Native peoples' "legal right to possess, occupy, and use their lands as long as they wished"; rather, "the planting flags or leaving objects to prove their presence, were sufficient to pass rights in these lands to the discovering European country."[36] In its first incantation, the need to protect "infidels" resounded in the rhetoric of the doctrine (rhetoric that exists throughout Native history, exemplified in Silko's play with the Angelita's Friends of the Indians notebooks).

As time passed, however, the doctrine became less about regulating European wars and more to control fights over the rich resources in the Americas. Through the Marshall decisions, the Doctrine of Discovery codified and justified the use of conquest to control Native populations, and the mark of "contact" was likely to be in written form from the perspective of the explorer, surveyor, or conquistador. In a sense, almanacs were instrumental to conquest, and the violence justified and supported under the settler state laws. Joanne Barker pinpoints the importance of the U.S.–focused Marshall trilogy, which enacts the foundational myth of the discovery doctrine, and its outreach on a global scale. She writes, "The way that the trilogy was taken up by England's Colonial Office in directing relations with the Indigenous peoples in Canada, New Zealand and Australia signifies much about the international exchange of ideas regarding the character and rights of sovereignty for the nations of Europe and North America as well as the attempt to justify the denial of that status and rights for indigenous peoples."[37] In Silko's almanac the push and pull of territorial claims are violent, global, and about reorganizing our knowledge about these first moments of early globalization rooted in the relationship between conquest and writing.

Almanacs did more than claim territory through marking coordinates; they were also incredibly influential in changing society's philosophies on religion, science, the occult, medicine, women's concerns, and government. From the earliest publication in Massachusetts by Stephen Daye (1639) to the widely circulated Ames Almanac, mathematical and astronomical elements were accompanied by political positions, personal barbs, and nationalist propaganda. In *Almanac* the writing of various characters reflects similar debates that are reoccurring in the present moment—such as those on global warming, environmental disasters, or even the ethics of medicine in the form of organ harvesting. Some characters in the text allude to the power and significance of early colonial writing that imagines land as property and Native peoples as demonic "Indians." Cotton Mather, the early colonist who saw Indians as part of a biblical unfolding and sought to make a "place" for the Puritans, was an important figure who used the press for his political gain and to fashion Indians and women as aligned with "evil forces." In fact, Harvard owned and operated the presses that printed not only the first map of New England, but also the first almanac, and Cotton Mather's father Increase Mather was a significant figure in publishing.[38] Though most commonly known for his part in the Salem witch trials, it was thought that he "likely disguised his continuing allegiance to supernaturalism after the mid-1690s in an effort to make his work seem more in tune with the scientific currents of the era."[39] He did this through producing his own almanac, *The Boston Ephemeris,* which included self-calculated mathematical charts particular to the locale of Boston. Cotton Mather also was a great rhetorician who used the power of words to condemn Native peoples and women, however, and it is for this that he is remembered. His imagining of Indians in place—the sublime wilderness—and as bodies in need of cleansing would circulate via print and have a terrible impact. It is also no coincidence that it coalesced with his position on women—white or Native.

It is no coincidence, either, that Mather and other prominent writers find themselves weaving in and out of the esoteric passages in *Almanac.* General J, the character who produces snuff films and leads an oppressive force to squelch the Indian "rebels," resorts to the comfort of early forms of writing, particularly those accepted in the canon. If the canon reflects society, a huge debate in the multicultural wars of the 1980s and 1990s, then the reflection that Silko provides us through the character of General J is horrifying. General J is simultaneously well educated and brutal. The classics become a source of inspiration for General J as he maps the state through both territorial claiming and violent biopolitics: "When deserters bolted off to the mountains to lead battalions of other stinking mestizos and Indians, the general had reread *Paradise Lost.* One had to take the philosophical view: the sky rained down dirty-brown angels over the rugged coastal mountains. Indians were the work of the devil" (328). By having one of the most despicable characters in the text reiterate a semblance of Mather's words and map bodies in the contemporary moment, Silko creates an awareness of the underlining power dynamics of the literary. Furthermore, later in the text the General reflects on how "reading the great literature of the world had prepared him for anything" (328). Silko unpacks some of what that "great literature" has taught General J.: "So when his child had married a faggot, General J. had simply reread *King Lear*. When deserters bolted off to the mountains to lead battalions of other stinking mestizos and Indians, the general had reread *Paradise Lost*." (328). The literary divisions expounded in the classics and popular literature consistently pitched Indians as the work of the devil, from its earliest form the almanac.

Perhaps the best-known almanac in American literary history is *Poor Richard's Almanack,* which, according to William Pencak, "became a key role in developing the politically involved private sphere—with all its limitations on class, race and gender—in provincial America." He continues that it is in the genre of an almanac that one of the first articulations of the self-made and hardworking man making his own destiny begins, supporting "the claim . . . that *Poor Richard's Almanack* played an important role in the international Enlightenments questioning of traditional institutions."[40] A nation of individuals possessing rights to prosper became an American mantra as the United States extended its territories and markets globally. Silko's almanac, as I demonstrate later, questions these very same institutions—specifically those of law and settler-governance—that Benjamin Franklin helped to construct, and haunting presence would affirm its subsequent ideologies.

While Franklin's almanac sought to unify a political entity in order for individuals to "prosper," other almanacs rose to testify to great American heroes. They were steeped in nationalism that only increased as the country expanded its reach. I cull the following excerpts from a variety of almanacs that span temporalities from 1498 to 2011, and these are but a few that demonstrate the link between writing and violent spatial restructuring of Native lands and bodies:

> I do not hold that the earthly Paradise has the form of a rugged mountain, as it is shown in pictures, but that it lies at the summit of what I have described as a stalk of the pear, and that by gradually approaching it one begins, at a great distance, to climb towards it. (Christopher Columbus, 1498)[41]

> Their reason for killing and destroying such an infinite number of souls is that the Christians have an ultimate aim, which is to acquire gold, and to swell themselves with riches in a very brief time and thus rise to a high estate

disproportionate to their merits. It should be kept in mind that their insatiable greed and ambition, the greatest ever seen in the world, is the cause of their villainies. And also, those lands are so rich and felicitous, the native peoples so meek and patient, so easy to subject, that our Spaniards have no more consideration for them than beasts. And I say this from my own knowledge of the acts I witnessed. (Bartolomé Des Las Casas, 1542)[42]

War brings Scars. (Benjamin Franklin, 1745)[43]

I go for Texas and Oregon, clear up to the gravel stone, for they both belong to Uncle Sam's plantation. (Davy Crockett, 1845)[44]

Andrew Hutton reflects on the Crockett almanacs, which at first propelled the adventurer turned politician (much like Franklin and Cotton Mather), into political power: "After 1841, however, a new political element was added as the almanacs became mouthpieces for Westward expansion and a wildly jingoistic nationalism."[45] The frontier heroes took shape as the almanac transformed into cheap dime store novels and magazines. What remained the same, however, were the jingoistic nationalism that supported manifest destiny and the racial hierarchies that became more and more entrenched as expansion became more violent and the state more repressive in terms of difference. "A true democratic spirit of insult animated the almanac writers, with no group spared," comments Hutton. "Blacks and Indians were treated with particularly mean-spirited bigotry meant to appeal to the middling and working class."[46] While the early nautical almanacs were used to actually map the land of the West and subjugate it to United States jurisdiction, Davy Crockett's immensely popular almanac claimed it by creating an American landscape filled with frontier heroes and wild Indians. The national imagination and geographies of imagination intersect in this history of colonial spatial restructuring achieved through the social cultural production of writing.

Spatial violence in the form of writing was manifested in conquest, which as Andrea Smith and others remind us is always a gendered process. In pushing forward an analysis of gendered spatial violence, it is important to interrogate the gendered technologies of colonial writing. "The project of colonial sexual violence," as Smith makes clear in her groundbreaking work *Conquest,* "establishes the ideology that Native bodies are inherently violable—and by extension, that Native lands are also inherently violable."[47] These examples of colonial diaries and almanacs are only a few from the vast corpus of colonialism and conquest literature to choose from; each, however, clearly establishes the connection between conquering land and bodies. In this chapter, I further Smith's assertion, examining closely patterns of spatial violence—which too are always gendered—and the relationship of writing and mapping.

Writing pulled various class and national settler identities together within and across spaces, producing a very different engagement with land and identity politics from the Native peoples whose lands were "discovered." The mappings of boundaries in colonial discourses coincide with writing the Native out of history and are mechanisms of control.[48] The maps of the nation-state do not represent real boundaries or settlement, but rather they become the tool of domination. In structuring colonial spatialities as forms of dominance, Indigenous people are erased in the cartographic imagination of European symbols and maps. However, the land and the people maintain their own image of the world, an image largely based on narratives that counter the myth of *complete loss*.[49]

The almanac form is instrumental to mapping the Americas, not only in history but also in Silko's reformulation of the structure of the almanac and map itself. Sterling, the Laguna Pueblo man who opens and closes the text, reads of Dillinger, Davy Crockett, Jesse James, and the heroes of the West who occupied nineteenth- and early twentieth-century almanacs, such as those quoted above, and continue to do so. These are the heroes who still haunt the American imagination and solidify narratives of conquest as past truths and axioms of American empire. These almanacs would eventually become magazines and later dime-store novels, and as technology progressed, movies. These cultural productions were of the sort that Sterling stores in his trunk and reads over and over again in order to make sense of his place in American culture.

Throughout the first chapters of the book other characters try to place Sterling, as though demarcating him by the boundaries of Arizona will lead them to an understanding: Seese asks if he is an "Arizona Indian," the bartender states, "you're not an Arizona Indian," and Ferro hires him for not knowing anyone in close vicinity. Sterling comments on this alienation, "He was still new to this place. Here the earth herself was almost a stranger" (36). Sterling is consistently adrift in this beginning narrative and looks to magazines and popular writings to explain his place in the world and connection to others. At one point, he turns to his magazines to get his mind off the subject of displacement and diaspora created through colonizing lands and exploiting bodies. Sterling reflects "that the people he had been used to calling Mexicans," such as in the case of Ferro in the text, "were really remnants of different kinds of Indians" (88). He begins to wonder about whether or not Mexicans had heroes like Pretty Boy Floyd or Geronimo or those who resisted American expansion and dominance. Silko repeats twice the need for Sterling to "get his mind off such thoughts," and he turns to the magazines so he doesn't have to think of the terrors of human actions and "Indians flung across the world forever separated from their tribes and from their ancestral lands— that kind of thing had been happening to human beings since the beginning of time" (88). Sterling understands that being phenotypically Indian is not enough as he becomes troubled by Mexicans as a racial category, especially as he connects his own situation of banishment to theirs: "But what remained of Indian was in appearance only. . . . They had lost contact with their tribes and their ancestors' worlds" (88). At the start of the novel, Sterling does not link his magazines and received narrative to the spatial restructuring of lands and bodies that confuses him. It is not until later, when he can link the various strains of spatial violence, that he begins to make the connections.

On one level, he is aware of the relationship between dominance and writing, even as he tries to seek solace through it: "Since it had all happened Sterling couldn't help thinking about the law, and what the law meant." If he can understand the law, in particular, he believes he can understand his place and the ordering of the world around him:

> Sterling had been interested in the law since he was a kid in Indian Boarding School. Because everything the white teachers had said and done to the Indian children had been 'required by law.' Reading his magazines, Sterling had made a modest study of the law on his own, the way Abraham Lincoln had. The *Police Gazette* and *True Detective* magazine gave the most detailed explanation of the law. Sterling had bought subscriptions to both magazines so he would never miss a single new development in the law. (26)

Yet the understanding of the law prompts further confusion throughout the text. As he wonders if Mexicans have hero outlaws or their "production of outstanding criminals," he also begins to ponder all those Mexican revolutions. "He knew that although the winning side usually executed and jailed the losers for being 'criminals,' both *Police Gazette* and *True Detective* magazines disqualified crimes committed during wars and revolutions" (89). In the early stages of the novel, Sterling believes that if he follows the idioms from *Reader's*

Digest or other such magazines, he will learn to be content, but "what happened to Sterling was in the category of things the magazine articles called 'irreparable' and 'better forgotten.' Water under the bridge" (24). These cute sayings, quips, and aphorisms are also part of what composed early almanacs, especially those of Franklin and Mather. The intertextual reference highlights how forms of writings as processes can also mask other relationships and obscure other forms of knowledge. Yet, as Sterling is acutely aware through his own experiences, the power of the state is limited in particular places and always contested.

The racialized, colonial, and displaced subject embodied in the character of Sterling gives up on writing toward the end of the novel by canceling his magazine subscriptions and instead looks toward the tiniest and most seemingly inconsequential of life-forms for answers: an ant. Sterling longs for a belonging that he realizes is not found through colonial law or through acceptance of colonial orderings of human bodies and land: "Sterling did not understand why, but the success of the ants had lifted his spirits. He wished he had listened more closely to Aunt Marie and her sisters, for he might have understood better the connections between human beings and ants" (758). The law, almanacs, and other writings do not provide the power that observation of the nonhuman does—in fact, in terms of this literary mappings and mapping of borders and laws, the nonhuman is rarely considered. Furthermore, by reorienting his relationship to writing, we also see a reorientation to balance between male/female relationships. The voices of the very women too often written out of History become the means to recognize the voices of Native futures.

THE VIOLENCE OF SETTLER TEMPORALITIES AND SPATIALITIES

The almanac form employed by Silko is a (re)mapping of the settler state and liberal ideologies; it is a countermap that presents us with complex renderings of the threads of history that hold the fabric of colonial society together. Native peoples' stories of land—whether violent or from time memorial—move us beyond the abstract state rendering of space as territory or property.[50] By elucidating the violence of struggles over land through play with textual forms, Silko strategically moves us beyond a celebratory multicultural viewpoint of inclusion that focuses on the individual. In doing so, she confronts the violence of neoliberalism while relating it to the colonial events that continue to haunt us and amnesiac structures that uphold systems of colonial and imperial power. The amnesia that characterizes settler histories must be remedied. According to several moments throughout the text, at stake in (re)mapping regimes of geographical power/knowledge is "the continents called the Americas" (133).

In a pivotal border-crossing scene entitled "The Indian Way," Zeta takes to task her nanny, an older woman who is attempting to scold her for using a child to smuggle illegal product back and forth across the border. Motherhood contains and disciplines in this moment, but rather than accept this gendered norm it is brought into relationship with the legal violence and fictions of the border. Zeta turns the cultural apparatus of gendered authenticity, "this is not the Indian way," on its head, and rather than question herself as a "good" Native woman, she questions the very logic of the border history itself and the organization of gendered logics that sustain it. She recalls the mandate of priests who declared smuggling a sin, "because smuggling was stealing from the government." "There was not, and there had never been, a legal government by Europeans anywhere in the Americas," Zeta states, "Not by any definition, not even by the Europeans' own definitions and laws" (133). Colonial, Indigenous, and historical intersections are pulled into a temporal, spatial, and gendered relationship by invoking settler spatial imaginaries into this Indian almanac. The almanac kept by the twins and their grandmother support Yoeme's "arguments and crazed legal theories." In utilizing the oldest Western form of a printed book in the United States and altering elements to also account for the Mayan Codices, the *actual oldest documented written form* in the Americas, Silko creates an alternative knowledge of the land based on confrontations between differing histories and power relations. Almanacs were a print form responsible for mapping the ideological dilemmas we face in the neoliberal moment; they were a technology used in what is referred to as the U.S. revolution and what the Haudenosaunee see as a betrayal, one of many that would soon follow in the wake of violence that is the U.S. nation-state.[51]

The point here, and one I believe Silko is making, is that the almanac, as a foundational colonial form of writing, is an originary document producing the myth of nations—myths that are foundational to abusive global economies. Walter Mignolo's work is pivotal in examining writings of the new world during the Renaissance, as he asks more explicitly about the connection between writing, the *organization* of knowledge, and the production of history. He concludes that the effect of organizing discourse in genre formats is vital to issues of authority, power, and the colonization of memory. If maps organize knowledge (as they assuredly do) and the literary genre of the *almanac* also has a stake in this organization, consider Mignolo's comments:

> In the first case [referring to letters written by the colonizer], genres as social practices worked toward the spread of Western literacy and the reconfiguration of the classical tradition. In the second case [letters written by Amerindians], genres as social practices work toward the preservation of Amerindian memories and the discontinuity of the classical tradition. In a colonial situation the conflict of interpretations is played out at the basic level of cultural conversion, on the one hand, and the transformation of cultural traditions that give rise to new and emergent identities.[52]

How we organize writing is important in understanding the way that territories and places emerge. Silko is intricately entwining maps, historic events, and pieces of knowledge in her almanacs to unsettle colonial imperatives. By rewriting the imagined and enforced social construction of the border as illegal and the history of the Americas as one constructed of war, not of divine discovery and manifest destiny, she further destabilizes the knowledge base of Western ideas about legal land rights. Through the women characters who are writing and written into the histories of conquest, she takes on the construction of colonial male violence manifested in separation between land and bodies as they are turned into property. The women in the text are often the dead, from the past and present, who speak throughout the lost almanac. Whether it is social or literal death, or the many forms death takes throughout the novel or in real life, those destined for death in the colonial story of America have their own tales to tell and prophecies to bring forth.

Yoeme, a name that means "the people" in Yaqui language, is a main character in the novel who continually disrupts the grand narrative with memories of violence and blood. Her historic memory, or memory of the people, is an Indigenous almanac. Most importantly, as an almanac, she contains reading, memory, and mapping practices that carry forth, teaching Lecha and Zeta how to look at the landscape in a new fashion and maintain the social production of territories. Rather than their tribal allegiance being too easily equated as inherent ownership of land in a Lockean fashion, which is about individual possession and passing down through patrilineal inheritance, Yoeme teaches an alternate imagining of territory that overrides the Doctrine of Discovery, the Treaty of Guadalupe Hidalgo, NAFTA, and state territories positioned in imaginary but material violent borders. From Yoeme they learn the land is soaked with blood. In a section entitled "Cottonwood Trees," we learn the history of the trees themselves, beginning with a conversation between the twins and their mother, Amalia, shortly after their grandmother's return. Yoeme's marriage to Guzman, a direct reference to the brutal Spanish landholder and slave trader Nuno Beltran de Guzman, could be perceived as a marriage of convenience: they married to cement a relationship between the Spanish and the Native people who occupied the land. In this vein, the marriage, one controlled through the precepts of Western gender logics discussed in previous chapters, was about ensuring Yaqui land and bodies as property. Yet from Yoeme's point of view this control was always meant to fail: "Guzman and my people had made an agreement. Why do you think I was married to him? For fun? Hah! To watch and make sure he kept the agreement" (116). Silko not only recalls a history of Indian–white relationships that are not romanticized by referencing the persecution of Yaquis; she also embeds it within an indigenized worldview.

Ellen Arnold's excellent analysis of the word and image in relation to this particular story clarifies the role Yoeme has within this almanac by recalling an oral creation myth in which the tribe splits off in order for one segment to protect traditional knowledge and the other to work toward combing the old and new worlds. In Arnold's analysis of this story, based on the work of Larry Evers and Felipe Molina, Yoeme stands for the translator who would "be found to understand the future in a language of the past."[53] Yoeme's memory and fearlessness in telling the stories of violence she has witnessed enable her to resurrect the land around her and her grandchildren's relationship to it. As Arnold states, "Through Silko's use of imagery, it becomes clear that the old world emerging into the New World not only suffuses the present with time-fullness and the written word with dynamism of the spoken/aural, but also permeates the technologies of objectification that have rendered the world inanimate and consumable."[54] The "technologies of objectification" are the very writings that map Yoeme as a "thing" of the past without relationship to the present generation.

The strategy of associating Yoeme's name with the trees appears throughout the story of Zeta and Lecha's childhood. She is intricately linked and at times embodied as the land itself. Yoeme tells the girls to ask their mother who birthed "them," refusing to let Amalia and the entire family off the hook from her Indian "flesh and blood," a term Silko repeats with chilling effect. The girls want to know why Yoeme left *and* the source of their family's fear and rejection of the Indian woman. Their mother tells them Yoeme ran away and abandoned her children after cutting down Guzman's prize cottonwood trees, but in her version she leaves out the details of rotting "flesh" and spilled "blood" of the Yaqui people, her own relations. What the girls did not learn from their received colonial history was the fact of how these trees came to line the homestead through their transportation by slaves. Yaqui slaves were denied water and rest in the terrible heat, and according to Yoeme, "these white men came and they began digging up the cottonwoods and moving them here and there for sinister purpose" (117). The hanging of women, men, and children from trees was common in times of enslavement and in times of colonialism. Todorov inveighs against the connection between enslavement and colonial governance (while recognizing the ahistorical framing), especially in regard to Las Casas, who provides a rich document witnessing the violence that Yoeme speaks to:

> Las Casas and the other defenders are not hostile to the Spanish expansion, but they prefer one of its forms [colonialism] over the other [enslavement]. . . . Enslavement . . . reduces the other to status of an object, which is especially manifested in conduct that treats the Indians as less than men: their flesh is used to feed the surviving Indians or even the dogs; they are killed in order to be boiled down for grease, supposed to cure the wounds of the Spaniards; all their extremities are cut off, nose, hands, breasts, tongue, sexual organs, thereby transforming them into hapless trunks, as one might trim a tree; it is suggested that their blood be used to irrigate the fields, as if it were the water of a stream.[55]

While Todorov provides examples of these exact events by reciting from the conquistador writings and clearly delineating how the rhetoric of Native land and bodies was conflated so as to justify violence, Yoeme employs her experiential memory of those days of her departure from Guzman. The old Indian woman refuses to be complicit in this form of enslavement leading to the death of the Yaquis. She also refuses the colonial structuring of mapping and marking Yaqui lands. Instead, she waits patiently for the days to line up again, the time when her recollection would be most powerful, and she "waited to see if any of you grandchildren might have turned out human" (118). The reference to "human," rather than a political allegiance to a state or specific nationalist identity, is very important here and holds true to Silko's cartographic (re)vision and problemitizing of state practices throughout the novel. "I still see this . . . very clearly, because I was your age then," Yoeme tells the girls, who realized without being told what hung from the cottonwood trees as "dark objects" both "large and small, swaying from the low, heavy branches . . . in the beautiful green leaves" (117). Yoeme sums up this story, "laughing loudly" at the Guzman family's rejection of their Indian "flesh" and at their refusal to acknowledge the Indian "blood" spilled on these borderlands. This conversation between generations exemplifies the loss of information and the decontextualization of how land came to be privatized in Cuilican. Indian presence is denied and subsumed in settler narratives. Yoeme, however, is the shadow of history that returns to haunt: "They would not get rid of her" (115).

Sources of knowledge are questioned in the story of Yoeme, and the trees that were the site of massacres and the responsibility for those atrocities will not be ignored but return in the present. The lost grandmother is cast as a bad woman, a bad *Indian* woman, who left her children, stole money, cursed, and would only be a bad influence on them. The girls at one point summarize to their mother why their grandmother left in the simplest of terms: "it was because she was an Indian, Grandpa Guzman's family didn't like Indians" (117). Amalia tries to dismiss this as the bad teachings of her errant *Indian* mother, but instead Lecha matter-of-factly states the source of her knowledge: "I just know. Nobody likes Indians" (116). Again motherhood, a gendered role, becomes entangled with the production of histories, borders, and power relations. Ingested racial and gendered norms, the lack of knowledge about their own Indian identity and ancestral history, and the amnesia about the landscape surrounding them need remedying. Whereas Amalia is sickly and weak, partly, if we are to listen to Yoeme, because of her living lies, the girls become stronger daily as they listen to their grandmother and come to respect the land and their history. The stories are sustenance in this instance (and literally in the story of the Death Eye Dog when pages of the almanac sustain three children on a long journey north). Through Yoeme's teachings and (re)mapping of the spatial imaginary, the twins find not only survival, but possibility for change.

Narrative apparatuses do more than reflect or represent colonial and later nation-building projects—they also are instrumental in (re)producing them. The conquest of land and bodies through a narrative mapping that disavows violence is instrumental to that of sustaining colonialism and developing patriarchal states. In *Almanac*, the language of violence becomes key to understanding the forcefulness of colonial mapping that is ongoing and permeating. Though the current liberal state disavows violence, both temporally, in ways that render the former as an unfortunate remnant of a violent past, and spatially, in which unjust spatial practices construct a racial and colonial distribution of property that in turn is normalized in settler cartographic languages, the material reality of these patterns nonetheless remains part of dispossessed peoples' everyday existence. And awareness of this, according to Silko, is just enough: "All around them, all their lives they had witnessed their people's suffering and genocide; it only took a few, the merest handful of such people, to lay the groundwork for the changes" (742).

Resistance, however, does not mean presenting an opposite story that can be easily incorporated into the hegemonic state as a "differing perspective," as the tale of the cottonwood trees exemplifies. Yoeme's story is like many within Silko's almanac. Some are recoverable and others fleeting, but all become interpretable through national mythology and a liberalism that relegates the violence to an unfortunate past without seeing the circumstances it introduces in the present. In portraying the reemergence of a set of days that resemble conquest in her grotesque novel, Silko provides an almanac that just may tell us what to aim for and be wary of in the future. The text incudes powerful acts of language providing a model for Native political theory that allows for a critique of gendered and racial distributions of private property and capitalist accumulation. It does so without endangering political viability for Native nations that are compelled to mimic the map of territorial claims, based on masculinist notions of male citizens with allegiance to the abstract state, in order for recognition from settler law and corresponding parts of the state. Through the over-the-top grotesque language and scenarios, which do not make them any less real, as we have seen in the years since *Almanac*'s publication, Silko compels us to question the relationship among land, memory, violence, and justice in the late twentieth century.

In his essay "The Victim's Tale," Peter Van Der Veer questions the narration of the nation as it concerns the absorption of the victim's stories into the nation's story of itself. In these moments of horror and violence Van Der Veer asks: "What does national history do with the victim's tale? Such history is the grand narrative of the modern nation-state. In it, the stories different groups have about their past, about inner differences within the nation, are incorporated, reinterpreted, farmed into History. 'History' as sign of the modern is central to the idea of 'progress' or 'development' and thus to both colonialism and the liberal nation-state."[56] Silko's tales of terror and bloodshed do not rest as part of the United States', Canada's, or Mexico's *past*, however. The stories told in Silko's text are not framed into nation-state narratives; the multiple stories we are told have many discrepancies and overlap with many territories. Rather than create a monolithic narrative history, as the United States and other nation-states attempt to do, Silko tells the tales of the victims—in their variety and reoccurring forms, albeit in a way that can be troublesome. These dead voices, or voices meant to be dead, weave the memories of violence into the fabric of late twentieth-century life. Silko wrote Yoeme's stories as coinciding with the conquistador narratives. In fact, many narratives in *Almanac* repeat, contradict, and present alternative stories. Important to remember, however, is that "there is no true story of violence. Violence is a total phenomenon, but it comes to us as fragment. . . . Something terrible has happened, and there is no plot, no narrative, only leads that go nowhere."[57] What the victim's tale does show us, however, "are the limits of historical knowledge." The violence within Yaqui territory is not something that is recent or prompted solely by twentieth-century policies such as NAFTA.[58] This violence has a long history. The dead rise in Silko's almanac to reorder, or at the very least question, the current global ordering of the world into empires and nation-states.

Almanac provides an insight into Indigenous politics in the last third of the twentieth century. It is an era that is post–cold war, termination, civil rights, and relocation in which a rise of neoliberalism and democratization, accompanied by an expansion of laissez-faire financial and social networks across borders, frames Indigenous politics. In particular, *Almanac* was written during a time when neoliberal economic and political projects were being pushed by the nation-states of Mexico, the United Sates, and Canada. Tenets of neoliberalism focus on the free flow of capital and removal of trade barriers (such as regulations on labor or environmental impacts, or legalities that might affect corporate actions). Unlike classic liberalism, privatization, deregulation, and liberal trade agreements have had a profound impact not only on the economic and political spheres, but also that of the social realm in which individuals, regardless of their histories that might make them more vulnerable to exploitation, are left to the forces of the market system. The body, as examined in gruesome detail in *Almanac,* is nothing more than a commodity that is part of an unwieldy and competitive market. As the United States pumps money into physical enforcement in the name of "securing" its borders, the laissez-faire, liberal policies that become manifest in NAFTA present us with a further destabilization of economies in Mexico and in Latin America. Silko links these violent and economic transformations to early colonial spatial restructuring, thus positioning the early crimes of the colonial nation-state as the precursor and foundation for current neoliberal political and economic order.

The violent impact of the neoliberal policy of NAFTA on Indigenous people is too often elided by the geographical containment of the nation-state, containment signified in the imaginary and real material effects of state-constructed borders. Indigenous people within these borders often become collapsed and defined as national citizens. As discussed, the way the state deals with Indigenous entities is constantly being redefined, but with the incorporation of neoliberal principles there is a push to construct Indigenous peoples as new "market citizens." In their important essay "Remapping Gender, Justice, and Rights in Indigenous Americas," feminist scholar Shannon Speed and her coauthors explore the effects of neoliberal policies on Indigenous peoples across borders.[59] The new regulations set into process by Mexico, the United States, and Guatemala reflect a reordering of Indigenous people and their land by the liberal state that recognizes them as private entities or land as property. These policies deeply affect relationships to the land. Instead of collective units, Indigenous peoples have become undermined by a state story of dehistorized individuality. The material effect of this has had consequences, resulting in mass migration of Indigenous people to the Americas: "The new international economic order has been characterized by a contradictory process of opening up borders to transnational capital and controlling and closing borders to people. . . . However, the movements of people continue to be regulated and controlled by the state, as is evident in the control and militarization of the Mexico–United States and Mexico–Guatemala borders."[60] Indigenous peoples have always migrated and maintained social relationships to land and communities, but the reordering in neoliberal politics has made it difficult for many to hold onto their land and support their families. This has led to mass migration as lands are privatized and labor without constraints is sought by companies as far away as North Carolina. Even while the decades of the 1980s and 1990s saw an increase in Indigenous global movements across borders, the emphasis of nation-to-nation relationships of federal Indian policy remained a fixture of resistance, though as some have argued also part of the structures of dominance. The moments preceding the implementation of NAFTA are important to recognize, as they represent a major shift in the ways that nation-states deal with Indigenous peoples and communal land holdings, albeit differently nation-state to nation-state. Yet even while the decades of the 1980s and 1990s saw an increase in Indigenous global movements across borders, the emphasis of nation-to-nation relationships of federal Indian policy remained a fixture of resistance, though as some have argued, also part of the structures of dominance.[61] This too in part fluctuates based on differing policies of multiculturalism: "The hierarchical ordering of society along racialized lines obscured, all members of society are presumed to be equal and social relations an open competition in which the most meritorious prevail. In this discursive framework, to the extent that Indian communities and tribes are suffering poverty and marginalization, it is not the responsibility of the government, but rather a failure of the tribes themselves to adequately compete with other sectors of U.S. society."[62]

NAFTA profoundly reorganized territories yet again in the Americas. As Jennifer Wolch and Michael Dear contend in *The Power of Geography*, as territories are restructured and assaulted they severely alter social reproduction and destabilize existing structures. If territories are places of exchange, as addressed in the introduction in regard to Walter Mignolo's definition of territoriality, and units of cultural organizations they serve as places where the "social production of daily life" comes into being, then what does the recent change of territories prompted by NAFTA do to the communities of which Silko writes?[63] T. V. Reed, focusing on the transnational blueprint for decolonial environmental justice movements, asserts that "in *Almanac*, a focus on Native 'free trade' across the U.S.–Mexico border, going back as it does for centuries, is at once a parody of NAFTA-style free trade and a serious critique of it."[64] Part of the critique is one of dispelling progressive myths that NAFTA is not part of an ongoing history of land dispossession. For Silko this alteration of an entire territory reflects the spatial violence of previous years. The violent testimonies of daily life that Silko offers up are subaltern forms of protest against the NAFTA policies that profoundly rearrange Indigenous spatialities. Though it is not often thought of as an Indigenous policy restructuring, I position NAFTA as part of a long line of U.S., Mexican, and Canadian policy that restructures Native land holdings by liquidating communal land into private property, displacing Indigenous bodies from their lands, and extracting the resources of land and labor in order to absorb them into the settler nation-state.

The stories that compose Silko's almanac are borderland stories that tell a complex tale of instability in the shift toward neoliberal spatial restructuring. Borders become significant signs and symbols of nation, both marking territorial limits and setting them off from one another in terms of difference. These state-constructed borders are significant players in the regulation of NAFTA, which bolsters their regulatory strength while seemingly making economies immune to its forces. Borders are "meaning-making and meaning

carrying entities, parts of cultural landscapes which often transcend the physical limits of the state and defy the power of state institutions."[65] For Native
peoples whose traditional lands are part of this borderland, the state constructions have always been shifting and have focused on economics and state
politics. Like Johnson's notion of borders that disappear, *Almanac* enables us
to address the regimes of geographical knowledge that produce and are productive of Native realities.

Throughout the text, the characters write and record what they witness
of the world around them. The social practices exposed through the various
writings that collude and collide in various places throughout *Almanac* tell
us a different side of the rise of the U.S. economy and subsequent nation-
building and imperial processes throughout the Americas from the vantage
of the dispossessed. By examining sexual violence, borders, and capitalism
as a matrix of domination, Silko ties older forms of colonialism to neocolonialism and global migration. By interpellating histories of the Indigenous
through various modes of time and space, and by intermingling Indigenous
and European forms of writing, she (re)maps settler landscapes by writing
a history where the juxtaposition between Native people as passive objects
marked for death is coupled with Native people's ongoing, organized, and
resilient resistance. Sadiya Hartman's work on black subjection is useful to
think about in the context of Silko, as she troubles the notion of rights granted
through "slave humanity and individuality" as a source of protection from
brutality, and suggests rather that the rhetoric worked to "tether, bind and
oppress": "It was often the case that benevolent correctives and declarations of
slave humanity intensified the brutal exercise of power upon the captive body
rather than ameliorating the chattel condition."[66] Hartman's problematizing
of the "compulsory contract" with the state as individuals is useful in speaking
through the colonial conditions in the present; just as "the barbarism of slavery did not express itself singularly in the constitution of the slave as object,"
nor did the making of Indians as objects under "ownership" by the nation-
state. Rather, violence toward Native people is exerted through the law and
often through benevolence toward Native people, evident when we explore
how the modalities of colonialism operate at various scales and the politics of
Indigenous people who become racialized in the moment of absorption into
the state. By examining the production of Native land and bodies through the
form of writing and mapping, the contradictions of subjection arise.

Silko's border stories in this sense are a tool to put forth important cultural and geographical imaginings and must be considered when we speak to

Native women's efforts to (re)map our nations. Like Harjo, Silko links early colonial mappings of Native lands and bodies to the current exploitation formed in neoliberal renderings of the globe. As the prolific forms of writing pepper this immense novel, the reader also comes to understand that writing remains essential to a continued production of landscapes of power. The almanac and forms of mapping in the text interrupt and expose an ongoing production of the nation-states. The local stories are also linked to the larger picture, and the redeployment of the tools of conquest—almanacs as a genre of writing and maps—reveals the gendered spatial violence enacted on Indigenous subjects in the Americas and (re)maps toward a Native futurity.

ROAMING PROPHECIES AND BORDER PERFORMANCES

Silko structures the novel as an almanac, a compilation of facts and figures relating to specific spaces in time, to point out various narratives that bring us to the present moment of colonization and imperialism. Furthermore, by pulling these written traditions of the map and almanac together, Silko unravels the spatial, temporal, and ideological space of the nation. The narratives in *Almanac* produce and recover Indigenous knowledge for the purpose of positing new ways of thinking vital to the process of decolonization, which is not an event so much as actions always in process. These narratives are related as traditional stories, gossip, humorous accounts, dreams, history, notebooks, glyphic representations, facts, figures, details, and memories. Just as an almanac is about cycles of time as well as geographical local spaces, Silko situates her characters in the locale of Tucson and records seemingly unconnected relationships among drug dealers, political figures, business people, strippers, psychics, and guerrilla activists to demonstrate the cycles of exploitation. She deals with the cycles of history and employs measures of time and space—such as epochs, continents, states, and cities—to arrive at the Indigenous concept of worlds. Edward Soja, however, reminds us that national and global projects are "constantly being localized in various ways and with different intensities at every scale."[67] Silko's work is exemplary of the various intensities of scale she works with to delineate a history of violence in this place and a connection to violences in other places. That is, while these stories have specific meaning to people in specific places and with specific histories of colonization in their repeated patterns of spatial violence, such as the Yaquis discussed in the earlier section, they develop on a glocalized scale. Silko's novel articulates the various scales of violence in the 1990s, just as the forms of early almanacs articulated a violent vision and map of the Americas.

Finding the patterns in innumerable details and fragmented facts and figures is an important component of making an almanac useful. This way of reading is important in unlocking the relationship between the larger historical narrative and the individual, messy histories produced through conflict. Patterns emerge as historical relationships of power and the stories that justify them repeat over and over again, and as they do so, the interconnections of various sets of narratives emerge. In other words, colonial stories' repetition of freedom, individuality, democracy, and liberation as well as the repeated absences of Native presence within these stories are, to borrow from Judith Butler, a "productive act"; the body of the state is similar to the bodies it produces in that it is comprised, not by one unilateral subject but in a myriad of valences that produce power, in *"a process of materialization that stabilizes over time to produce the effect of boundary, fixity, and surface we call matter."*[68] The body, whether it is that of the Indian or the settler and the state, becomes an old, familiar constituent who allows for new and ongoing material possibilities. The repeated stories of violent conquest and progression into liberal democracy are essential for the materialization of a new state with new imperial subjects, new global futures, and a renewed faith in capitalist development. However, in *Almanac* there is a focus on the absented stories as well as a narrative of capitalist declension and an awareness of the reality of the intersections of capitalism and colonialism. These repeated and ignored signifiers have always existed along with the dominant narrative. Silko's map represents this convergence of history and people by not excluding the destroyers from its surface and by writing-in the absent Native. In an interview Silko states, "I wanted it to be an almanac. But it's an almanac made of narrative." She then proceeds to talk about the strategic value of creating it this way. She didn't want people to say "well, that happened in 1492 what can we do about it now"—rather, she wanted to point out that people do experience those events from five hundred years ago, or even in time immemorial, in the present. Nor are these events experienced meant to be mystical in nature; rather past violences on the body, land, and peoples set up the structures that allow current violence to perpetuate. Silko is pointing out that "things aren't lost, the dead aren't lost."[69] Yet, for the colonized the trick is to recollect and remember the stories but escape many of the pitfalls that essentialist nostalgia presents, as only "the image of a memory exists in the present moment" (574). Rather than present homogenous space on a map of the nation-state or one counterhistory and spatialization from the perspective of the colonized in the almanac, Silko restructures these forms to recall the history of Indigenous and colonial *interactions*. In positing the reading of history as a moment of interpretive dislocation and interpretive unsettlement, Silko (re)maps the making of nation and the bodies of those subsumed under its spatial rubrics.

The form of the almanac in the text is used to branch out from a specific locale to a more inclusive global vision that is necessary in accounting for cultural and political change in the twenty-first century. In Silko's words, she was not trying to tell the histories of multiple characters in individual narratives, rather she "was trying to give history a character."[70] An ambitious goal for sure, but a spatial examination of *Almanac* allows us to locate the "character." History's role as protagonist and antagonist in the text (re)conceptualizes time and history by making the convoluted narrative of colonization come to life in the present. A (re)writing/telling of history with an awareness of the particular problems of "us" versus "them," inclusion and exclusion, and identity politics is necessary to move beyond models that do not reconfigure power relations. As Guidotti-Hernandez clarifies, "historically, extreme violence has been tolerated and in fact legitimated and reinforced by both nations [Mexico and the United States] precisely because of their interlocking colonial legacies."[71] It is the national imaginaries of both states, fortified in what becomes History, and repeated state violence enacted through ever-changing technologies of violence, that are addressed in Silko's almanac— a literary map. By working with history as the main character, recalcitrant space, and a "mosaic" of interpretive history, Silko moves us through narrative from the small kitchen in the specific locale of Tucson to the broader project of addressing the socioscapes of global capitalism.

Silko's worlding of space through the almanac and map is based on a variety of understandings of the mapping of history. Her repetition of myths and histories—as well as their confluence—presents an alternative epistemology and historical archive. For instance, Silko articulates that in order to make it to the next world, her characters must watch for what will come in the repetition of "arcane symbols" and "old narratives."[72] Arnold Krupat discerns the meaning of history and myth:

> Historical narratives tell of events nearer to the present in time, while mythical narratives relate an eventfulness very far from the present in time, when the world was young and "soft," or not fully formed. But both mythical and historical stories are true, and both are history in the sense that [Greg] Dening defines

the term. History, Dening writes, "is public knowledge of the past public in the sense of being culturally shared." "Histories are ways of knowing what happened in the past" and, conversely, those ways of knowing the past that are culturally and communally confirmed are history.[73]

Silko's text is an example of Krupat's assertion; it collapses myth and traditional Western forms of history. Whether recognized by the state or not, and in most cases not, the histories exist to challenge colonial spatialities of Native lands and bodies. The telling of history, however, like the writing of the almanacs on the text, is always in process. For instance, the once very public Yaqui hangings in the trees discussed by Yoeme become misplaced and misinterpreted in Mexican state narratives and accepted histories, but the residue of subaltern versions is constantly threatening to unravel national imaginaries.

The character of Menardo, the Mexican/Indigenous security man who exploits the fear of the Native other, denies the history of the Americas for money and power. He has profited from the fear of uncontrolled borders and Indians prompted by NAFTA. Like many of the destroyers in the novel, he is unable or unwilling to heed the world around him. Menardo embraces power at the subjugation of others and his Indigenous past. Disassociation from his Indian grandfather, hatred of his nose, and ultimately a hatred of himself take the form of separation from the stories his grandfather used to tell him as a child. The more he separates himself from his own narrative history or genealogical base, the more he slips into the culture of the destroyers. It is his security forces that enable an encroachment into Native lands and the South, providing a sense of security for economic development to the benefit of non-Natives. Menardo's massing of weapons and a personal air force would "*be there* to offer complete protection to clients" in the case of "revolution, mutiny, uprising, or guerilla war" (292). This private army is geared to maintaining possession of land conceived of as private property and resources of the privileged. As a security salesman whose profit depends on violence, danger, and fear, Menardo puts himself in a position that counters the Indigenous people's reclamation of the land or view of it as something to be allocated to the highest bidder.

If Menardo had continued to listen to the stories of his Indigenous grandfather, then perhaps he, too, could understand the message of the snake. The story of his descent into a morbid fascination with death counsels the reader to beware of separation and abstractions of the living both human and nonhuman, as Silko warns: "A great many fools like Menardo would die pretending they were white men; only the strongest would survive. The rest would die by the thousands along with the others; the disappearance would take place over thousands of years and would include massive human migrations from continent to continent" (511). In Menardo's narrative the snake appears as a warning sign, but he chooses to ignore it, unlike the sister twins who learn the secrets of the snake. His inability to read the signs around him, his willful intent to ignore surrounding details, his averted glances from the suffering of those around him, and his severing of his relationship to the people and the land in order to gain wealth ultimately end in his demise. His obsession with a bulletproof vest prompts him to ask the rebel Indian spy, Tacho, to shoot at him in order to test the material. The bullet penetrates through a rare flaw in the vest. Menardo's demise began, however, with his discovery and consequent rejection of the knowledge passed on by his Indigenous grandfather. The individual and collective narratives that form this novel are like the snake that so easily moves from place to place and is called back by memory and telling. Only by acknowledging "the Indian connection," outlined in the legend and the messages of the ancient snake depicted in the "Five Hundred Year Map," can there be a space for renewal.

However, Silko's repeated symbols and created narratives in the text do not just assert the destruction of "all things European," but rather, her performative use of language brings about a series of moments leading to an apocalyptic imagining. The map, for instance, lists characters that exist in the present with those of the dead; the stories connect them to the place now called Tucson. The dead, as Renee Bergland demonstrates in her book *The National Uncanny,* occupy a particular place in the creation of an American subject. They are powerful figures in the trope of American literature because "national ghosts threaten rationalist hegemony, and hence they threaten the nation."[74] The normalization of borders, for instance, is disrupted as Silko tells an abundance of stories regarding transgression of settler state laws. Borders are not a natural structure and must be maintained by brutal force—but then they were never concrete spaces. By the end of the text, this play with borders becomes an understandable sign of instability. Although borders are commonly comprehended as a physical marker between Mexico and the United States, Silko's use of language now associates borders with cruelty, subjugation, greed, perverse sexualities, and violence that separate human beings from one another and sustain structures of domination. The normative geographic language of borders is disrupted, as at the end of this long text, we have come to interpret borders as always unstable. In using the dead, Silko questions the originary moment of the nation and its futurity.

A new relationship to spatial consciousness is imagined in the reification of the history of the Americas when the dead can inhabit the same terrain as the living and when their narratives converge. The map poignantly initiates new associations of meanings by shifting the signs to new spatial planes where the spatial is not "objective" representations of geographic space but rather a hyper geopolitical account of colonial attempts to confine space. Silko's constant implementation of spatial tropes continues the process of breaking down the conventional concepts of borders and ideology of the nation-state. Menardo's business blooms in the wake of trying to stabilize the Chiapas border. The building of mansions in the jungle lays claim to Indigenous land as fabricated spatial constructions. Yet, the land has its own plans, and in the case of Menardo's house in the jungle, it creeps in on him as he nears death. In a conversation between Menardo and Tacho, his Indian servant and confidant who is actually part of the leadership of the Indigenous forces seeking reclamation of the land, Silko writes, "Menardo thought Tacho had finished on the subject [of blood, sacrifice, and spirits], but then Tacho had blamed all the storms with landslides and floods, all the earthquakes and erupting volcanoes, on the angry spirits of the earth fed up with the blood of the poor" (337). This moment in which Menardo faces a gap in Western knowledge of humanity controlling nature as normal is an important turning point in the story's trajectory and what the sign of borders means. Borders are performative acts of language that rely on constative practices such as repetition to secure their dominance.

The above constative practices of the state—that is, practices that supposedly simply state information or inform of what ought to be—are reversed into performative acts by Silko. Through repetitive stories and narrative accounts found in media, history, academic assertions, and so forth, the border is seen not only as tangible, but also as ahistorical. It has been a constant in the national imaginary, and the violence that enables this action has been erased in American history and mainstream consciousness. Anthropologist Donald Carter, who examines immigrant diasporas and nation-states, talks about the link among documents, media, academics, and mapping in Italian propaganda: "Like the cartographers' map of the nation, the document maps vast territories of the imagination cast between the identified and the unknown, life and death, and normalcy and divergence."[75] Silko makes the same connection between different forms of knowledge and relates bits and pieces of information while constantly calling into question their legitimacy. By making use of language to create new associations with borders as unreal and history as not yet finished, she reflects a map without borders. The prophecy referred to in the binding, then, is not a magical happening *but rather the processes of language and communal sharing.*

The repetition of numerous uprisings and Native symbols articulate the inner differences within the nation-states. The United States asserts its border with Mexico by ignoring these multiple histories, such as the occupation of the land by Native people before Europeans began their explorations into the new world, migration back and forth among Indigenous people, and the legal claims of Native people. Mainstream society comes to *know* and, more importantly, comes to *believe* that borders are stable, tangible, and controllable geographical places. Menardo's belief that the vest will protect him is similar in nature. He obsesses over its form, its shape, and the technical manual, and he even "had taken to sleeping in the bulletproof vest" (335). Yet in the end, it is his request for Tacho to shoot him and his beliefs that his wealth will buy him protection and superiority that result in his death. The vest fails. Those in an exterior position are not to be defined as proper subjects of the state. Obscured in categories of race and citizenship are the structures of dominance and oppression that consider the constative practices of making of geohistorical and geopolitical spaces. Silko's spatializing of the nation's history, by recovering Indigenous narratives that testify to the brutality of nation-building and reject its very foundation, engenders a (re)mapping of how difference is incorporated into certain spaces. Language does not merely reflect the world as many politicians, scientists, historians, and geographers represent in their discourse; it also has the power to organize it as Silko so aptly strives to do in *Almanac*. This is not a natural process, as Silko demonstrates, but one in which it is important to acquire a new literacy.

In bringing the Native into a forceful existence by narrating events of the past through collective memories and through collective imaginings, such as the snake notebooks and various tellings in the novel, Silko is generating a sense of belonging based on acknowledging the relations around us. In Silko's world on the brink of chaos, relationships are essential. In these relationships "no outsider knows where Africa ends or America begins" (421). The forms of the text clarify Silko's assertions: on the map the arrows point toward other continents in a continuous dotted line that connotes movement, and in the almanac the collection of data, events, narratives, and information supersedes the boundaries of nation and time. The arcane symbols and narratives arrive in Tucson from Africa, the Caribbean, pre-contact, and during mass migrations in which people overlapped spatially and socially. Colonial truths of these borders, those defined by a variety of intersections such as gender, race, nationality, and geography, are upset in a narrative in which the events of the past continue to influence the present.

ROUTED STORIES

If one overarching theme can be derived from *Almanac of the Dead,* and Silko's work in general, it is that stories are powerful; they are the cornerstones of political viability. Stories converge in the moment, and as they do so they provide strategies of resistance. Robert Warrior, in addressing Edward Said's treatise of the circulation of cultural and intellectual life, observes the following regarding the life of stories:

> The routes that ideas follow in their travels are oftentimes the same ones that trade goods follow from their points of origin to markets. Through extended visits by voyagers and even the idle chatter of merchants and caravaners, ideas have moved from time immemorial along the same paths as foodstuffs, medicines, textiles, tools, and toys. Books, too, have played an enormous role as goods and vessels for ideas. The process of transporting ideas has often been as informal as formal, and the equation of knowledge and power has been evident throughout history in the favorable relationships between some nations and the inequitable, exploitive ones between others.[76]

This aptly applies to the eclectically routed stories in *Almanac.* Though Warrior is speaking to the travel of Native nonfiction, his words regarding the ability of ideas to travel across time and space are important in rethinking the complexity of the roots and routes that Silko is working to remember in her text. Oftentimes, capitalism and the desires of the state have forced the story forward or may have resulted in its secrecy until the time is right again for its telling.

Rather than accept a grand narrative of history, a reading of *Almanac* suggests that we examine the transmission and reception of stories. The dead in the text do speak, and the presence of those deemed lost actually "remain[s] the same over hundreds of years" (119). Land is not a blank space awaiting conquering, such as in the idea of *Terra nullius* or other modes of creating blank space ready to be possessed (discussed in the introduction), nor does it develop in a linear fashion; its dimensions are intertwined in human and nonhuman relationships that have been formed over time. Likewise, human identity and relationships are tied to the land, a concept at the forefront of much American Indian writing. Elaine Jahner speaks to the importance of this path of questioning in her analysis of the way the Stone Boy narratives constitute a "textual community" by asking the reader, "What kinds of communal agreements create the pragmatic conditions that enable a group to function as a narrating community? That last question points to the originary authority of local communities and the processes of self-reflection that sustain communities."[77]

In the course of this chapter, I have pointed to the ways that Silko takes up the challenge of textual communities and various powers within them. Cheyfitz speaks to our awareness of the connections between textual communities and the ways in which they travel: "Concomitantly, following *Almanac,* because the European theft of Indian land *in the name of the law* founds the modern Americas (accompanied by the theft of Indian and African labor), it makes no sense to ground a postcolonial American studies, including the reading of *all* national literatures in the Americas, in anything but an historical understanding of the legal machinations of the ongoing Euro-American colonial war against the indigenous peoples of the Americas."[78] General J.'s philosophical foundations, after all, are not far off from the juridical mechanisms of federal Indian law or Mexico's legal relationship to Indigenous people. Particularly in *Almanac,* Silko tackles colonizing forces that dictate relationships to the land through borders and other geographical signifiers; to humans through their separation as autonomous beings from animal and plant life and through racializing humans into unequal groups; to history and away from various versions and overlapping of events. The foes are a necessary part of the stories that make up the almanac; they attempt to erase the analogue, break apart the mosaic, and obscure the details until one narrative of history exists. The story of the nation-state circumscribes relationships to the land, disrupts already existing relationships, and defines human beings in narrow categories that isolate people from one another, such as by race, sexuality, gender, and nation. For Silko, as with many other American Indian writers and other colonized peoples, remembering, creating, and sharing multiple stories establishes Native discourses countering the monolithic history supported by the destroyers.

Leslie Marmon Silko enables the reader to see that forging a freedom based on the oppression of others results in the further destruction of humanity.

As Silko's character Clinton tells us: "Ignorance of the people's history had been the white man's best weapon" (742). *Almanac of the Dead's* multivocal, multitemporal, and simultaneously juxtaposed narratives converge to produce alternative mappings to the nation-state. By raising the forgotten dead and highlighting the ongoing violence and perpetuation and extension of colonial power, teaching us how to read and watch for the signs around by reconstructing the forms of the map and almanac, examining revolution and complicating forms of resistance, *Almanac* asserts that the destruction of a patriarchal nation-state must be considered as part of reframing the project of decolonization and globality. We must be able to read the stories around us and negotiate the power they contain. These literary acts become real-world necessities—and not just for Indians.

Conclusion:
"She Can Map Herself Like a Country She Discovers"

I N WRITING ABOUT OCCUPY WALL STREET MOVEMENT, JOANNE BARKER recalls the particular history of Wall Street and its relationship to claiming Lenape land through enforcing settler forms of spatial constructions. She reminds us that the street itself was named after the physical wall built by the Dutch to claim the land base of Mana hata and to keep the Lenape and their then allies, the English, out. However, the Dutch would lose their foothold, and "the English would be defeated by the Americans. The Americans would preserve 'Wall Street'—and all of Manhattan—as their own."[1] This is similar to the ways in which the geographies the women in this project capture the context of their lived realities, such as Leslie Marmon Silko living on the border in Tucson, Arizona, or Joy Harjo traveling from city to city across Native lands.

The violent history of colonialism and Wall Street is forgotten, and in its place the state becomes naturalized as a center of wealth distribution. The ever-shifting construction of the state relies on producing such geographies that attempt to stabilize settler/imperial powers. Barker's blog continues and reminds the readers that "Wall Street is only possible because of this history of land fraud and treaty violation. The 'United States' is only possible because of its still imperial-colonial relations with Native peoples."[2] As I have argued, American, Canadian, and Mexican wealth and power dynamics are only possible by consistently shifting policies that deal directly with Native peoples while simultaneously erasing their histories and knowledges or even such policies' effects on Native people's everyday reality. Although

I did not have time to develop it here, the spatial injustices that occur in the case of the Pacific Islands speaks volumes to how our spatial imaginary becomes limited as much through absence as it does through presence. The erasure from a national map of those deemed "territorial lands" and the people who have inhabited them since time immemorial exists simultaneously with intense military occupation and incorporation of Native bodies into the military.[3]

(Re)mapping our nations, both the nation-state and Native nations, requires us to engage in past modes of knowledge production as well as to examine how it informs policies and laws—and yes, even our own resistance to colonialism and imperialism. We must recognize how the injustices that coupled a mapping of the Americas materializes in all our lives—Native and non-Native alike—on a daily basis. What we now know as Wall Street was once a tribal center, and, as such, is disputed space in a settler context. Wall Street isn't the only place where conflicting geographies come into play, however, as we have seen throughout: the city of Chicago as discussed in Harjo's poem, or Los Angeles in Belin's poetry.

In addressing claims to the right to spatial justice, many Native activists and writers have suggested asking, whose land is it that is deemed public by interests that have always been about the privatization of land and bodies? How might we (re)map the social, historical, political, and economical in these moments to include a critique of colonialism and imperialism? The geographic language employed in our work toward spatial justice has the potential potency of unpacking neoliberal accumulations of private wealth, but recognition of colonial restructuring of land and bodies must be recognized. Complicating the history of spatial restructuring in settler societies not only enables us to perceive the Americas as layered with complex histories and enduring struggles, but also permits us to imagine forms of resistance that do not perpetuate violence.

Ultimately, we must question our mental and material maps. What geographies have we been taught and then normalized that hinder a movement toward spatial justice? Heid Erdrich's poem "The Girl in Geography Class" reminds us of the processes by which we learn our place in the world:

> The girl in geography class takes nice, legible notes
> in capital letters, in pencil. The teacher ticks off facts
> on another world she can't quite grasp though she

herself might have been FOUNDED thirteen years ago
by religious order and BORDERED by sisters on all sides.
The CAPITOL of her love? Fear.[4]

Erdrich's geography lesson reminds us that we cannot be fearful of confronting how we are spatialized as Native peoples. The state has marked our lands and our bodies through the process of creating a geopolitics in which "BORDERS" enforce state violence and enact settler colonial biopolitics that materialize in the interpersonal. The small girl in the poem is representative of Native children or all of us who have gone through a colonial education. I understand this interpersonal violence as the force of "religious order" or other ideologies that manifest themselves through cultural production and technologies of rule exerted through nuns, teachers, and geographic "facts." Part of mapping the settler state was and continues to be the shifting of Native lands to resources or that which produces capital. In Erdrich's poem, the double play on words links the making of state capitals and accepted geographies to the making of profit from Native lands. These geographic hubs, or urban centers, are the places where bureaucratic decrees are issued, exports and industry are regulated, goods transported, populations managed, and land as a life force becomes abstracted as property.

As I have been arguing throughout this book, however, the geographies foundational to Native communities have not disappeared but are waiting to be (re)mapped and "grasped." Erdrich's transitioning sentence in the poem, "she can map herself like a country she discovers," is a poetic force imagining new geographies that account for the violence of gendered spatial restructuring. I bring into juxtaposition the personal violence felt by a small girl in her geography class who has been denied her "landmarks" or ways of guiding herself with tribal knowledges with the worldwide Occupy Wall Street movement, which is concerned with the effects of "industry," in order to demonstrate possibilities in connecting the various scales of spatial injustice. Erdrich's poem continues to address the gendered spatial connections between geographic knowledge production and settler violence:

In perfect blocks she quizzes:
LANDMARKS? Ancient forces left a chain of depressions
now known as Lazy Lake, Lake of the Shy, Care Less Lake.
EXPORT? The main export of her sex is shame.

INDUSTRY? Pressure treatment processes rage
into a soft, slow-burning fuel.
TRANSPORTATION? Any bike, any train, any boat, truck, or plane.[5]

The state's reformulations of gender and race relations brings into emergence
new forms of organizing space—from the body noted in "her sex" to the mapping of nation—in order to absorb Native lands and break up tribal communities. It is in this context that Native women strive to bring into balance the
negative impact of the political, economic, and cultural colonial restructuring, signified in one girl's affective mapping of her place in geography class.
I contend that in close examinations of literary spatial imaginary, possibilities are opened in making the connection between state spatial violence and
interpersonal violence.

On a daily basis, women in all of our variously conceived communities
strive to keep the connections among family, stories, histories, and the land
alive and well. The maps we write illuminate the power of incorporating spatial practices from Native frameworks. Rather than mapping space as homogenous, bounded, and temporally linear, the Native writers I discuss see the
land as having a history that must be respected; it is not a contained space but
has connections to multiple other spaces, histories, and people. In her qual-
itative study, Faye Lone examines the interviews of twenty-one Haudenosaunee people of various ages, and points toward the meanings of space in
conceiving of identity. She very clearly delineates the differences between
racial identities—those she sees as in flux due to constantly changing external pressures—and national identities—those she sees as arising from geographical temporalities and artificially bounded land. In her conclusion, she
declares, "Perhaps we would do well to create a framework for indigenous
research from this [spatial] perspective. A structure based on connected
spaces, not bounded by geography, but by territories that speak from a life
of their own, from ageless stories and intergenerational depth of meanings
and interpretations. A framework that allows relatedness to a flexible spatial
community, one that allows for strong, mobile, symbolic identity that underlies, and perhaps even belies, external influences."[6] Land is conceived of as
interconnected and inhabited through "ageless stories" and "intergenerational
depth." Silko's cartographic web in *Almanac* carries with it the stories of
Laguna Pueblo that ground Silko in her perceptions of land and history, but
it also includes histories of the dispossessed who are connected to Tucson

through political and economic forces. It is our research, as Lone suggests, that must follow this lead.

Where possible, I have made connections among seemingly disconnected histories by (re)mapping the materiality and symbolism of the violence of colonization, but there is much work to be done in this area. Native women engage with the world around them and, starting with this premise, redirect our attention to the artifactualization and delimitation of oppositional spaces, such as in the reserve or reservation dichotomy. Native women writers make visible the contradictions of dominant social formations. Creating histories that exclude or make "others" will not liberate us from bounded race, gender, and national norms. By engaging with "flexible spatial communities," Johnson, Silko, Belin, and Harjo are dealing directly with the history of colonization and continuing policies of spatial restructuring to provide vital tools with which to maintain the strength of communities and rethink our connection with humanity. In a land where Natives are objects in geography lessons to be "founded," "discovered," "exported" from our lands, and used for cheap labor, positioning Native geographies to work through acts of colonial spatial violence is of upmost importance and vital to creating healthy communities.

In the narratives of Native women mapped out in creative forms, we can begin to further promote an analysis that accounts for differences within communities, how these communities adhere, and the relationship between colonization, writing, and our present-day intracommunity and intercommunity relationships that exist in many multiscalar forms. Literary scholar Ramon Saldivar addresses the connections between narrative and ideology in his book *Chicano Narrative,* declaring that the possibilities art and writing open up are important, as they "put ideology to work" and "reveal the heterogeneous systems that resist the formation of a unitary base of truth."[7] The narratives discussed throughout are examples of a writer's ability to disrupt the "truths" of settler colonialism. I have concentrated mainly on writings that rearticulate our spatial relations, but there are many more examples of writing that disrupt the "naturalness" of settler structures found in modalities of race, gender, and contemporary nation-states. I consider these texts great art; and, as Saldivar informs us, "great art distances ideology by the way in which, endowing ideology with figurative and narrative articulations, the text frees its ideological content to demonstrate the contradictions within which ideologies are created."[8] Contradictions are at the foundation of intersecting concepts of geographies that have a great impact on the world in which we live.

Examining Native spatialities in the work of Native women proves fruitful in many ways: first, this examination points out the spatial injustice that forms the many contradictions in settler colonialism; second, it provides a history of Native women's refusal to be defined, erased, or subjugated to colonial law, reminding readers that colonialism was and is a gendered process and that efforts to decolonize must address it as such; and third, it demonstrates the ways that women have engaged with spatial production to produce places of their own making that are vital to Native communities.

These women mark twentieth-century American literature by creating a spatial imaginary through language that carries the weight and contradictions of history and living into the present moment. Whether it be Christie's and Esther's refusal to be bound in unequal marriages and union with the nation in Johnson's stories at the turn of the century, Belin reconnecting to her Navajo subjectivity despite years of policies that would have it otherwise, Harjo's ability to keep with her "the smallest talking drum" in her global travels at the end of the twentieth century and encounters with Indigenous people on a global scale, Silko's ability to expose and connect the violence of settler-colonial spatial restructuring in policies such as NAFTA, or Erdrich's poetic reminiscing of the origin of settler education in her elementary geography class, mark their words for these authors provide the key for (re)mapping our futures.

Acknowledgments

These pages are perhaps the easiest and simultaneously the most difficult to write. I have been very fortunate in my life to have the support of friends, family, and colleagues who have helped me through the years and across the myriad geographies I have traveled. As such, support has come in many fashions, and I worry about leaving one of you out or not expressing enough how significant your help has been. I am truly grateful for those who have entered my life and helped to shape this book.

Elaine Jahner's class in Native American literature would set me on this road, just as her mentorship and belief in my abilities at such a young age would open up the possibilities of graduate school and teaching. My community of NAADS and NADS would provide a rich context in which I learned a lot about other Nations, their various struggles and resistances, as well as the importance of all our collective and individual stories. NADS, you are too numerous to name, but know that many of you have touched my life as friends, classmates, and students and continue to do so. A special shout-out goes to Randy Quinones Akee. A special nod also goes to Carol Atkinson-Palombo, who is the best of friends.

At Stanford University in the Modern Thought and Literature Department, I was very fortunate to have wonderful cohorts. Thank you, Raul Cornado, Manishita Dass, Nicole Fleetwood, and Celine Parrenas-Shimizu, Mattie Stevens, and Sandra Shagat. I am especially thankful for your continued friendship, love, and support, as well as for being my children's aunties! Special thanks also go to Magdalena Barrera, who provided countless hours of laughter. I would also like to thank members of my writing group in MTL, who read through the very first drafts of this book and provided me with excellent feedback: Lisa Arellano, Shona Jackson, Yael Ben-zvi, Kyla

Thompkins, and Evelyn Asultany. The intellectual vigor of my MTL experience helped me to become a better scholar, while the positive energy helped me to maintain my sanity.

I was also privileged to have a great working community of Native scholars and their families at Stanford who provided guidance; readings of one another's work, dinners, talks about things small and large, and community. Thank you, Renya and Gil Ramirez, Anne Medicine (now deceased), Denni Woodward, the Tovars, Victoria Bomberry, Stephanie Fryberg, Verna St. Denis, Tiffany and Ivan Lee, Kenric Tsethlikai, Renee Watchman, and Beth Hege-Piatote.

To my dissertation adviser, Yvonne Yarbro-Bejarano, I owe a huge debt, as she took me on at a critical time and was willing to work, read, and guide me through the first drafts of this book. She was a wonderful adviser, and I treasure the nurturing and intellectual quality of that relationship. I also would like to extend a thank-you to my two other committee members, Mary Louise Pratt and Richard White. Your comments and help were instrumental to my project. I also appreciated the advice given by Renato Rosaldo, Teresa LaFromboise, and Matt Snipp, and my early classes with Sharon Holland, Paula Moya, Nicholas De Genova, and Cherrie Moraga. Finally, Monica Moore, David Palumbo-Liu, and Jan Hafner, I thank you for your administrative help and always warm presence.

My time at Dartmouth as an assistant professor was incredibly important in finishing this book. I would like to thank all my colleagues in NAS and in English who provided important advice, support, and intellectual engagement. Ivy Schweitzer and Mellissa Zeiger were excellent mentors and invested so much time. A special thanks to Alex Halasz, Sam Vasquez, Soyica Diggs, Michael Chaney, Bed Giri, Jeffery Santa Ana, Colleen Boggs, Pat Mckee, Peter Travis, Colin Calloway, Bruce Duthu, George Edmondson, and the most lovely Hazel-Dawn Dumpert. Special cheers to Dale Turner, whose intellect, jokes, breakfasts at Lou's, and advice were always helpful. As I have said many times before while stuck in an airport trying to get back to Hanover—I am so very glad to have been stuck with you! Vera Palmer, your presence in my life has had an incredible impact on my intellectual work and in my heart as you set the bar for how to do this difficult work. Nya:weh.

My move to UCLA has provided a depth of community I had not previously imagined. I especially thank Grace Hong, whose style of mentorship is exactly what I needed! My colleagues have been generous in reading and supporting my work. Sondra Hale, Beth Marchant, Sharon Traweek, Kate

Norberg, Juliet Williams, Purnima Mankekar, Chris Littleton, Aisha Finch, and Michelle Erai, I appreciate your presence in these pages. I also love the fact that there is a community of wonderful American Indian studies scholars with whom to work and extend thanks to those of you at UCLA. Particularly, I have appreciated the Settler Colonialism and Sovereignty Reading Group and would like to thank Jessica Cattelino, David Shorter, Joseph Bauerkemper, Maylei Blackwell, Keith Camacho, Pamela Grieman, Angela Riley, Joanne Barker, and Addie Rolnick. My other reading group in the wider Southern California area has helped me in numerous ways and was pivotal to my finally letting the manuscript go. I appreciate all you LOUDies for sharing knowledge, in-depth readings, camaraderie, and, most importantly, for providing a vision and space in academe that takes seriously the intersections of race, colonialism, sexuality, and gender.

Beyond the institutions of which I have been part, I have benefitted immensely from other scholars who are committed to Native American/American Indian studies. Robert Warrior was a huge help in my first years in graduate school, later as a reader for the Dickey Manuscript Review program at Dartmouth, and he continues to be so. Your successful work to develop Native studies has benefited me greatly, as I have met other Indigenous scholars from around the globe. Eric Cheyfitz provided generous feedback through the manuscript workshop and provided excellent advice for each chapter. Chapter 2 benefited greatly from Kehaulani Kaunui's input: I appreciate your advice, help, fabulous radio voice, and great taste in music. Mark Rifkin also provided a reading on my introduction and chapters through the First Peoples manuscript workshop, although he is always willing to help me through any issue that my research may raise. Andrea Smith also helped immensely in providing feedback throughout the manuscript process.

I am also fortunate to have met along the way others who have touched my work: Vince Diaz, Chris Anderson, Rick Monture, Scott Morgenson, Kimberely Robertson, Noelani Arista, Dian Million, John Bowes, Lourdes Guiterraz, Lisa Hall, and I am sure many others who have helped me to shape this book. Jennifer Nez Denetdale, you always make me laugh, and I truly admire your fierce attitude toward your work and conviction that we can change the relationship between academia and the public. Audra Simpson, my Mohawt conspirator (spelling and its implication intentional), I am sure this is just one of many projects that you will help me plow through.

Through financial, administrative, and research backing, I was fortunate to be supported by a UCLA Faculty Career Development Award, Dartmouth

Junior Faculty Fellowship, Dartmouth's Walter and Constance Burke Research Initiation Award, Susan Kelly Power and Helen Hornbeck Tanner Newberry Library Fellowship, Stanford University's Research Institute of Comparative Studies in Race and Ethnicity Graduate Dissertation Fellowship, and the Michele Clayburn Institute for Research on Women and Gender Graduate Dissertation Fellowship. This support enabled my research. The University of California Presidential Postdoctoral Fellowship deserves special thanks, as I benefit so much through the continued community of scholars that the program engenders. I also would like to thank my host department of UC Berkeley Ethnic Studies. Special thanks also go to Rosie Bermudez and Jodi Guinn, who were research assistants instrumental in prepping the manuscript. A deep gratitude goes to my neighbor, Alanna Gibbons, who helped me in a read-through of these pages.

Especially important to starting and finishing this project was my mom, Debra Jean Re, who always provided fortitude and a dose of reality to the situation when it was especially needed. You taught me to be brave. My brother, Mishuan Goeman, was always there to instigate, back me up, or provide hours of laughter. I also thank Louise Palmer Goeman for taking him off my hands, as well as being a great sister-in-law whom I have grown to love and appreciate incredibly over the years. Degan, I love you. Peter Re, thank you for your ceaseless support. I extend a very special thanks to my families, both the Goemans and the Olivers, who are too numerous to name but have provided me with much encouragement, love, and memories throughout the years.

Finally, and most importantly, all my love and gratitude go to Keith Shulsky who has given me more than I can express. Besides unquestionable love, unfaltering friendship, and limitless belief in my ability to finish or accomplish any goal, I appreciate the dinners and wine, hours of listening, fixing of all the things that needed fixing, and the amount of patience it required to go through the start of grad school, caring for two children, the constant moving across the country, and the very different institutions and geographic regions. Our life journey began in our early twenties and was solidified with our move to Stanford with nothing but our clothes and a couple boxes of books. Very shortly thereafter, our beautiful and wise daughter, Sedonna, joined us; she provides me the passion and will power to continue on this path. My son, Theo, would later supply even more hearty laughter, bright smiles, warmth, and determination to make it better. With them, the world is right. Simply, I love you all and couldn't have done this without you.

Notes

1. I will use "Native," "American Indian," "Native American," and "Indigenous" intermittently throughout depending on the context. I use "Native" when referring to those indigenous to North America and "Indigenous" to refer to indigenous people on a global scale. I use the term "American Indian" to connote people that have a tribal base in the geographical region currently known as the United States. I use "Native American" when referring to the field of Native American studies or academia in general, or in the context of someone's work who utilizes the term. "Aboriginal" and "First Nations" originate in Canada, and I will employ them when it is necessary. While the inconsistent use of terms may be confusing in places, I do believe that it is evident of how geography and identifiers are fluid, dynamic, and inconsistent, and how they mark the power of language. I have tried to be as specific as possible, but there are many intersections involved in these labels.

2. In an effort to recognize the recovery and extension of precolonial constructions of space in Native writing, I use the parentheses around "re" in "(re)mapping" to acknowledge connections to cultural concepts. While Native women continue to construct alternative mappings of space, reflected in their work is an understanding of space passed down through generations, and it is often only the presentation of spatial concepts in new formats that are contemporary formulations. Even this format, however, contains elements of the traditional.

3. Planetary consciousness is defined in Mary Louise Pratt's *Imperial Eyes: Travel Writing and Transculturation* (New York: Routledge, 1992), as "a shift that coincides with many others including the consolidation of bourgeois forms of subjectivity and power, the inauguration of a new territorial phase of capitalism propelled by searches for raw materials, the attempt to extend coastal trade inland, and national imperatives to seize overseas territory in order to prevent its being seized by rival European powers" (9).

4. Linda Tuhiwai Smith, *Decolonizing Methodologies: Research and Indigenous Peoples* (New York: St. Martin's, 1999), 28.

5. Edward Soja, *Seeking Spatial Justice* (Minneapolis: University of Minnesota Press, 2010), 1.

6. Ibid., 18.

7. The legacy of Iroquois men as ironworkers began at the turn of the century. These men were known to have worked on most of the New York skyline.

8. Doreen Massey, *For Space* (Thousand Oaks, Calif.: Sage Publications, 2005), 6–7.

9. Ibid., 11.

10. For more information regarding the 2000 census statistics and Native Americans, see "American Indian and Alaska Native Resources," *U.S. Census Bureau,* http://www.cen sus.gov/aian/. The links to maps and geographic statistics are of interest. Looking at space in the light of dislocation from reservation areas or community centers also provides a direction for discussing relationships that move back and forth from on-reservation to off-reservation that would break with notions of authenticity dictated by linear, progressive ideas of space and racial hierarchies.

11. Gloria Bird, "Breaking the Silence: Writing as Witness," in *Speaking for the Generations,* ed. Simon J. Ortiz (Tucson: University of Arizona Press, 1998), 47.

12. See Renya Ramirez, *Native Hubs: Culture Community, and Belonging in Silicon Valley and Beyond* (Durham: Duke University Press, 2007).

13. In Martin Heidegger, *Being and Time* (Oxford: Blackwell, 1962), Heidegger writes of dwelling and the idea of "being in the world." For further humanistic geographers' definitions of place, see Yi-Fu Tuan, *Topophilia: A Study of Environmental Perception, Attitudes and Values* (Englewood Cliffs, N.J.: Prentice Hall, 1974); Yi-Fu Tuan, *Space and Place: The Perspective of Experience* (Minneapolis: University of Minnesota Press, 1977); and Edward Relph, *Place and Placelessness* (London: Pion, 1976).

14. For information on Maine crime statistics that cover the era to which I refer see *The Disaster Center,* http://www.disastercenter.com/.

15. Bird, "Breaking the Silence," 44.

16. Katherine McKittrick, *Demonic Grounds: Black Women and the Cartographies of Struggle* (Minneapolis: University of Minnesota Press, 2006), 3.

17. Irene Watson, "Settled and Unsettled Spaces: Are We Free to Roam?" in *Sovereign Subjects: Indigenous Sovereignty Matters,* ed. A. Moreton-Robinson (Crows Nest, N.S.W.: Allen and Unwin, 2007), 15.

18. Michel Foucault, *Discipline and Punish: The Birth of a Prison,* trans. A. Sheridan (New York: Vintage Books, 1995).

19. Ruth Wilson Gilmore,"Fatal Coupling of Power and Difference: Notes on Racism and Geography," *The Professional Geographer* 54, no. 1 (2002): 15.

20. Ibid., 15–16.

21. Robert Warrior, *Tribal Secrets* (Minneapolis: University of Minnesota Press, 1995), 2.

22. Ibid., 114, 124.

23. Kimberlé W. Crenshaw, "Mapping the Margins: Intersectionality, Identity Politics, and Violence against Women of Color," *Stanford Law Review,* 43, no. 6 (1991): 1241–42.

24. I use "Indian policies" to refer to the policies instituted by the United States and Canada, which named them as such during much of the time period I am addressing. In the United States, "American Indian," "Alaskan Native," and "Native Hawaiian" are used by the state to address policy, while Canada uses "First Nation," "Aboriginal," and "Métis."

25. Édouard Glissant, *Caribbean Discourse: Selected Essays,* trans. Michael M. Dash (Charlottesville: University Press of Virginia, 1989).

26. See Lisa Brooks, *The Common Pot* (Minneapolis: University of Minnesota Press, 2008); Cole Harris, *Making Native Space* (Vancouver: University of British Columbia Press, 2002); and Barbara Mundy, *The Mapping of New Spain* (Chicago: University of Chicago Press, 2000).

27. Denis Cosgrove, *Mappings* (London: Reaktion Books, 1999), 1–2.

28. Ricardo Padrón, *The Spacious Word* (Chicago: University of Chicago Press, 2004), 11–12.

29. Edward Said, *Orientalism* (New York: Random House, 1978).

30. Padrón, *The Spacious Word*, 20.

31. In fact, this very idea is foundational to Federal Indian Policy that shapes the borders of and legal jurisdictions throughout Indian country. See N. Duthu Bruce, *American Indians and the Law* (New York: Viking, 2008), 82–90.

32. Ned Blackhawk, *Violence over the Land* (Cambridge, Mass.: Harvard University Press, 2008); James P. Ronda, "'A Knowledge of Distant Parts': The Shaping of the Lewis and Clark Expedition," *Montana: The Magazine of Western History* 41, no. 4 (1991): 4–19.

33. Thomas Jefferson, *The Journals of Lewis and Clark*, ed. Frank Bergen (New York: Penguin Classics, 1989), xxiv.

34. See D. W. Meinig, *The Shaping of America: A Geographical Perspective on 500 Years of History*, vol. 2, *Continental America 1800–1867* (New Haven: Yale University Press, 1993); and James Ronda et al., *Finding the West: Explorations with Lewis and Clark* (Albuquerque: University of New Mexico Press, 2006).

35. See Harris, *Making Native Space*; Pratt, *Imperial Eyes*; Sherene H. Razack, *Race, Space, and the Law: Unmaping a White Settler Society* (Toronto: Between the Lines, 2002); Edward Said, *Culture and Imperialism* (New York: Vintage Books, 1994); Smith, *Decolonizing Methodologies*; Tzvetan Todorov, *The Conquest of America* (New York: Harper Perrenial, 1984); and Robert Young, *Writing History and the West* (New York: Routledge, 1990).

36. Colin Calloway, *One Vast Winter Count: The American West before Lewis and Clark* (Lincoln: University of Nebraska Press, 2006), 33. It would be interesting in this assertion of Native people as the first "pioneers" to think about the gendered dynamics in the hypermasculine pioneer as an American origin tale in relation to Native creation stories in which women were often very empowered and powerful.

37. See Keith R. Widder, "The 1767 Maps of Robert Rogers and Jonathan Carver: A Proposal for the Establishment of the Colony of Michilimackinac," *Michigan Historical Review* 30, no. 2 (2004): 35–75. Widder provides excellent historical references in his reading of Carver's maps in particular and of the change that next editions of the map underwent as Europeans stakes dug deeper into Native soil. For instance, he speaks to "Carver's references to kingdoms and a republic" that "reflect the Indians' assumption that they, not the British or French, were sovereign over their lands and people" (73). Kingdom becomes land, republic becomes country after American independence. See G. Malcolm Lewis, "First Nations Mapmaking in the Great Lakes Region," *Michigan Historical Review* 30, no. 2 (2004): 31–34, for an analysis of a First Nations map that was enclosed in a letter to the deputy minister of Indian affairs in Ottawa, Canada. He states, "One map was of the boundary as it had been surveyed after the Robinson Treaty of 1850, and the other was a 'true map' drawn by the chief as evidence of how the tribe had been 'wronged'" (31).

38. Lewis, "First Nations Mapmaking," 6–7.

39. Cole Harris, "How Did Colonialism Dispossess: From the Edges of Empire," *Annals of the Association of American Geographers* 94, no. 1 (2004): 165–82.

40. In Canada land designated by the state as Native land is called a reserve, while in the United States it is referred to as a reservation. "Reserve/ation" is shorthand to acknowledge common methods of settler colonial displacement.

41. Harris, "How Did Colonialism Dispossess."

42. Andrea Smith, "Heteropatriarchy and the Three Pillars of White Supremacy: Rethinking Women of Color Organizing," in *Color of Violence: The Incite! Anthology*, ed. Incite! Women of Color against Violence (Boston: South End Press, 2006), 66–73.

43. Denis Cosgrove, ed., *Mappings* (London: Reaktion Books, 1999), 25.

44. Eric Bulson, *Novels, Maps, Modernity* (New York: Routledge, 2007); Padrón, *The Spacious Word*; Richard Phillips, *Mapping Men and Empire* (London: Routledge, 1997); Said, *Culture and Imperialism*; and Alan Trachtenberg, *Shades of Hiawatha* (New York: Hill and Wang, 2004).

45. See J. B. Harley, *The New Nature of Maps: Essays in the History of Cartography*, ed. Paul Laxton (Baltimore: Johns Hopkins University Press, 2001), 79.

46. Since Harley's publication, others have explored the terrain of literature and mapping as part of empire, most notably Padrón, *The Spacious Word*; Phillips, *Mapping Men and Empire*; and Said, *Culture and Imperialism*.

47. On women and the fur trade, see Nancy Shoemaker, *Negotiators of Change* (New York: Routledge, 1995); Susan Sleeper-Smith, *Indian Women and French Men: Rethinking Cultural Encounter in the Western Great Lakes* (Amherst: University of Massachusetts Press, 2001); Sylvia Van Kirk, *"Many Tender Ties": Women in Fur-Trade Society in Western Canada* (Norman: University of Oklahoma Press, 1980).

48. Marc Warhus, *Another America: Native American Maps and the History of Our Land* (New York: St. Martin's Griffin, 1997), 3.

49. Ibid., 3.

50. Brooks, *The Common Pot*.

51. Diane Schenandoah, "Mark My Words," in *Iroquois Voices, Iroquois Visions: A Celebration of Contemporary Six Nations Arts*, ed. Bertha Roger (Treadwell, N.Y.: Bright Hill Press, 1992), 100.

52. Peter J. Taylor, *Modernities: A Geohistorical Interpretation* (Minneapolis: University of Minnesota Press, 1999), 102–3.

53. See Winona La Duke, *All Our Relations: Native Struggles for Life and Land* (Cambridge, Mass.: South End Press, 1999).

54. See Derek Gregory, "Geographical Imagination," in *The Dictionary of Human Geography*, ed. D. Gregory and D. M. Smith (Oxford: Blackwell, 1994), 217.

55. Harley, *The New Nature of Maps*, 79.

56. "Map, n.1," *OED Online*, http://dictionary.oed.com.

57. Patrick Wolfe, "Settler Colonialism and the Elimination of the Native," *Journal of Genocide Research* 8, no. 4 (2006): 401.

58. See Derek Gregory, *Geographical Imaginations* (Cambridge: Blackwell, 1994), 356.

59. Brooks, *The Common Pot*.

60. Wolfe, "Settler Colonialism," 402.

61. Schenandoah, "Mark My Words," 100.

62. I use the term "spatial restructuring" because it connects various moments together rather than isolating them as separate moments unrelated in time.

63. See Henri Lefebvre, *The Production of Space*, trans. Donald Nicholson-Smith (Oxford: Oxford University Press, 1974), 285. This groundbreaking work is crucial to the unfixing of space, demonstrating the intricacies bound up in power relations. It is also a crucial text to cultural geographers who examine the power relations at work in the mapping of social, economic, and political space, many of whom are engaged throughout this text.

64. Andrea Smith, *Conquest: The Sexual Colonization of the Americas* (Boston: South End Press, 2003).

65. Robert Sack, *Human Territoriality: Its Theory and History* (Cambridge: Cambridge University Press, 1986).

66. Razack, *Race, Space, and the Law,* 3.

67. Basil Johnston's work on Manitous is helpful in understanding Anishinabeg place-making and societal constructions. Manitous are directly rooted to a geographic location, but the lessons contained in the teachings of the stories are ongoing and not rooted in time, such as Sack's premodern. See Basil Johnston, *Manitous: The Spiritual World of the Ojibwe* (New York: Harper Collins Publishers, Inc., 1995).

68. See Mishuana Goeman, "From Place to Territories and Back Again: Centering Storied Land in the Discussion of Indigenous Nation-Building," *International Journal of Critical Indigenous Studies* 1, no. 1 (2008): 23–34.

69. Walter Mignolo, *The Darker Side of the Renaissance: Literacy, Territoriality, and Colonization* (Ann Arbor: University of Michigan Press, 1995), xv.

70. Watson, "Settled and Unsettled Spaces," 20.

71. Here Scott quotes from the Epic of Gilgamesh, "I would conquer in the Cedar Forest . . . I will set my hand to it and will chop down the cedar." James Scott, *Seeing Like a State* (New Haven: Yale University Press, 1999), 13.

72. Denis Woods, *The Power of Maps* (New York: Guilford Press, 1992), 45.

73. Aileen Moreton-Robinson engages with the juxtaposition of immigrant and Indigenous belonging in the state of Australia particularly as it concerns the Mabo case, which "affirms the nation-state's sovereignty by creating in law a hybrid of settlement that diminishes but does not erase Terra Nullius." In speaking to the state's intent to diminish the ontological relationship of Indigenous people to land, Moreton-Robinson makes clear that the severing of Native belonging that derives from the relationship of Native bodies in place is necessary to the settler state that structures the legal regime to give itself a place and sense of belonging to its immigrant citizens. See Aileen Moreton-Robinson, "I Call Australia Home: Indigenous Belonging and Place in a White Postcolonizing Society," in *Uprootings/Regroundings: Questions of Home and Migration*, ed. Sara Ahmed, Claudia Castañeda, Anne-Marie Fortier, and Mimi Sheller (Oxford: Berg Publishers, 2004), 35–36.

74. Smith, *Conquest,* 15.

75. Jace Weaver. "Leslie Marmon Silko" *Leslie Marmon Silko's Ceremony: A Casebook,* ed. Allan Chavkin (New York: Oxford University Press, 2002), 213 (emphasis mine).

76. "Project Naming," Library and Archive Canada, http://www.collectionscanada.gc .ca/.

77. Phillips, *Mapping Men and Empire,* 168.

78. For a foundational example of the relationship among land, language, place, and cultural practices, see Keith Basso, *Wisdom Sits in Places* (Albuquerque: University of New Mexico Press, 1996).

1. "Remember What You Are"

1. Sharon Venne and Gail Hinge, *Indian Acts and Amendments 1868–1975: An Indexed Collection* (Saskatoon: University of Saskatchewan Native Law Centre, 1981), 107.

2. The Indian Act of 1906, for instance, defined "Indian Lands" as "any reserve or portion of a reserve which has been surrendered to the Crown." When the land did become surveyed as such, the surveys were not paid for by the Canadian government or individuals who benefited, but rather with the monies held in trust "for" Indians. The slippery act of defining land and peoples in terms of property accounts for the continuously shifting language of the law. See Venne and Hinge, *Indian Acts and Amendments*, 107–8.

3. Ethel Brant Monture, *Famous Indians: Brant, Crowfoot, Oronhyatekha* (Toronto: Clarke, Iwin, 1960).

4. Elizabeth Povinelli, *The Empire of Love: Toward a Theory of Intimacy, Genealogy, and Carnality* (Durham: Duke University Press, 2006), 17.

5. In the Indian Act, the superintendent general "shall be the sole and final judge as to the moral character." This was especially true in cases of inheritance laws. See Venne and Hinge, *Indian Acts and Amendments*, 183.

6. E. Pauline Johnson, "As It Was *in the Beginning*," in *The Moccasin Maker* (Norman: University of Oklahoma Press, 1998), 156; further citations will appear in the text.

7. See Rick Monture, "'Beneath the British Flag': Iroquois and Canadian Nationalism in the Work of Pauline Johnson and Duncan Campbell Scott," *Essays on Canadian Writing* 75 (Winter 2002): 118–41.

8. Joanne Barker, "Gender, Sovereignty, and the Discourse of Rights in Native Women's Activism," *Meridians: Feminism, Race, Transnationalism* 7, no. 1 (2006): 149.

9. Povinelli, *The Empire of Love*, 17. Also see Ivy Schweitzer, *Perfecting Friendship: Politics and Affiliation in Early American Literature* (Chapel Hill: University of North Carolina Press, 2006). While there is a distinction between love and friendship, Schweitzer's text is useful in examining the "tropes of equality and similarity" (14). By tracing the roots of Western notions of friendship, she examines the development of democracy in the settler context through the "perfecting" of friendship between women and men, cross-gender friendship, marriage, and interracial relationships between individuals and nations. She asks: "What affective or discursive force can render social and physical differences imperceptible, creating a single figuratively con/fused body as the dwelling for spiritually fused souls? To translate this into political terms, what affiliative mode can constitute 'a single corporate or juridical body, a legal fiction creating an operative unity' ..., transforming the 'many' of a diverse population into the 'one' of a collective political body?" (15).

10. Povinelli, *The Empire of Love*, 17.

11. Here I would like to emphasize that I am referring specifically to settler colonialism, as work by such scholars as Ann Stoler is instrumental in exploring intimate relationships and colonial rule. See Ann Laura Stoler, *Race and the Education of Desire: Foucault's History of Sexuality and the Colonial Order of Things* (Durham: Duke University Press, 1995).

12. Cheryl Harris, "Whiteness as Property," *Harvard Law Review* 16, no. 8 (1993): 1707–91. See also Aileen Moreton-Robinson, "Writing Off Treaties: White Possession in the United States Critical Whiteness Studies Literature," in *Transnational Whiteness Matters*, ed. A. Moreton-Robinson, M. Casey, and F. Nicoll (Plymouth: Lexington Press, 2008).

13. Venne and Hinge, *Indian Acts and Amendments*, 107–8.

14. Bonita Lawrence, *"Real" Indians and Others: Mixed-Blood Urban Native Peoples and Indigenous Nationhood* (Lincoln: University of Nebraska Press, 2004), 41.

15. Ibid.

16. Venne and Hinge, *Indian Acts and Amendments*, 26, 183.

17. See Razack, "Gendered Racial Violence and Spatialized Justice: The Murder of Pamela George," in *Race, Space, and the Law*, 121–56.

18. Report of the Royal Commission on Aboriginal Peoples, "Perspectives and Realities," vol. 4 (Ottawa: The Commission, 1996), 27.

19. See Harris, "Whiteness as Property"; Moreton-Robinson, "Writing Off Treaties."

20. Harris, "Whiteness as Property," 1724.

21. Report of the Royal Commission on Aboriginal Peoples, 1:185.

22. Quoted in ibid., 4:29.

23. Lawrence, *"Real" Indians and Others*, 32. She provides an in-depth account of enfranchisement and its current result of large urban populations.

24. Macdonald qtd. in Report of the Royal Commission on Aboriginal Peoples, 1:179.

25. Goeman, "From Place to Territories," 23–34.

26. Veronica Strong-Boag and Carole Gerson, *Paddling Her Own Canoe: The Times and Texts of E. Pauline Johnson Tekahionwake* (Toronto: University of Toronto Press, 2000), 34–35.

27. E. Pauline Johnson, "Brant: A Memorial Ode," in *E. Pauline Johnson Tekahionwake: Collected Poems and Selected Prose*, ed. Carole Gerson and Veronica Strong-Boag (Toronto: University of Toronto Press, 2002), 21.

28. R. Monture, "Beneath the British Flag," 181.

29. Ibid., 181–84.

30. Razack, "When Place Becomes Race," in *Race, Space, and the Law*, 3.

31. See Lawrence, *"Real" Indians and Others*, 49. See also Van Kirk, *"Many Tender Ties"*; Sleeper-Smith, *Indian Women and French Men*.

32. E. Pauline Johnson, "A Red Girl's Reasoning," in *The Moccasin Maker* (Norman: University of Oklahoma Press, 1998), 102; further citations will appear in the text.

33. Johnson, *E. Pauline Johnson Tekahionwake*, 203.

34. Ibid., 183.

35. Phillips, *Mapping Men and Empire*, 15.

36. Ibid., 13.

37. While the Gradual Enfranchisement Act of 1857 was voluntary and met with little participation, it was the first step in incorporating gendered morality, education, and reduction of land base. By 1869 the Indian Act came to rely on a gendered and raced identity in order to obtain and erase Native nations' claims.

38. See Razack, "Gendered Racial Violence," for an excellent analysis of the spatiality of whiteness and consequent affirmation of privileged personhood through excursions into areas outside the space of justice. She contends that the historical mapping and policing

of Indigenous people "maintain all the characteristics of the nineteenth-century colonial encounter" (191).

39. This tactic of asserting humanity is similar to the emotional pull and activist rhetoric of Sojourner Truth, whose famous question "Ain't I a woman?" promoted the humanity, and thus rights, of black women. Truth's words were well circulated within feminist circles. Strong-Boag and Gerson (*Paddling Her Own Canoe,* 216–17) also point to the common reframing and its contemporary use in Beatrice Culleton, *In Search of April Raintree* (Winnipeg: Portage and Main Press, 1999).

40. Maria Cotera, *Native Speakers: Ella Deloria, Zora Neale Hurston, Jovita Gozales and the Poetics of Culture* (Austin: University of Texas Press, 2008), 137–38.

41. J. R. Miller, *Skyscrapers Hide the Heavens: A History of Indian–White Relations in Canada* (Toronto: University of Toronto Press, 1989).

42. Glenda Laws, "Women's Life Courses: Spatial Mobility, and State Policies," in *Thresholds in Feminist Geography: Difference, Methodology, Representation,* ed. John P. Jones, Heidi J. Nast, and Susan Roberts (Lanham, Md.: Rowman and Littlefield, 1997).

43. See Judith Butler, *Gender Trouble: Feminism and the Subversion of Identity* (New York: Routledge, 1990). Butler's concentration on dress as "corporeal styles that constitute bodily significations" is useful to an extent in the context of gender impositions, morality, and settler colonialism.

44. I would like to thank Mary L. Pratt for pointing out that state is the derivative of statistics. Census data has been pivotal to spatial conceptions since the early 1900s.

45. Nancy Fraser, "Rethinking the Public Sphere: A Contribution to the Critique of Actually Existing Democracy," in *Habermas and the Public Sphere,* ed. Craig Calhoun (Cambridge, Mass.: MIT Press, 1997), 109–42.

46. Anne McClintock, *Imperial Leather: Race, Gender, and Sexuality in the Colonial Contest* (New York: Routledge, 1995), 241.

47. Ibid., 45.

48. See Smith, *Conquest.*

49. Barker, "Gender, Sovereignty, and the Discourse," 149.

50. Povinelli, *The Empire of Love,* 197.

51. Ibid., 197.

52. See Harris, "Whiteness as Property"; and Aileen Moreton-Robinson, "The House That Jack Built: Britishness and White Possession," *Australian Critical Race and Whiteness Studies Association Journal* 1 (2005): 21–29.

53. Strong-Boag and Gerson, *Paddling Her Own Canoe,* 44.

54. Ibid., 21.

55. Ibid., 44.

56. Robert K. Thomas and Tom Holmes define "peoplehood" as the interrelating four factors: language, sacred history, religion, and land. Others, such as Vine Deloria Jr., have artfully wrestled with the term "Nation" to part from a statist definition; see Vine Deloria Jr., *Custer Died for Your Sins* (Norman: University of Oklahoma Press, [1969] 1988); Vine Deloria Jr., *God Is Red* (New York: Gosset and Dunlap, 1973); Francis Jennings, *The Invasion of America: Indians, Colonialism, and the Cant of Conquest* (Chapel Hill: University of North Carolina Press, 1975); David E. Wilkins, *American Indian Sovereignty and the United States Supreme Court: The Masking of Justice* (Austin: University of Texas Press,

1997). Still others disregard the concept of a nation based on forms of state sovereignty, which they see as unable to escape its European articulations; see Alfred Taiaiake, *Peace, Power and Righteousness: An Indigenous Manifesto* (Don Mills, Ont.: Oxford University Press, 1999); Jeff Corntassell, *Forced Federalism: Contemporary Challenges to Indigenous Nationhood* (Norman: University of Oklahoma Press, 2008); and Robert A. Williams Jr., *Like a Loaded Weapon: The Rehnquist Court, Indian Rights, and the Legal History of Racism in America* (Minneapolis: University of Minnesota Press, 2005).

57. For more information on the legal rights of Native women in Native communities compared to those of Anglo society, see Johnson's nonfiction article, aptly named "The Stings of Civilization." She elaborates on her stance that "more civilized" is a step back for most Native women. See E. Pauline Johnson, "The Strings of Civilization," in *E. Pauline Johnson Tekahionwake*, 283–88.

58. Karen Piper, *Cartographic Fictions: Maps, Race, and Identity* (New Brunswick: Rutgers University Press, 2002), 9.

59. See Bruce McLeod, *The Geography of Empire in English Literature, 1580–1745* (Cambridge: Cambridge University Press, 1999), for an early history of the ties between British geography and literature in the production of empire in the transatlantic world.

60. Ibid., 6.

61. Lauren Berlant, "Intimacy: A Special Issue," in *Intimacy* (Chicago: University of Chicago Press, 2000), 285–86.

62. See Audra Simpson, "Captivating Eunice: Membership, Colonialism, and Gendered Citizenships of Grief," *Wicazo Sa Review* 24, no. 2 (2009): 105–29.

63. For an in-depth discussion of the impact of bill C-31 see Audra Simpson, "Paths toward a Mohawk Nation: Narratives of Citizenship and Nationhood in Kahnawake," in *Political Theory and the Rights of Indigenous Peoples*, ed. D. Ivison, P. Patton, and W. Sanders (Cambridge: Cambridge University Press and Status of Women of Canada, 2000), 113–36; and *Aboriginal Women's Roundtable on Gender Equality* (Ottawa: Status of Women of Canada, 2000).

64. See Sarah Carter, *The Importance of Being Monogamous: Marriage and Nation Building in Western Canada to 1915* (Edmonton: University of Alberta Press; Athabasca: Athabasca University Press, 2008); Karlen Faith, Mary Gottriedson, Cherry Joe, Wendy Leonard, and Sharon MacIvor, "Native Women in Canada: A Quest for Justice," *Social Justice* 17, no. 3, (1990): 167–89; and Wendy Moss, *History of Discriminatory Laws Affecting Aboriginal People* (Ottawa: Library of Parliament Research Branch, 1987), 1–29.

65. See Cari M. Carpenter, *Seeing Red: Anger, Sentimentality, and American Indians* (Columbus: Ohio State University Press, 2008); Franca Iacovetta, "Gendering Trans/National Historiographies: Feminists Rewriting Canadian History," *Journal of Women's History* 19, no. 1 (2007): 206–13; Margo Lukens, "'A Being of a New World:' The Ambiguity of Mixed Blood in Pauline Johnson's 'My Mother,'" *MELUS* 27, no. 3 (2002): 43–56; Cecilia Morgan, "Private Lives and Public Performances: Aboriginal Women in a Settler Society, Ontario, Canada, 1920s–1960s," *Journal of Colonialism and Colonial History* 4, no. 3 (2003): 125–27; and Sylvia Van Kirk, "From 'Marrying-In' to 'Marrying-Out': Changing Patterns of Aboriginal/Non-Aboriginal Marriage in Colonial Canada," *Frontiers* 23, no. 3 (2002): 1–11; and A. LaVonne Brown Ruoff, "Justice for Indians and Women: The Protest Fiction of Alice Callahan and Pauline Johnson," *World Literature Today* 66, no. 2 (1992): 249–55.

2. (Re)routing Native Mobility, Uprooting Settler Spaces

1. Philip J. Deloria, *Indians in Unexpected Places* (Lawrence: University of Kansas Press, 2004), 27.

2. Cognitive mapping in this instance refers to Cosgrove, *Mappings*, 7.

3. Donna Landry and Gerald MacLean, *Material Feminisms* (Oxford: Blackwell Press, 1993), 12.

4. For an historical account of the frontier and the rise of American individualism, see the groundbreaking work Richard Slotkin, *Regeneration through Violence: The Mythology of the American Frontier 1600–1860* (Middleton: Wesleyan University Press, 1973).

5. Charles Wilkinson, *Blood Struggle: The Rise of Modern Indian Nations* (New York: W. W. Norton, 2005), 57; Donald L. Fixico, *Termination and Relocation: Federal Indian Policy, 1945–1960* (Albuquerque: University of New Mexico Press, 1986), 183.

6. Jodi Kim, *Ends of Empire: Asian American Critique and the Cold War* (Minneapolis, University of Minnesota Press, 2010), 3.

7. Ibid., 4.

8. Ibid., 23.

9. See Setsu Shigematsu and Keith L. Camacho, eds, *Militarized Currents: Toward a Decolonized Future in Asia and the Pacific* (Minneapolis: University of Minnesota Press, 2010); and Vince Diaz, *Repositioning the Missionary: Rewriting the Histories of Colonialism, Native Catholicism, and Indigeneity in Guam* (Honolulu: University of Hawai'i Press, 2010).

10. John R. Finger, *Cherokee Americans: The Eastern Band of Cherokees in the Twentieth Century* (Lincoln: University of Nebraska Press, 1991), 89–120.

11. While head of household could be a woman, as designated recipients of property, this was rare. The mechanism for this occurring was still through notions of patrilineal inheritance and property laws—such as a widowed woman being named head of household. Even when a woman may be designated as head of household, upon marriage her property would transfer.

12. Kevin Bruyneel, *Third Space of Sovereignty* (Minneapolis: University of Minnesota Press, 2007), 126.

13. Ibid., 129.

14. To emphasize, however, the language of sovereign nations had long been used before this time. For instance, Deskaheh (1872–1925) in 1923 petitioned the League of Nations to influence Canada's atrocious policies toward Indigenous peoples, and though he did not succeed, his work carried on in important ways, resulting in the passage of the albeit controversial UN Rights of Indigenous Peoples Declaration. For Deskaheh's speech, see Chief Deskaheh, *Petition to the League of Nations from the Six Nations of the Grand River.* Communicated by the Government of the Netherlands, C.500.1923.VII, 3 (August 7, 1923); and for an analysis of the pros and cons of this discourse, see Jeff Corntassel, "Toward a Sustainable Self-Determination: Rethinking the Contemporary Indigenous-Rights Discourse," *Alternatives* 33 (2008): 105–32.

15. See "The American Indian and Alaska Native Population," *U.S. Census Bureau, 2010 Census Redistricting Data (Public Law 94-171)* Summary File, Table P1.

16. Esther Belin, *From the Belly of My Beauty* (Tucson: University of Arizona Press, 1999), 68; further citations will appear in the text.

17. John A. Price, "The Migration and Adaptation of American Indians to Los Angeles," *Human Organization* 27, no. 2 (1968): 168–75.

18. See K. Tsianina Lomawaima, *"They Called It Prairie Light": Oral Histories from Chilocco Indian Agricultural Boarding School* (Lincoln: University of Nebraska Press, 1994).

19. For further information on the federal relocation program and related history, see Larry W. Burt, *Tribalism in Crisis: Federal Indian Policy, 1953–1961* (Albuquerque: University of New Mexico Press, 1982); Fixico, *Termination and Relocation;* and Kenneth R. Philip, *Termination Revisited: American Indians on the Trail to Self-Determination, 1933–1953* (Lincoln: University of Nebraska Press, 1999).

20. Jack O. Waddell and Michael Waddell, *The American Indian in Urban Society* (Boston: Little, Brown, and Co., 1971).

21. H.Res. 108, 83rd Cong., 1st Sess., 67 Stat. B132 (1953).

22. Edward W. Soja, *Postmodern Geographies: The Reassertion of Space in Critical Social Theory* (New York: Verso, 1989), 112.

23. For information on the Los Angeles Indian population, demographics, and making of the "Indian Community of Los Angeles" see Joan Weibel-Orlando, *Indian Country L.A.* (Urbana: University of Illinois Press, 1991).

24. Glen Emmons, "Bureau of Indian Affairs," *1954 Annual Report,* ed. Douglas McKay (Washington: U.S. Government Printing Office, 1976), 227.

25. James B. LaGrand, *Indian Metropolis: Native Americans in Chicago, 1945–1975* (Urbana: University of Illinois Press, 2002), 48–49.

26. See Genevieve Chato and Christine Conte, "Legal Rights of American Indian Women," in *Western Women: Their Land, Their Lives,* ed. Lillian Schlissel, Vicki L. Ruiz, and Janice Monk (Albuquerque: University of New Mexico Press, 1988), 229–46; and Tressa Berman, *Circle of Goods: Women, Work, and Welfare in a Reservation Community* (New York: State University of New York Press, 2003).

27. Bureau of Indian Affairs Relocation Records in Edward E. Ayer Manuscript Collection, Newberry Library, Chicago.

28. Carole Goldberg-Ambrose, *Planting Tail Feathers: Tribal Survival and Public Law 280* (Los Angeles: American Indian Studies Center, 1997), 50.

29. Timothy J. Droske, "The New Battleground for Public Law 280 Jurisdiction: Sex Offender Registration in Indian Country," *Northwestern University Law Review* 101, no. 2 (2007): 898.

30. See Goldberg-Ambrose, *Planting Tail Feathers,* for an in-depth study of Public Law 280, specifically as it played out in the state of California.

31. This is particularly the case with sexual assault on reservations. See Amnesty International's important assessment *Maze of Injustice: The Failure to Protect Indigenous Women from Sexual Violence in the USA* (New York: Amnesty International USA, 2007). The recently enacted Tribal Law and Order Act also contains major issues because it relies on the very spatialities I am talking about throughout this project. For an in-depth look at the issues, see Kimberly Robertson, "Righting the Historical Record: Violence against Native Women and the South Dakota Coalition against Violence and Sexual Assault," *Wicazo Sa Review* 27, no. 2 (2012): 21–47.

32. Nicholas Blomley, "Law, Property, and the Geography of Violence: The Frontier, the Survey, and the Grid," *Annals of the Association of American Geographers* 93, no. 1 (2003): 121–41.

33. See Valerie Lambert, "Political Protest, Conflict, and Tribal Nationalism: The Oklahoma Choctows and the Termination Crisis of 1959–1970," *American Indian Quarterly* 31, no. 2 (2007): 283–309, for a particular account of how termination was discussed in one reservation community as not giving up political rights and ending tribal life, but rather as a form of creating new economies and growth.

34. See, e.g., Susan Hardy Aiken, Ann Brigham, Sallie A. Marston, and Penny Waterstone, eds., *Making Worlds: Gender, Metaphor and Materiality* (Tucson: University of Arizona Press, 1998); Mona Domosh and Joni Seager, *Putting Women in Place: Feminist Geographers Make Sense of the World* (New York: Guilford Press, 2001); and Linda McDowell and Joanne P. Sharp, *Space, Gender and Knowledge: Feminist Readings* (London: Edward Arnold, 1997).

35. Doreen Massey, *Space, Place, and Gender* (Minneapolis: University of Minnesota Press, 1994), 166.

36. Gillian Rose, *Feminism and Geography: The Limits of Geographical Knowledge* (Minneapolis: University of Minnesota Press, 1993).

37. See Smith *Conquest,* 7–33.

38. Berman, *Circle of Goods,* 120.

39. Massey, *Space, Place, and Gender,* 166.

40. Elided in this are ways that some, Ella Deloria for instance, both traveled and sought to document the Dakota tradition for future generations. See Cotera, *Native Speakers.* Jace Weaver is one critic whose assessment of the field was instrumental to upsetting this binary notion. Weaver holds that the common trait that traditionalists and progressives held was their commitment to their community, though these groups imagined survival differently. This dichotomy has elided complex historical and social implications, as well as causing exclusion from a "Native American Literary Canon." Literary critics such as Robert Warrior, Jace Weaver, Bernd Peyer, A. LaVonne Brown Ruoff, Cheryl Walker, and others have revived early writers and looked at their works in new and complex ways, especially concerning race and nation.

41. Susan Lobo, "Urban Clanmothers: Key Households in Cities," *American Indian Quarterly* 27, nos. 3–4 (2003): 505–22.

42. Ramirez, *Native Hubs,* 58. Ramirez credits the word "hub" to Laverne Roberts, but throughout her book does an excellent job at exploring how the hubs in urban areas have incredible "potential to support political change" across Indian country (2).

43. Myla Carpio, *Indigenous Albuquerque* (Lubbock: Texas Tech University Press, 2011).

44. Interview with Floria Forcia, Chicago American Indian Oral History Project, 1982, Newberry Library and NAES (Native American Education Services) College Library, Chicago (emphasis mine).

45. Trudy Griffin-Pierce, *Earth Is My Mother, Sky Is My Father* (Albuquerque: University of New Mexico Press, 1992), 72.

46. Ibid.

47. María Josefina Saldaña-Portillo, *The Revolutionary Imagination in the Americas and the Age of Development* (Durham: Duke University Press, 2003), 7.

48. Ibid.

49. Ibid., 27.

50. Ibid., 7.

51. Gerald Vizenor, "Shadow Survivance," in *Manifest Manners: Narratives on Post-indian Survivance* (Lincoln: University of Nebraska Press, 1999), 63–106. Vizenor's work is very useful in discussing the way spatial simulations of the real operate, such as the rez or borders. Play with language, tribal stories, imagination, and communal memory are necessary to escape the trap of colonialism as "tragic figures" and "terminal creeds."

52. David Murray, "Crossblood Strategies in the Writings of Gerald Vizenor," *Yearbook of English Studies* 24 (1994): 213–27.

53. See Carpio, *Indigenous Albuquerque,* for a comprehensive look at the ways that the termination and relocation policies during this era continue to influence the way that urban Indian communities are handled in relation to employment, healthcare, education, welfare, etc.

54. Luci Tapahonso's poem "This Is How They Were Placed for Us," in *Blue Horses Rush In: Poems and Stories* (Tucson: University of Arizona Press, 1997), 39–42, also uses the four directions, moving from east to west. The poems are linked by the importance of the mountains to place both women, who experience different geographical, historical, and generational subjectivities.

55. Clara Sue Kidwell and Alan Velie, *Native American Studies* (Lincoln: University of Nebraska Press, 2005), 83.

56. Washington Matthews, *Navajo Legends* (Salt Lake City: University of Utah Press, 1994), 71.

57. Klara B. Kelly and Francis Harris, *Navajo Sacred Places* (Bloomington: Indiana University Press, 1994), 20.

58. Maureen Trudelle Schwarz, *Molded in the Image of Changing Woman: Navajo Views on the Human Body and Personhood* (Tucson: University of Arizona Press, 1997), 21–23.

59. Susan J. Scarberry, "Land into Flesh: Images of Intimacy," *Frontiers: A Journal of Women's Studies* 6, no. 3 (1981): 26.

60. Ibid., 25.

61. Paul G. Zolbrod, *Diné bahane': The Navajo Creation Story* (Albuquerque: University of New Mexico Press, 1984).

62. James McNeley, "The Pattern Which Connects Navajo and Western Learning," Paper presented at the seventh annual Navajo Studies Conference, Tsaile, Arizona, October 7, 1993, qtd. in Schwarz, *Molded In the Image of Changing Woman.* 78.

63. Ursula K. Heise, "Ecocriticism and the Transnational Turn in American Studies," *American Literary History* 20, nos. 1–2 (2008): 384–85.

64. Warhus, *Another America,* 3.

65. Jeff Berglund, "'Planting the Seeds of Revolution': An Interview with Poet Esther Belin," *Studies in American Indian Literature* 17, no. 1 (2005): 64.

66. Lloyd Lee, "Reclaiming Indigenous Intellectual, Political, and Geographic Space," *American Indian Quarterly* 32, no. 1 (2008): 101.

67. Faye Lone-Knapp, "Rez Talk: How Reservation Residents Describe Themselves," *American Indian Quarterly* 24, no. 4 (2000): 640.

3. From the Stomp Grounds on Up

1. Joy Harjo, *A Map to the Next World: Poetry and Tales* (New York: W. W. Norton, 2000), 135.

2. Linda McDowell, *Gender, Identity, and Place: Understanding Feminist Geographies* (Minneapolis: University of Minnesota Press, 1999), 34.

3. Azfar Hussain, "Joy Harjo and Her Poetics as Praxis: A "Post-colonial" Political Economy of the Body, Land, Labor, and Language," *Wicazo Sa Review* 15, no. 2 (2000): 29.

4. Ibid., 35.

5. Yi-Fu Tuan, "Language and the Making of Place: A Narrative-Descriptive Approach," *Annals of the Association of American Geographers* 81, no. 4 (1991): 685.

6. Joy Harjo, *The Woman Who Fell from the Sky* (New York: W. W. Norton, 1996).

7. The United States at the turn of the century set about creating a Federal Indian Bureau that, instead of dealing with Native people on a Nation to Nation basis, sought to homogenize Native people under the racial rubric of "Indian." Native people have dealt with the repercussions of federal legislation, scholarship, and society in which the dominant image of one kind of Indian exists, and it is loosely based on Plains culture. Maintaining cultural specificity while collaborating with many "Indian" communities takes skills that are learned over decades and with the many failures and successes that come with this experience.

8. Craig S. Womack, *Red on Red: Native American Literary Separatism* (Minneapolis: University of Minnesota Press, 1999), 26.

9. Mishuana Goeman, "Tools of a Cartographic Poet: Joy Harjo's Poetry and the (Re)-mapping of Settler Colonial Geographies," *Settler Colonial Studies* 2, no. 2 (2012): 69–88.

10. Domosh and Seager, *Putting Women in Place,* 112.

11. For a full account of the history and geographical nature of this shift, see Ruth Wilson Gilmore's *The Golden Gulag: Surplus, Crisis, and Opposition in Globalizing California* (Berkeley: University of California Press, 2007). In it, she examines the rise of the prison industry in relation to neoliberalism and those deemed surplus populations.

12. Grace Hong, *The Ruptures of American Capital: Women of Color Feminism and the Culture of Immigrant Labor* (Minneapolis: University of Minnesota Press, 2006), xii.

13. In fact, in her acknowledgments to *In Mad Love and War* (Hanover, N.H.: Wesleyan University Press, 1990), Joy Harjo references Audre Lorde and Leslie Marmon Silko, while Adrienne Rich provides a blurb for the back flap. These women were instrumental in using their writings to push forth activist agendas that account for the multiple-layered experiences of a subjectivity layered with gender, race, class, sexuality, and colonial experiences.

14. Harjo, *In Mad Love and War,* 9–10; further citations will appear in the text.

15. Audre Lorde, "Poetry Is Not a Luxury," *Sister Outsider: Essays and Speeches* (Berkeley, Calif.: Crossing Press, 1984), 38–39.

16. Joy Harjo and Gloria Bird, eds. *Reinventing the Enemy's Language* (New York: W. W. Norton, 1998), 1.

17. Womack, *Red on Red,* 240.

18. Watson, "Settled and Unsettled Spaces," 15.

19. See Robert Warrior, "Your Skin Is the Map: The Theoretical Challenge of Joy Harjo's Erotic Poetics," in *Reasoning Together: The Native Critics Collective,* ed. Janice Acoose et al. (Norman: University of Oklahoma Press, 2008), 345.

20. While speaking to black inclusion as lip service or omission in multiculturalism rather than a restructuring of systems, see Patricia Hill Collins, *Black Feminist Thought: Knowledge, Consciousness, and the Politics of Empowerment* (London: Routledge, 2000); and Lorde, *Sister Outsider;.* these texts offer useful insights into how multiculturalism in the

context of Native people is fraught with issues that do not recognize the political realities of the everyday.

21. Laura Coltelli, *Winged Words: American Indian Writers Speak* (Lincoln: University of Nebraska Press, 1990), 57.

22. Joy Harjo, *How We Became Human* (New York: W.W. Norton, 2002), 141; further citations will appear in the text.

23. Walter D. Mignolo, *Local Histories/Global Designs: Coloniality, Subaltern Knowledges, and Border Thinking* (Princeton: Princeton University Press, 2000), 21.

24. Gregory, "Geographical Imagination," 7.

25. Mignolo, *Local Histories*, 22.

26. Ibid.

27. Harjo, *Map to the Next World*, 39.

28. While minority status is being considered in globalization studies, I would like to point out the difference in dealing with an Indigenous group that often has legal claims to land and resources. Certainly this is true in the case of First Nations people in Canada, the Inuit, many American Indian nations, the Maori of New Zealand, and Aborigines of Australia, to name a few. While these legal issues are not ideal and are often points of contention between governments, they do exist and define the politics of globalization in a different manner than looking at minority status within a nation-state.

29. Geraldine Pratt delves into the importance of examining the spatial metaphors we use to depict the connections between production of space and inequalities in "Geographic Metaphors in Feminist Theory," in Aiken et al., *Making Worlds*, 13–30.

30. Henri Lefebvre, *The Production of Space* (Malden, Mass: Blackwell, 1991), examines how humans influence the way that space is conceived of ideologically, as well as how it is used, and how this produces an effect on the way we conceive of ourselves and each other.

31. Massey, *Space, Place, and Gender*.

32. Soja, *Postmodern Geographies*, 6.

33. Tyron P. Woods, "Globalizing Social Violence: Race, Gender, and the Spatial Politics of Crisis," *American Studies* 43, no. 1 (2002): 125.

34. Ibid, 127.

35. While the 2002 United States Census recognized that over 60 percent of American Indians in fact reside in urban areas, social constructions of race and a culture that imagines Indians as dead or living in remote areas of the Southwest completely erase them from urban landscapes. Susan Lobo and Kurt Peters, *American Indians and the Urban Experience* (Walnut Creek, Calif.: Altamira Press, 2001), is an excellent collection of essays that speaks to the historical, contemporary, and personal presence of Indians in various U.S. major cities.

36. Although not discussed in this chapter, the opening up of the U.S.–Mexico border in the 1992 NAFTA Act under the rhetoric of free trade is just one example of how Native communities' rights were jeopardized. This will be discussed in the next chapter.

37. Frederick Jameson and Misao Miyoshi, eds., *The Cultures of Globalization* (Durham: Duke University Press, 1998), 18.

38. Harjo played in the band Poetic Justice and has released several CDs that combine her poetry and music.

39. Harjo, *The Woman*, 52; further citations will appear in the text.

40. Smith, "Heteropatriarchy and the Three Pillars of White Supremacy."

41. Womack, *Red on Red*, 238.

42. For more information on the importance of dance and American Indian history, see David Whitehorse, *Pow-wow, The Contemporary Pan-Indian Celebration* (San Diego: Dept. of American Indian Studies, San Diego State University, 1988).

43. While I do not have the space to address it within this chapter, performance theory offers useful insights into the importance of dance in creating relationships, sustaining memory, and political protest. See David Delegado Shorter, *We Will Dance Our Truth: Yacqui History in Yoeme Performances* (Lincoln: University of Nebraska Press, 2009); Mark Franco, *Dancing Modernism/Performing Politics* (Bloomington: Indiana University Press, 1993); and Randy Martin, *Critical Moves: Dance Studies in Theory and Politics* (Durham: Duke University Press, 1998).

44. Leslie Marmon Silko, *Almanac of the Dead* (New York: Simon & Schuster, 1991), 578.

45. Elizabeth Deloughrey, "Heliotropes: Solar Ecologies and Pacific Radiations," in *Postcolonial Ecologies: Literatures of the Environment*, ed. E. Deloughrey and G. B. Handley (Oxford: Oxford University Press, 2011), 237.

46. It would be too vast a task to name all the writers who use myth, story, and narrative to "return" home, but some of the important authors are Louise Erdrich, Scott Momaday, Elizabeth Woody, Luci Tapahonso, Gerald Vizenor, Beth Brant, Simon J. Ortiz, Ofelia Zepeda, Esther G. Belin, and Victor D. Montejo. Harjo has always had a concern with the return home, and Womack postulates that her poetry increasingly makes strides toward this imaginative homecoming. See Womack, *Red on Red*, 224.

47. William Bevis, "Native American Novels: Homing In," in *Recovering the Word*, ed. Brian Swann and Arnold Krupat (Berkeley: University of California Press, 1987), 580–620.

48. Ibid., 602.

49. Domosh and Seager, *Putting Women in Place*, 99, 98.

50. Harjo and Gloria Bird edited a volume of contemporary Native women's poetry under this title. In the introduction Harjo speaks of differences as well as influences we have on each other: "As we read stories and poems to each other, we were excited to discover the many similarities in our work. Native women in the Americas share similar concerns based on community. . . . We too appreciated the differences between us, and recognized that though differences may sometimes be difficult (which can include old tribal enmities and divergent customs) these were to be appreciated, for our differences add dimension to any knowledge." See Harjo and Bird, *Reinventing the Enemy's Language*, 23.

51. Holly Youngbear-Tibbetts, "Making Sense of the World," in Aiken et al., *Making Worlds*, 42.

4. "Someday a Story Will Come"

1. Ella Shohot and Robert Stam write of absence as "an ambivalently repressive mechanism [that] dispels the anxiety in the face of the Indian, whose very presence is a reminder of the initially precarious grounding of the American nation-state itself. . . . In a temporal paradox, living Indians were introduced to 'play dead,' as it were, in order to perform a narrative of manifest destiny in which their role, ultimately, was to disappear." See Ella Shohat and Robert Stam, *Unthinking Eurocentrism* (London: Routledge, 1994), 118–19.

2. Matthew Sparke, "Political Geography: Political Geographies of Globalization III—Resistance," *Progress in Human Geography* 32, no. 3 (2008): 423–40.

3. In Janet St. Clair, "Death of Love/Love of Death: Leslie Marmon Silko's *Almanac of the Dead*," *MELUS* 21, no. 2 (1996): 141–56, St. Clair writes of the homophobic tone and misogyny within *Almanac of the Dead*, arguing that in many ways it replicates the egocentrism and individualism of Western liberal tradition and its devastating consequences.

4. bell hooks, *Belonging: A Culture of Place* (New York: Routledge, 2009), 122. For a further critique of aesthetics in the text, see Sharon Patricia Holland's work with the grotesque, *Raising the Dead: Readings of Death and (Black) Subjectivity* (Durham: Duke University Press, 2000).

5. Silko, *Almanac of the Dead*, 129; further citations will appear in the text.

6. Peter Eisenstadt, "Almanacs and the Disenchantment of America," *Pennsylvania History* 65, no. 2 (1998): 147.

7. Leslie Marmon Silko, *Storyteller* (New York: Seaver Books, 1981).

8. Quoted in Carren Irr, "The Timliness of *Almanac of the Dead*, or a Postmodern Rewriting of Radical Fiction," in *Leslie Marmon Silko*, ed. Louise Barnett and James Thorson (Albuquerque: University of New Mexico Press, 2001), 223–26. She continues a worthy critique of the premises and assumptions upon which Birkerts relies by exploring developing concepts of time in American society and literature.

9. Eric Cheyfitz, "The (Post)Colonial Predicament of Indian Country: U.S. American Indian Literature and Federal Indian Law," *Interventions: International Journal of Postcolonial Studies* 4, no. 3 (2002): 420. Huhndorf, however, decides ultimately that she is interested largely in the question of the "tensions and contradictions between nationalism and transnationalism." See Shari Huhndorf, *Mapping the Americas* (Ithaca: Cornell University Press, 2009), 143.

10. Huhndorf, *Mapping the Americas* 161.

11. Rachel Adams, *Continental Divides: Remapping the Cultures of North America* (Chicago: University of Chicago Press, 2010), 9.

12. See, for instance, Eric Wolfe, *Europe and the People without History* (Berkeley: University of California Press, 1982), who presents a world that is connected and mobile, rather than contained and static.

13. Sparke, "Political Geography," 16.

14. Ibid.

15. See Padrón, *The Spacious Word*, 21.

16. Warhus, *Another America*, 4.

17. Cosgrove, *Mappings*, 3.

18. Ibid., 2.

19. Scott Michaelsen and David E. Johnson, eds., *Border Theory: The Limits of Cultural Politics* (Minneapolis: University of Minnesota Press, 1997), 15.

20. Harley, *The New Nature of Maps*, 112.

21. Ibid, 113.

22. Laura Cotelli, *Winged Words: American Indian Writers Speak* (Lincoln: University of Nebraska Press, 1990), 119.

23. Warhus, *Another America*, 37–43.

24. Ibid., 43.

25. Ibid., 8.

26. Padrón, *The Spacious Word*, 21.

27. Soja, *Seeking Spatial Justice*, 6.

28. Mignolo, *The Darker Side of the Renaissance*, 216.

29. For an in-depth analysis of the etymology of "almanac" and its relationship to the Mayan Codices, see Paul Beekman Taylor, "Silko's Reappropriation of Secrecy," in *Leslie Marmon Silko* ed. Louise Barnett and James Thorson (Albuquerque: University of New Mexico Press, 2001), 23–62.

30. Allison Chapman, "Marking Time: Astrology, Almanacs, and English Protestantism," *Renaissance Quarterly* 60, no. 4 (2007): 1257–90.

31. Arlen Large, "How Far West Am I? The Almanac as an Explorer's Yardstick," *Great Plains Quarterly* 13 (Spring 1993): 117.

32. Patrick Spero, "The Revolution in Popular Publications: The Almanac and *New England Primer*, 1750–1800," *Early American Studies* 8, no. 1 (2010): 44.

33. Ibid., 55 (emphasis mine).

34. Ibid., 56.

35. Ibid.

36. Robert J. Miller and Elizabeth Furse, *Native America, Discovered and Conquered: Thomas Jefferson, Lewis and Clark, and Manifest Destiny* (Lincoln: University of Nebraska Press, 2008), 11, 15.

37. Joanne Barker, "For Whom Sovereignty Matters," in *Sovereignty Matters*, ed. Joanne Barker (Lincoln: University of Nebraska Press, 2005), 6.

38. Michael Garibaldo Hall, *The Last American Puritan: The Life of Increase Mather* (Middletown: Wesleyan University Press, 1988), 131–40.

39. Eisenstadt, "Almanacs and the Disenchantment," 158.

40. William Pencak, "Politics and Ideology in Poor Richard's Almanack," *Pennsylvania Magazine of History and Biography* 100, no. 2 (1992): 210–11.

41. Christopher Columbus, "Narrative of the Third Voyage," in *The Four Voyages of Christopher Columbus*, trans. J. M. Cohen, (New York: Penguin, 1969), 220–22.

42. Bartolomé De Las Casas, *The Devastation of the Indies: A Brief Account*, ed. Bill M. Donovan (Baltimore: Johns Hopkins University Press, 1992), 117.

43. Quoted in Pencak, "Politics and Ideology," 205.

44. Quoted in Paul Hutton, "'Going to Congress and Making Allmynacks Is My Trade:' Davy Crocket, His Almanacs, and the Evolution of a Frontier Legend," *Journal of the West* 37, no. 2 (1998): 20.

45. Ibid., 20. Hutton's close look at the Davy Crockett almanacs are particularly interesting in the context of raising dead voices. They were so popular that they continued after Crockett's death. In fact, his legend grew immensely as the almanac writers "invented a hard-edged hero for the masses, the popular audience that at first parodied but soon eclipsed Cooper's romanticized Leatherstocking as the frontier ideal" (20).

46. Ibid.

47. Smith, *Conquest*, 12.

48. The analysis of Johannes Fabian, *Time and the Other: How Anthropology Makes Its Object* (New York: Columbia University Press, 1983), is useful in discussing how the Native is written out of history. As a thorough discussion of time and its relationship to cultural

production, it sheds light on the crucial conception of time (influenced by the terms of Enlightenment) coinciding with travel and social evolution that creates a chronological history excluding the Native from "true knowledge" of meaningful society. In this universalizing project, the Native is "mapped" out of spaces now occupied by the "more evolved" colonizer. Time and space exclude the other or what is deemed pagan.

49. See Goeman, "From Place to Territories," 23–34.

50. For a more in-depth analysis of this, see ibid.

51. Patrick Spero's examination of early print culture, especially woodcuts, which were used for the first educational primer in the colonies, recalls writing as potential revolution and way to form new identities. He states: "*The New England Primer* became the primary text through which North American children, especially those in living in the Northeast, learned to read" ("The Revolution in Popular Publications," 68). The primers would also reflect various changes in political pressures and religious doctrine at the local level. Teaching children to learn and read the signs and indoctrinating them as colonial citizens depended on these educational modes. While a majority of primers rested on biblical sayings, two of the letters, O and K, in the original colonial primer carried with them overt political messages of divine monarchy and rule of England. Thus, after the Revolutionary War, changing the letters to reflect a new liberal democracy proved to be a conundrum for the printers because of the material reality of the woodcuts, which were not as malleable as the almanacs. Spero states, "Just as printers reshaped the interpretation of the civil war in the almanac's historic calendar, they refashioned the meaning of these letters to meet the ideological demands of the new nation" (70). It was not an easy task to transform the picture of the king embedded into the woodcut into the new forms of democracy in woodcuts. The K, however, maintained its image, but the original rhyme, "King Charles the Good / No man of Blood" became "A King *should* be good / No man of blood" (70–71). In positing the role of the woodcut letters alongside the Mayan Codices that are vital to the almanac in the story, we begin to see the correlation between writing forms as political apparatuses. The assumed permanency and natal origins of the United States are also vexed in this moment of juxtaposition. Just as these primers used the visual and the narrative to map out their place in the Americas, we see Yoeme attempting to use old forms of literacy to uproot her granddaughters from these colonial orderings by teaching them how to read the signs around them.

52. Mignolo, *The Darker Side of the Renaissance*, 216.

53. Ellen Arnold, "The World Made Visible: Leslie Marmon Silko's *Almanac of the Dead*," in *American Indian Rhetorics of Survivance: Word Medicine, Word Magic*, ed. Ernest Stromberg (Pittsburgh: University of Pittsburgh Press, 2006), 225.

54. Ibid.

55. Todorov, *The Conquest of America*, 175.

56. Peter Van Der Veer, "The Victim's Tale: Memory and Forgetting in the Story of Violence," in *Violence, Identity, and Self-Determination*, ed. Hent de Vries and Samuel Weber (Palo Alto: Stanford University Press, 1997), 186–87.

57. Ibid., 199.

58. For a more in-depth history of the violence, Shorter, *We Will Dance Our Truths*, provides an excellent history of Yaqui encounters and unique method of converging dominant histories and the history from Yaqui oral history. For a broader focus on violence in

these border histories, see Nicole M. Guidoti-Hernandez, *Unspeakable Violence: Remapping U.S. and Mexican National Imaginaries* (Durham: Duke University Press, 2011).

59. Shannon Speed et al., "Remapping Gender, Justice, and Rights in Indigenous Americas: Toward a Comparative Analysis and Collaborative Methodology," *Journal of Latin American and Caribbean Anthropology* 14, no. 2 (2009): 300–331.

60. Ibid., 312.

61. For a look at both the political and psychological issues of dominance at work in the politics of recognition, see Glen Coulthard, "The Subjects of Empire: Indigenous Peoples and the 'Politics of Recognition' in Canada," *Contemporary Political Theory* 6 (2007): 437–60.

62. Speed et al., "Remapping Gender," 311.

63. Jennifer Wolch and Micahel Dear, eds., *The Power of Geography: How Territory Shapes Social Life* (Boston: Unwin Hyman, 1989), 4.

64. T. V. Reed, "Toxic Colonialism, Environmental Justice, and Native Resistance in Silko's *Almanac of the Dead*," *MELUS* 34, no. 2 (2009): 37.

65. Hastings Donnan and Thomas M. Wilson, *Borders: Frontiers of Identity, Nation and State* (Oxford: Berg, 1999), 4.

66. Sadiya Hartman, *Scenes of Subjection: Terror, Slavery, and Self-Making in Nineteenth-Century America* (Oxford: Oxford University Press, 1997), 5.

67. Edward Soja, *Postmetropolis: Critical Studies of Cities and Regions* (Oxford: Blackwell, 2000), 200.

68. Judith Butler, *Bodies That Matter: On the Discursive Limits of Sex* (New York: Routledge, 1993), 9.

69. Ray Gonzalez, "The Past Is Right Here and Now: An Interview with Leslie Marmon Silko," in *Conversations with Leslie Marmon Silko*, ed. Ellen L. Arnold (Jackson: University Press of Mississippi, 2000), 103.

70. Linda Niemann, "Narratives of Survival," in Arnold, ed., *Conversations with Leslie Marmon Silko*, 108.

71. Guidotti-Hernandez, *Unspeakable Violence*, 27.

72. As critic Deborah Horvitz notes about the use of repetition in her psychoanalytic reading of *Almanac of the Dead*, Silko merges Freud's idea of repetition with Paula Gunn Allen's views of repetition in Native American literature. Freud views repetition as a matter of repeating an unresolved memory as a contemporary experience rather than a memory of the past. Horvitz states: "Perhaps she attributes the intergenerational evil inflicted by the destroyers, who are without histories/stories/memories from their ancestors, to their repression of all links to their pasts" ("Freud, Marx, and Chiapas in Leslie Marmon Silko's *Almanac of the Dead*," *Studies in American Indian Literature* 10, no . 3 [1998]: 51). This links the prophecy box with the discussion of the "Indian Connection" box in the previous section.

73. Arnold Krupat, *Red Matters: Native American Studies* (Philadelphia: University of Pennsylvania Press, 2002), 49.

74. Renee L. Bergland, *The National Uncanny: Indian Ghost and American Subjects* (Hanover, N.H.: University Press of New England, 2000), 17.

75. Donald Carter, *States of Grace: Senegalese in Italy and the New European Immigration* (Minneapolis: University of Minnesota Press, 1997), 101.

76. Robert Warrior, *The People and the Word* (Minneapolis: University of Minnesota Press, 2005), 182.

77. Elaine Jahner, "Traditional Narrative: Contemporary Uses, Historical Perspectives," *Studies in American Indian Literature* 11, no. 2 (1999): 6.

78. Cheyfitz, "The (Post)Colonial Predicament."

Conclusion

1. Joanne Barker, "Manna-hata," *Tequila Sovereign*, October 12, 2011, http://tequila sovereign.blogspot.ca/2011/10/manna-hata.html.

2. Ibid.

3. See Lisa Hall, "Navigating Our Own 'Sea of Islands': Remapping a Theoretical Space for Hawaiian Women and Indigenous Feminism," *Wicazo Sa Review* 24, no. 2 (2009): 15–38; and Shigematsu and Camacho, *Militarized Currents*.

4. Heid E. Erdrich, "The Girl in Geography Class," in *The Mother's Tongue* (Cambridge: Salt Publishing, 2005), 34.

5. Ibid.

6. Lone-Knapp, "Rez Talk," 640.

7. Ramon Saldivar, *Chicano Narrative: The Dialectic of Difference* (Madison: University of Wisconsin Press, 1990), 206, 207.

8. Ibid, 213.

Index

Heidegger, Martin, 214n13
Heise, Ursula, 113
heliotropes, Deloughrey's concept of, 146–47
heteropatriarchy: colonialism and, 22; Native women and, 14–15
history: Native erasure in, 230n48; Silko's collapsing of, 195–200; Silko's "Five Hundred Year Map" and, 168–71
Hong, Grace, 127
hooks, bell, 159–60
Horvitz, Deborah, 232n72
house imagery, in Harjo's poetry, 131–33
House Resolution 108, 90–96
"How Far West Am I?" (Large), 174
How We Became Human (Harjo), 4
hozho, Diné philosophy of, 117
Hudson Bay Company, in Johnson's writing, 53, 72–73, 83
Huhndorf, Shari, 162–63, 229n9
humanistic geography, relocation and, 100–104
Human Territoriality (Sack), 33–34
Hussein, Azfar, 121–22
Hutton, Andrew, 179, 230n45
hyperspatialization, Native experience with, 10

Igbo culture, in Harjo's poetry, 144–54
immigrants and immigration: community destruction and, 141–42; erasure of indigeneity through, 138–40; Native connections with, 142–54
Imperial Eyes: Travel Writing and Transculturation (Pratt), 213n3
"imperial hermeneutic," 121
imperialism: almanacs as reflection of, 173–82; mapping and creation of, 16–23; Native termination policies and, 90–96; relocation and ideology of, 96–97
inclusion politics, spatial production and, 27–28
Indian Act (Canada), 15, 41; bifurcated taxonomy in, 76–78; colonialism and, 42–46, 81–83; dispossession and, 46–51; domesticated space and flesh in provisions of, 59–70; gender and race identity in, 219n37; impact on women of, 46–51,

84–85; land defined in, 218n2; moral judgment in, 218n5; Riel Rebellion and, 61
"Indian Mom" (Belin), 101–2
Indian policies: borders and legal jurisdictions in, 215n31; definition of, 214n24
Indian Reorganization Act (IRA), 91
Indigenous Albuquerque (Carpio), 103
Indigenous identity: assimilation pressures on, 144–45; Australian immigrant/indigenous juxtaposition, 217n73; globalization and, 134–40, 227n28; land recovery and, 3; musical genres and, 140–54
Indigenous people, defined, 213n1
inheritance laws: colonial concepts of, 222n11; Indian Act concepts of, 49–51, 218n5
In Mad Love and War (Harjo), 127–33, 226n13
intersectionality, feminist theory of, 14
intimacy, Native concepts of, 84–85
ironworkers, Iroquois men as, 4–7, 214n7
Iroquois Confederacy, 41. *See also* Haudenosaunee culture

Jahner, Elaine, 201
James, Jesse, 180
Jameson, Fredric, 139
jazz: in Harjo's poetry, 143–54; slave origins of, 140–41
Jefferson, Thomas, 18–19
Johnson, E. Pauline, 15, 38, 192; dispossession in work of, 84–85; domesticated space and flesh in writing of, 59–70; fantasized and state-implemented concepts of space and, 51–59; gender and dispossession in work of, 46–51; historical context for writing of, 41–46; marital uneasiness in writings of, 70–83
Johnston, Basil, 217n67

Keeling, Kara, 164–65
Kelly, Klara, 111
Kidwell, Clara Sue, 110
Kim, Jodi, 90–91
Kinaaldá Diné womanhood ceremony, 99–100

MISHUANA GOEMAN is assistant professor of gender studies at University of California, Los Angeles.